TIM LaHaye

your

Temperament:

DISCOVER
ITS POTENTIAL

Tyndale House Publishers, Inc.
WHEATON, ILLINOIS

All Scripture quotations are taken from the King
James Version of the Bible, unless otherwise noted.

First printing, October 1984

Library of Congress Catalog Card Number 84-51516
ISBN 0-8423-8752-8, cloth
Copyright © 1984 by Tim LaHaye
Printed in the United States of America

CONTENTS

PART *One*

THE POWER OF TEMPERAMENT

CHAPTER
ONE

Temperament Influences Everything You Do

When I was in high school, there was a pair of identical twins in my class. We could hardly tell them apart. They tested out identically on their I.Q. scores (128). But that is where the similarities stopped. One was personable; the other withdrew from people. One loved sports, history, and literature; the other preferred math, physics, and language. Interesting to me was the fact that their grade-point averages were almost identical at the end of their four years in high school. Yet they did not get the same grades in most subjects. What made the difference between these young men? Their temperaments!

Temperament influences everything you do—from sleep habits to study habits to eating style to the way you get along with other people. Humanly speaking, there is no other influence in your life more powerful than your temperament or combination of temperaments. That is why it is so essential to know your temperament and to be able to analyze other people's temperaments, not to condemn them, but so you can maximize your potential and enable them to maximize theirs.

Sit with me in the counseling room and you will see what I mean. The sanguine talks about the weather, friends, and a hundred things before facing the real problem. The choleric gets right to the point. He (or she) wants you to straighten out his partner so he can have a good home life. The melancholy sighs deeply as he sits down with depression, self-pity, and unhappiness etched on his face. The phlegmatic rarely gets around to making an appointment, and when she does it takes most of the first half hour just to prime her conversational pump.

These people are not the temperament they are because they do

these things. Rather, they act the way they do because of their
temperaments. Some of our acts are subtle, like tastes or preferences,
while others involve outlooks and attitudes or even styles of thinking.
There is hardly a function in life that is not influenced by temperament.
Thus, you had better determine your temperament and consistently
direct it into the best life-style for you and your family. Otherwise your
temperament will subconsciously direct you.

TEMPERAMENT AND EATING HABITS

I can almost judge a man's temperament by his eating habits. Sanguines eat everything in sight—and usually look it. In a restaurant they so enjoy talking that they almost never look at a menu until the waitress arrives. Cholerics—stereotyped eaters—seldom vary their menu from one day to the next; and when it arrives, they bolt it down in big chunks, often talking while chewing their food. Melancholies are very picky eaters. It takes them forever to make up their minds about what to order, but once it arrives they savor every bite. Phlegmatics are the most deliberate eaters of all and are invariably the last ones through eating. That is the main reason they rarely gain weight. (All weight specialists warn obese patients to eat slowly, for it takes twenty minutes for food passing into the mouth to shut off hunger pangs.)

TEMPERAMENT AND DRIVING SKILLS

Sanguines are erratic drivers. Sometimes they speed, then for no apparent reason lose interest in driving fast and slow down. They are so people-oriented that they want to look you in the face when talking, even while driving.

Cholerics are daring speed demons who dart in and out of traffic constantly. They always try to get more accomplished in a given period of time than is humanly possible and attempt to make up time by driving furiously between appointments.

Melancholy motorists never leave home without preparing for the trip well in advance. They study the map and know the best route from A to Z. Of all the temperaments, they are the most likely to keep a complete log of their driving history, including gas and oil consumption and car repairs. Legalists by nature, they rarely speed.

Phil Phlegmatic is the slowest driver of all. The last one to leave an intersection, he rarely changes lanes and is an indecisive danger when joining the flow of freeway traffic from an entrance ramp. He is a pokey "Sunday driver" seven days a week. He gets few tickets and rarely has accidents, but he can be a road hazard.

TEMPERAMENT
AND THE WAY
YOU SHOP

Sanguines are not price conscious, but select for visual satisfaction. They are drawn by colorful packaging and advertising. In the grocery store, theirs is the most overloaded cart.

Cholerics, particularly men, are not fond of shopping. They only go to the store when they need something and want to purchase it and get out. Like sanguines, they usually overbuy but not quite as much.

Melancholies are deliberate and decisive shoppers who compare prices and quality quite carefully. They run their hands over the item, try it on two or three times, leave the store a time or two, and if it isn't sold by the time they return, they buy it. They create traffic jams waiting to make up their mind. In the grocery store they know where everything is and save all the coupons from every manufacturer.

Phlegmatics, particularly women, enjoy shopping. They take longer, shop slower, and are probably more frugal than any other type. They are almost as indecisive as the melancholy. They have to shop more frequently than any other type because they don't get enough on the first trip.

TEMPERAMENT
AND YARD CARE

As incredible as it may seem, you can almost decipher a person's temperament by the way he does the yard work around his home.

Sparky Sanguine gets up early Saturday morning to fix his yard. With great gusto he lines up all his tools (he has every gadget known to man because he totally lacks sales resistance) and prepares to cut, trim, shear, and prune. However, within thirty minutes he is chatting joyfully with a neighbor. Before the day is over, he orders his son to "put my tools away" and decides to fix the yard next week. Sparky is clearly one of the world's great procrastinators.

Rocky Choleric hates yard work, and therefore when he does it at all it is with a vengeance. He works at a frenzied pace in order to get the job done, and neatness is not his hallmark. One can usually spot the choleric's yard while driving through the neighborhood. Just look for miniature hedges and dwarf trees.

Martin Melancholy has a natural aptitude for growing things and usually maintains the best yard in the neighborhood. He is the one who talks to and babies his plants, and on almost any weekend we will find him on hands and knees, "manicuring" his lawns and hedges.

The phlegmatic's lawn usually suggests that its owner is still in the house late on a Saturday morning, sipping his third cup of coffee—

because he is. Capable of superior lawn care, Phil will scrupulously attend to "the old plantation," however, because his desire to rest is overcome by his drive to do the accepted thing.

TEMPERAMENT AND STUDY HABITS

Melancholies are usually good students who enjoy learning. They have inquisitive minds and if taught to read well will have a ferocious appetite for books. They are blessed with keen retentive minds that enable them to remember a multitude of details. As a rule they are good spellers because they take mental pictures of each word. Although they have messy files and a desk top that is impossible to organize, they have an amazing concentration regardless of the mess, interruptions, or noise going on around them.

Phlegmatics can be good students if their procrastination doesn't catch up with them. They need a series of short-term assignments rather than long-term projects. They work best under pressure, though they claim they don't like it. They have orderly minds capable of analysis and deductions. They are prone to get their news more from TV than magazines and newspapers. They have good memories and can be intelligent people if somehow motivated to learn.

Cholerics are clever as a rule but not brilliant. They like the people-oriented subjects such as history, geography, literature, and psychology. They may not be good spellers, because they skim over things so quickly. They are adept at speed-reading and have curious minds. They constantly ask "Why?" Cholerics love charts, diagrams, and graphs; they like to know where everything fits in the main scheme of things. They may have a difficult time concentrating on anything that reminds them of other goals or projects that get their minds off on a tangent and then may have a difficult time getting back to the subject at hand.

Sanguines, unless endowed with a high I.Q., are not usually good students. They can be if they are motivated, because they are often bright enough, but they are very restless and undisciplined. They have a short interest span and anything can be a distraction, from a bird flying overhead to a picture on the wall. These people have incredible potential but usually squander it because they don't discipline themselves. Concentration for long periods of time is difficult for them.

HANDWRITING AND YOUR TEMPERAMENT

I am not an authority on handwriting, but I have observed that temperament and handwriting analysis are very similar. Our penmanship usually follows our temperament.

Everything a sanguine does is expressive and flamboyant, and he writes that way. The choleric usually has poor handwriting. Everything he does is fast; consequently, he does not take time to write legibly. The phlegmatic usually has a small but neat handwriting. Melancholies have the most unpredictable handwriting of all. They are extremely complex people and usually write that way.

COMMUNICATION SKILLS AND TEMPERAMENT

Thinking skills and communication skills are not based solely on the brain. They also involve temperament. Sanguines are intuitive speakers. They are overly expressive and use exaggeration freely. Cholerics are extroverted enough to speak freely, but usually are more deliberate than sanguines. They are debaters and argumentative; no one can be more biting or sarcastic. Melancholies never start talking until they have thought out precisely what they want to say. They don't like to interrupt others, but once they get started they go on until they have unloaded their entire message. Phlegmatics are quiet about everything and seldom enter into debates or thrust themselves into conversations. They will respond to questions with wit and good humor, but rarely volunteer anything unless asked.

Peter was told, "Your speech betrays you" (Matt. 26:73). That is often true of your temperament; your speech patterns are a giveaway of your temperament.

BILL PAYING AND TEMPERAMENT

Paying bills is a necessary part of life, and it seems to get more complex all the time.

Believe it or not, unless you are a trained bookkeeper, the way you tackle that problem will be a reflection of your temperament.

Sanguines are terrible record-keepers. They dislike detail and can get momentarily depressed with their overspending habits. Their method of handling deficit spending is rarely to cut down on their standard of living, but simply to try to make more money. They pay their bills, but it usually takes several reminders.

Cholerics like to pay bills on time. They aren't very detailed unless they have a melancholy or phlegmatic secondary temperament, but they like things orderly. Their style is to put all the bills in one place and pay them all the same night each month. They aren't "bugged" if their checkbook doesn't balance, just so they keep the bank honest. For $5 or $10 they will accept the bank's balance—they figure their time spent hassling over the details is worth more than that.

Melancholies are perfectionists. Their conscientious nature makes them difficult to live with if they don't pay all their creditors on time. Their bill cabinet is a mess, but they know what each statement and receipt is. They usually have every receipt for the past five years, but in no set order. They pride themselves on balancing their checkbook to the penny. If there is a mistake, it will be the bank's. They usually have a triple "A" credit rating.

Phlegmatics systemize everything. They have a detailed budget and keep matching records. They not only pay bills on time, they like to get them in early wherever it saves an additional 2 or 4 percent. (Sanguines don't even realize there are companies that do this.) To some phlegs, balancing their checkbook is the highlight of their month. It is the one clear signal that their life is in order and they are ready to launch into the next month.

CHILD DISCIPLINE AND YOUR TEMPERAMENT

Child discipline is largely a result of family tradition, religious training, culture, and temperament. In recent years there have been a number of books written on this subject, some good, some very harmful. Those who base their philosophy on humanistic values or humanistic psychology have produced a permissive society that tends toward lawlessness. Books based on biblical principles have, on the other hand, been very valuable. My three favorite books on child discipline are two by my friend Dr. James Dobson (*Dare to Discipline* and *The Strong-Willed Child*) and one by my wife, Beverly: *How to Develop Your Child's Temperament*. These three books should be in every Christian parent's library. If you study them, you will be equipped to be a maximum parent.

Having said all of that, however, you will find that unless you learn what is right in disciplining your children, you will respond to them according to your temperament. Even when you know what to do, your temperament will influence the way you do it. Consider these four familiar styles.

Everything a sanguine does in life is spontaneous, and discipline is usually no exception. He is loud in his instruction and correction, and a woman sanguine is apt to be a screamer. Since sanguines are not disciplined themselves, their threats are rarely carried out; so Johnny knows he never has to answer the first time he is called or told to do something. He waits until the pitch of the scream or the volume of the call gets to a certain intensity before he comes home.

When it comes to spankings, sanguines must do it immediately, while

they are angry or frustrated, or they probably won't do it at all. Their
tender heart and forgiving spirit make delayed punishment no
punishment. Their leniency leads to permissiveness, which in turn
encourages lawlessness. And inconsistent parents usually raise
inconsistent children.

One thing is commendable about sanguines: after they have
disciplined their children, they take time to love and comfort them.
Sanguines never carry grudges (we could all do with a bit of that).
Another thing about these fun-loving people is that they will often take
time to play with their children, particularly as they get older.

Cholerics, being authority-prone, want to run their homes like a
Marine boot camp. This may produce good robots, but it doesn't do
much for kids. The child of a choleric parent never lacks knowledge of
what his parent requires in the way of obedience and rules—he is
told regularly. Cholerics love to give out orders. Choleric spankers tend
to spank too hard too often and too many spanks per discipline. Masters
of the overkill in all that they do, their motto is, "If a little helps, a lot
will cure." (In reality, no parent should spank a child when angry. He
makes the child feel he is just a release valve for the parent's frustration.)

Cholerics can be good parents, but they have to work at it. They are
hard to please at best, and if a child is a "late bloomer" or of a less
activist temperament, such parents are apt to make her feel inferior and
constantly disapproved. Such parents need to encourage their children,
approve them, and build up their self-image, going out of their way to
show their love.

Melancholy parents were perfectionists before they became parents,
and having children won't change that. They have high-to-unreal
expectations for their young and dole out praise sparingly (although
most children need it lavishly). Academically, their children know that
anything less than an "A" is a failure—in every subject. Legalistic by
nature, they usually have rules for everything and procedures that must
be followed. If they say they will spank for a particular offense, they
usually follow through; but rarely do they overspank, unless they see
their own shortcomings in their child. Then they may take out on the
child the frustrations they have toward themselves.

It is hard for melancholies to be approving, because their standard is
so high and because they are afraid their child will become complacent
with approval. They are the last temperament to learn that everyone
needs praise and that most people thrive better on approval than on
condemnation. They have a great capacity to love their children, but
they need to learn how to express it. One of the biggest parental failings

is that they never forget anything wrong the child has done, and if not trained out of the habit will bring it up again and again.

Phlegmatics can be good parents if they learn to be more assertive and confrontive when necessary. They are patience personified. They love children and probably feel more comfortable with little children than anyone else. They take time with them, play with them, and can be patient trainers. As choleric children get older, phlegmatic parents may be intimidated by them and look the other way, thus undermining in the teen years the good training they gave in childhood. However, the one thing they may indulge in (melancholies can be guilty of this also) is to permit their children to sass them. No parent should accept this. The Bible says children are to honor their parents. If they don't honor them with their mouths, they must at least be forced not to dishonor them. Parents who lose that battle in childhood seldom gain control in the teen years.

The phlegmatic is the least likely to spank. He usually waits until the more extroverted parent does it. When the teen years come and the child needs a forceful father figure, it is sad when Dad goes to the garage and putters at his workbench to avoid unpleasant confrontations. I once counseled a phlegmatic man whose conflict with his wife arose because she wouldn't forbid the kids to watch certain TV shows he felt were objectionable. Children need two parents to agree on rules and to enforce them, applying whatever punishment is appropriate or promised. Phlegmatics can be good parents but, like the rest of us, they have to work at it.

SUMMARY   We could go on giving illustrations of how
                     temperament influences the way you exercise,
sleep, decorate, select clothes, have hobbies, and everything else in your life. But these are enough to get you started in the right direction. As you become more familiar with the temperament theory, you will see it at work in your own life and that of your friends.

Why You Act the Way You Do

Everyone is interested in human behavior. That is why over 80 percent of our nation's thirteen million college students voluntarily take psychology classes; they are fascinated by what makes people tick. And most of all, they are interested in why they think, feel, respond, explode, and act the way they do.

Nothing answers those questions better than the theory of the four temperaments. It explains differences in people—their tastes, their creative capabilities, their strengths and weaknesses. It explains why some people conflict with others and why others are attracted to each other.

TEMPERAMENT—
YOU'RE BORN
WITH IT

Humanly speaking, nothing has a more profound influence on your behavior than your inherited temperament. The combination of your parents' genes and chromosomes at conception, which determined your basic temperament nine months before you drew your first breath, is largely responsible for your actions, reactions, emotional responses, and, to one degree or another, almost everything you do.

Most people are completely unaware of this extremely powerful influence on their behavior. Consequently, instead of cooperating with it and using it, they conflict with this inner power and often try to make something of themselves that they were never intended to be. This not only limits them personally, but affects their immediate family and often spoils other interpersonal relationships. It is one of the reasons so many people say, "I don't like myself" or, "I can't find myself." When a person discovers his own basic temperament, he can usually figure out rather easily what vocational opportunities he is best suited for, how to get along with other people, what natural weaknesses to watch for, what kind of wife he should marry, and how he can improve the effectiveness of his life.

WHAT IS
TEMPERAMENT?

Temperament is the combination of traits we inherited from our parents. No one knows where it resides, but I think it is somewhere in the mind or emotional center (often referred to as the heart). From that source it combines with other human characteristics to produce our basic makeup. Most of us are more conscious of its expression than we are its function.

It is a person's temperament that makes him outgoing and extroverted or shy and introverted. Doubtless you know both kinds of people who were born to the same parents. Similarly, it is temperament that makes some people art and music enthusiasts while others are sports- or industry-minded. In fact, I have met outstanding musicians whose siblings were tone-deaf.

Temperament is not the only influence upon our behavior, of course. Early home life, training, education, and motivation also exercise powerful influences on our actions throughout life. Temperament is, however, the Number One influence on a person's life, not only because it is the first thing that affects us, but because, like body structure, color of eyes, and other physical characteristics, it escorts us through life. An extrovert is an extrovert. He may tone down the expression of his extroversion, but he will always be an extrovert. Similarly, although an introvert may be able to come out of his shell and act more aggressively, he will never be transformed into an extrovert. Temperament sets broad guidelines on everyone's behavior—patterns that will influence a person as long as he lives. On one side are his strengths, on the other his weaknesses. The primary advantage to learning about the four basic temperaments is to discover your most pronounced strengths and weaknesses so that with God's help you can overcome your weaknesses and take advantage of your strengths. In this way you can fulfill your personal destiny to the maximum.

Temperament is passed on through the genes and no doubt was influenced by the Adamic fall. That is why we all identify with the desire to do good while at the same time we possess a desire to do evil. The Apostle Paul no doubt felt that same way when he said, ". . . for to will is present with me; but how to perform that which is good I find not. For the good that I would I do not: but the evil which I would not, that I do. Now if I do that I would not, it is no more I that do it, but sin that dwelleth in me" (Rom. 7:18-20).

Paul differentiated between himself and that uncontrollable force within by saying, "It is no more I that do it, but sin that dwelleth in me." The "I" is Paul's person—the soul, will, and mind of man. The "sin" that dwelled in him was the human nature that he, like all human beings, inherited from his parents.

This basic nature that we have all inherited from our parents is called several things in the Bible: "the natural man," "the flesh," "the old man," and "corruptible flesh," to name a few. It provides the basic impulses of our being as we seek to satisfy our wants. To properly understand its control of our actions and reactions, we should distinguish carefully between temperament, character, and personality.

Temperament is the combination of inborn traits that subconsciously affect man's behavior. These traits are arranged genetically on the basis of nationality, race, sex, and other hereditary factors. These traits are passed on by the genes. Some psychologists suggest that we get more genes from our grandparents than our parents. That could account for the greater resemblance of some children to their grandparents than to their parents. The alignment of temperament traits is just as unpredictable as the color of eyes, hair, or size of body.

Character is the real you. The Bible refers to it as "the hidden man of the heart." It is the result of your natural temperament modified by childhood training, education, basic attitudes, beliefs, principles, and motivations. It is sometimes referred to as "the soul" of man, which is made up of the mind, emotions, and will.

Personality is the outward expression of ourselves, which may or may not be the same as our character, depending on how genuine we are. Often personality is a pleasing facade for an unpleasant or weak character. Many people go through life acting a part on the basis of what they think they should be, or how they want people to see them, rather than as they really are. This is a formula for mental and spiritual chaos. It is caused by following the human formula for acceptable conduct, which places the emphasis on externals. The Bible tells us, "Man looks on the outward appearance, but God looks on the heart"; and, "Out of the heart proceeds the issues of life." The place to change behavior is inside man, not outside.

In summary, temperament is the combination of traits we were born with; character is our "civilized" temperament; and personality is the "face" we show to others. Since temperament traits are received genetically from our parents and hence are unpredictable, one should keep in mind some of the factors that influence temperament. Nationality and race probably play the most significant part in formulating one's inherited temperament.

While on a missionary tour to Mexico, I noticed the vast differences in the tribes that I observed. One tribe of Indians impressed me greatly. Many tribes had been shiftless, indifferent, and careless in their mode of life. These people, however, were a very industrious and often ingeniously capable tribe. In one city we visited, they were actively pursuing the technical trade of weaving, and their sense of responsibility was in sharp contrast to anything we had observed in other tribesmen. The skills were learned, but adaptability and desire to learn were so universal throughout the tribe that it could only be an inherited trait.

A person's sex will also affect temperament, particularly in the realm of the emotions. Women are usually considered to be more emotionally expressive than men. Even the hardest of women will weep at times, whereas some men never weep.

Temperament traits, whether controlled or uncontrolled, last throughout life. The older we get, however, the softer and more mellow our harsh and hard traits tend to become. Man learns that if he is to live at peace with his fellow man, it is best to emphasize his natural strengths and subdue his weaknesses. Many are successful in developing their character and improving their personality, but comparatively few are able to change their temperament. It is possible, however, to so modify your temperament that you seem like an entirely different person. To do so, however, requires outside help, and that will be addressed thoroughly in a later chapter. But first we should meet the four temperaments.

Meet the Four Temperaments

The heart of the temperament theory, as first conceived by Hippocrates over twenty-four hundred years ago, divides people into four basic categories, which he named sanguine, choleric, melancholy, and phlegmatic. Each temperament type has both strengths and weaknesses that form a distinct part of his makeup throughout life. Once a person diagnoses his own basic temperament, he is better equipped to ascertain what vocational opportunities he is best suited for and what natural weaknesses he must work on to keep from short-circuiting his potential and creativity. The temperament chart on page 24 summarizes these strengths and weaknesses, revealing ten of each per temperament.

The following brief descriptions of the four basic temperaments will introduce you to these four different types of people. No doubt you will identify several of your friends in one or another of these classifications, and if you look carefully, you may even discover one that reminds you of yourself.

MEET SPARKY SANGUINE

Sparky Sanguine is a warm, buoyant, lively, and "enjoying" person. Receptive by nature, external impressions easily find their way to his heart, where they cause an outburst of response. Feelings rather than reflective thoughts predominate to form his decisions. Sparky is so outgoing he is usually considered a superextrovert. Mr. Sanguine has an unusual capacity for enjoying himself and usually passes on his fun-loving spirit. The moment he enters a room he tends to lift the spirits of everyone present by his exuberant conversation. He is a fascinating storyteller and his warm, emotional nature almost helps you relive the experience as he tells it.

Mr. Sanguine never lacks for friends. He can genuinely feel the joys and sorrows of the person he meets and has the capacity to make him feel important, as though he were a very special friend—and he is, as long as he is looking at you. Then he fixes his eyes with equal intensity on the next person he meets.

The Apostle Peter in the Bible was much like Sparky Sanguine. Every time he appeared in the Gospels he was talking. In fact, I read through the Gospels one time to verify my suspicion and found that Simon Peter talked more than all the other disciples put together. That is typical for Sparky. As my sanguine minister friend Ken Poure says, "A sanguine always enters a room mouth first." His noisy, blustering, friendly ways make him appear more confident than he really is, but his energy and lovable disposition get him by the rough spots of life. People have a way of excusing his weaknesses by saying, "That's just the way he is."

MEET ROCKY CHOLERIC

Rocky Choleric is hot, quick, active, practical, strong-willed, self-sufficient, and very independent. He tends to be decisive and opinionated, finding it easy to make decisions both for himself and other people. Like Sparky Sanguine, Rocky Choleric is an extrovert, but is not nearly so intense.

Mr. Choleric thrives on activity. He does not need to be stimulated by his environment, but rather stimulates his environment with his endless ideas, plans, goals, and ambitions. He does not engage in aimless activity, for he has a practical, keen mind, capable of making sound, instant decisions or planning worthwhile projects. He does not vacillate under the pressure of what others think, but takes a definite stand on issues and can often be found crusading against some social injustice or subversive situation. Rocky is not frightened by adversities; in fact, they tend to encourage him. His dogged determination usually allows him to succeed where others have failed.

Mr. Choleric's emotional nature is the least developed part of his temperament. He does not sympathize easily with others, nor does he naturally show or express compassion. He is often embarrassed or disgusted by the tears of others and is usually insensitive to their needs.

He reflects little appreciation for music and the fine arts, unless his secondary temperament traits are those of the melancholy. He invariably seeks utilitarian and productive values in life. Not given to analysis, but rather to quick, almost intuitive appraisal, the choleric tends to look at the goal for which he is working without recognizing the potential pitfalls and obstacles in the path. Once he has started toward his goal, he may run roughshod over individuals who stand in his way. He tends to be domineering and bossy and does not hesitate to use people to accomplish his ends. He is often considered an opportunist.

MEET MARTIN MELANCHOLY

Martin Melancholy is the richest of all the temperaments. He is an analytical, self-sacrificing, gifted, perfectionist type with a very sensitive emotional nature. No one gets more enjoyment from the fine arts than the melancholy. By nature, he is prone to be an introvert; but since his feelings predominate, he is given to a variety of moods. Sometimes they will lift him to heights of ecstasy that cause him to act more extroverted. However, at other times he will be gloomy and depressed, and during these periods he becomes withdrawn and can be quite antagonistic.

Martin is a very faithful friend, but unlike the sanguine, he does not make friends easily. He seldom pushes himself forward to meet people, but rather lets them come to him. He is perhaps the most dependable of all the temperaments, for his perfectionist and conscientious tendencies do not permit him to be a shirker or let others down when they are counting on him. His reticence to put himself forward is often taken as an indication that he doesn't enjoy people. Like the rest of us, he not only likes others but has a strong desire to be loved by them but finds it difficult to express his true feelings. Disappointing experiences make him reluctant to take people at face value; thus he is prone to be suspicious when others seek him out or shower him with attention.

His exceptional analytical ability causes him to diagnose accurately the obstacles and dangers of any project he has a part in planning. This is in sharp contrast to the choleric, who rarely anticipates problems or difficulties, but is confident he can cope with whatever crises may arise. Such a characteristic often finds the melancholy reticent to initiate some new project or in conflict with those who wish to do so. Occasionally, in a mood of emotional ecstasy or inspiration, he may produce some great work of art or genius. But these accomplishments are often followed by periods of great depression.

Martin Melancholy usually finds his greatest meaning in life through personal sacrifice. He seems desirous of making himself suffer, and he will often choose a difficult life vocation involving great personal sacrifice. But once it is chosen, he is prone to be very thorough and persistent in his pursuit of it and more than likely will accomplish great good if his natural tendency to gripe throughout the sacrificial process doesn't get him so depressed that he gives up on it altogether. No temperament has so much natural potential when energized by the Holy Spirit as the melancholy.

MEET PHILIP PHLEGMATIC

Philip Phlegmatic is the calm, easygoing, never-get-upset individual with such a high boiling point that he almost never becomes angry. He is the easiest type of person to get along with and is by nature the most likeable of all the temperaments.

Philip Phlegmatic derives his name from what Hippocrates thought was the body fluid that produced that "calm, cool, slow, well-balanced temperament." Life for him is a happy, unexcited, pleasant experience in which he avoids as much involvement as possible. He is so calm and unruffled that he never seems agitated, no matter what circumstances surround him. He is the one temperament type that is consistent every time you see him. Beneath his cool, reticent, almost timid personality, Mr. Phlegmatic has a very capable combination of abilities. He feels more emotion than appears on the surface and appreciates the fine arts and the beautiful things of life. Usually he avoids violence.

The phlegmatic does not lack for friends, because he enjoys people and has a natural, dry sense of humor. He is the type of individual who can have a crowd of people "in stitches," yet never cracks a smile. Possessing the unique capability for seeing something humorous in others and the things they do, he maintains a positive approach to life. He has a good, retentive mind and is capable of being a fine imitator.

Phil Phlegmatic tends to be a spectator in life and tries not to get very involved with the activities of others. In fact, it is usually with great reluctance that he is ever motivated to any form of activity beyond his daily routine. This does not mean, however, that he cannot appreciate the need for action and the predicaments of others. He and Rocky

Choleric may confront the same social injustice, but their responses will be entirely different. The crusading spirit of the choleric will cause him to explain, "Let's get a committee organized and campaign to do something about this!" The phlegmatic would likely respond, "These conditions are terrible! Why doesn't someone do something about them?" Usually kindhearted and sympathetic, Phil Phlegmatic seldom conveys his true feelings. When once aroused to action, however, his capable and efficient qualities become apparent. He will not volunteer to leadership on his own, but when it is forced upon him, he proves to be a very capable leader. He has a conciliating effect on others and is a natural peacemaker.

Four Basic Temperaments Chart

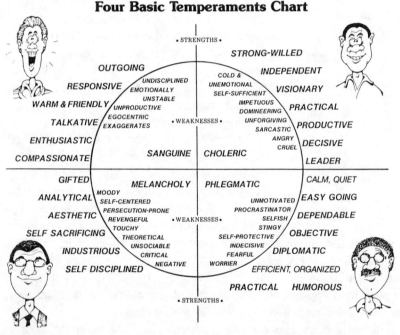

Now that you have been briefly introduced to the four basic temperaments you should study the above chart, which includes ten strengths and ten weaknesses for each temperament.

SUMMARY: There you have it! In just a few pages we have
WHICH ARE YOU?   presented the centuries-old theory of the four
                     basic temperaments. I say *basic* because no one
is 100 percent sanguine, choleric, melancholy, or phlegmatic. We are all a combination of at least two and perhaps three temperaments (more on that intriguing subject later).

However, your predominant or basic temperament, the one that influences you the most, should not be too difficult to diagnose. Just ask yourself a few questions while looking at the following illustrations.

Sanguine   Choleric   Melancholy   Phlegmatic

1. Are you an extrovert? If so, you are predominantly sanguine or choleric.
2. If "yes" to 1, ask yourself, "Do I lean toward being a superextrovert?" That is, are you generally the first to speak? If so you are a sanguine.
3. If "yes" to 1, ask yourself if you are a good salesman type. If so, you are predominantly sanguine.
4. If "yes" to 1, but "no" to 2 and 3, ask, "Am I a 'strong natural leader?' " If so, you are probably a choleric.
5. If you answered "no" to 1—that is, you are not an extrovert—then ask yourself, "Am I a perfectionist, analytical, and somewhat critical?" If so, you are probably predominantly melancholy.
6. If you answered "no" to 1, ask yourself if you are known by others as "very quiet." Do you rarely get angry but experience many fears and worries? If so, you are probably phlegmatic.

This, of course, is an oversimplified test, and it only considers your predominant temperament. But it will help you even at this point to have a strong indication of which temperament you are. As we progress through the book you will find more confirmation of what your basic temperament is, or you may find that learning more details about the various temperaments will reveal that your first selection is really your secondary temperament. But that usually happens only when a person is balanced between his primary and secondary temperaments.

More thorough temperament testing will be given later in the book, but first you need to know more about this fascinating subject.

PEOPLE ARE
DIFFERENT

Now that you have met the four temperaments, you no doubt realize why "people are individuals." Not only are there four distinct types of temperaments that produce these differences, but the combinations, mixtures, and degrees of temperament multiply the possible differences. In spite of that, however, most people reveal a pattern of behavior that indicates they lean toward one predominant temperament.

Recently I had an experience that graphically portrayed the difference of temperament. It was necessary for me to find a Thermofax machine while speaking at a summer high school camp. In the small town nearby, the only one available was in the education center. When I arrived by appointment, I found nine people hard at work. The calm, orderly, and efficient surroundings made me realize that I was in the presence of individuals of a predominantly melancholy or phlegmatic temperament.

This was later confirmed as the superintendent carefully computed my bill and refused my money because it was "against the rules." Instead he took me to the meticulous treasurer, who took us to the bookkeeper, who in turn relayed us to the cashier, who finally arranged for me to give my $1.44 to the switchboard operator, who kept the petty cash, lest some of their bookkeeping records would have to be altered. The clincher was the petty cash box, which clearly revealed the touch of a perfectionist. The change had been carefully stacked in neat piles of quarters, dimes, and nickles.

As I surveyed the placid environment and noted their calm but definite concern for this minor problem, my mind flitted hilariously to the scene of the sales office where they had sold the overhead projector. There the sales staff, chief executive, and all the employees were predominantly of the extrovertish choleric or sanguine temperaments. The place was a disorganized mess! Papers were strewn everywhere, telephones and desks were unattended, the office was a hubbub of noisy activity. Finally, above the din of voices, I heard the sales manager say to the staff, with a look of desperation, "One of these days we are going to get organized around here!"

These two scenes show the natural contrast of the inherited traits that produce human temperament. They also point out the fact that all four of the basic temperaments we have described are needed for variety and purposefulness. No single temperament can be said to be better than another. Each one contains strengths and richness, and yet each one is fraught with its own weaknesses and dangers. How to improve yourself by overcoming your weaknesses is the purpose of this book.

PART Two

WHAT TEMPERAMENT ARE YOU?

CHAPTER TWO

The Twelve Blends of Temperament

The chief objection to the theory of the four temperaments as advocated by the ancients is that it was overly simplistic in assuming every person could be characterized by only one of the four temperaments. As I have said in my previous books on temperament, that just is not true. We are all a blend of at least two temperaments; one predominates, the other is secondary. In an attempt to make the temperament theory more practical and true to life, we shall briefly examine twelve possible blends of temperament. In all probability, it will be easier for you to identify yourself in one of the blends than in one of the four basics.

A Variety Of Blends

Essentially, each person is capable of possessing twenty strengths and twenty weaknesses to one degree or another (ten for the predominant and ten for the secondary temperament). Some of them, as we shall see, cancel each other out, some reinforce each other, and some accentuate and compound others, accounting for the varieties of behavior, prejudices, and natural skills of people with the same predominant temperament but with different secondary temperaments. This will become clearer as you study the following twelve blends of temperament.

THE SANCHLOR

The strongest extrovert of all the blends of temperaments will be the SanChlor, for the two temperaments that make up his nature are both extroverted. The happy charisma of the sanguine makes him a people-oriented, enthusiastic, salesman type; but the choleric side of his nature will provide him the necessary resolution and character traits that will fashion a somewhat more organized and productive individual than if he were pure sanguine. Almost any people-oriented field is open to him, but to sustain his interest it must offer variety, activity, and excitement.

The potential weaknesses of a SanChlor are usually apparent to everyone because he is such an external person. He customarily talks too much, thus exposing himself and his weaknesses for all to see. He is highly opinionated. Consequently, he expresses himself loudly even before he knows all the facts. To be honest, no one has more mouth trouble! If he is the life of the party, he is lovable; but if he feels threatened or insecure, he can become obnoxious. His leading emotional problem will be anger, which can catapult him into action at the slightest provocation. Since he combines the easy forgetfulness of the sanguine and the stubborn casuistry of the choleric, he may not have a very active conscience. Consequently, he tends to justify his actions. This man, like any other temperament, needs to be filled daily with the Holy Spirit and the Word of God.

Simon Peter, the self-appointed leader of the twelve apostles, is a classic example of a New Testament SanChlor. He obviously had mouth trouble, demonstrating this repeatedly by speaking up before anyone else could. He talked more in the Gospels than all the others put together—and most of what he said was wrong. He was egotistical, weak-willed, and carnal throughout the Gospels. In Acts, however, he was a remarkably transformed man—resolute, effective, and productive. What made the difference? He was filled with the Spirit.

THE SANMEL

SanMels are highly emotional people who fluctuate drastically. They can laugh hysterically one minute and burst into tears the next. It is almost impossible for them to hear a sad tale, observe a tragic plight of another person, or listen to melancholic music without weeping profusely. They genuinely feel the griefs of others. Almost any field is open to them, especially public

speaking, acting, music, and the fine arts. However, SanMels reflect an uninhibited perfectionism that often alienates them from others because they verbalize their criticisms. They are usually people-oriented individuals who have sufficient substance to make a contribution to other lives—if their ego and arrogance don't make them so obnoxious that others become hostile to them.

One of the crucial weaknesses of this temperament blend prevails in SanMel's thought-life. Both sanguines and melancholies are dreamers, and thus if the melancholy part of his nature suggests a negative train of thought, it can nullify a SanMel's potential. It is easy for him to get down on himself. In addition, this person, more than most others, will have both an anger problem and a tendency toward fear. Both temperaments in his makeup suffer with an insecurity problem; not uncommonly, he is fearful to utilize his potential. Being admired by others is so important to him that it will drive him to a consistent level of performance. He has a great ability to commune with God, and if he walks in the Spirit he will make an effective servant of Christ.

King David is a classic illustration of the SanMel temperament. An extremely likable man who attracted both men and women; he was colorful, dramatic, emotional, and weak-willed. He could play a harp and sing, he clearly demonstrated a poetic instinct in his Psalms, and he made decisions on impulse. Unfortunately, like many SanMels, he fouled up his life by a series of disastrous and costly mistakes before he gained enough self-discipline to finish out his destiny. All SanMels, of course, are not able to pick up the pieces of their lives and start over as David did. It is far better for them to walk in the Spirit daily and avoid such mistakes.

THE SANPHLEG   The easiest person to like is a SanPhleg. The overpowering and obnoxious tendencies of a sanguine are offset by the gracious, easygoing phlegmatic. SanPhlegs are extremely happy people whose carefree spirit and good humor make them lighthearted entertainers sought after by others. Helping people is their regular business, along with sales of various kinds. They are the least extroverted of any of the sanguines and are often regulated by their environment and circumstances rather than being self-motivated. SanPhlegs are naturally pro-family and preserve the love of their

children—and everyone else for that matter. They would not purposely hurt anyone.

The SanPhleg's greatest weaknesses are lack of motivation and discipline. He would rather socialize than work, and he tends to take life too casually. As an executive remarked about one, "He is the nicest guy I ever fired." He rarely gets upset over anything and tends to find the bright side of everything. He usually has an endless repertoire of jokes and delights in making others laugh, often when the occasion calls for serious-ness. When Jesus Christ becomes the chief object of his love, he is transformed into a more resolute, purposeful, and productive person.

The first-century evangelist Apollos is about as close as we can come to a New Testament illustration of the SanPhleg. A skilled orator who succeeded Paul and others who had founded the churches, he did the work of stirring the churches with his Spirit-filled preaching and teaching. Loved by all, followed devotedly by some, this pleasant and dedicated man apparently traveled a great deal but did not found new works.

THE CHLORSAN

The second-strongest extrovert among the blends of temperament will be the reverse of the first—the ChlorSan. This man's life is given over completely to activity. Most of his efforts are productive and purposeful, but watch his recreation—it is so activity-prone that it borders on being violent. He is a natural promoter and salesman, with enough charisma to get along well with others. Certainly the best motivator of people and one who thrives on a challenge, he is almost fearless and exhibits boundless energy. His wife will often comment, "He has only two speeds: wide open and stop." Mr. ChlorSan is the courtroom attorney who can charm the coldest-hearted judge and jury, the fund-raiser who can get people to contribute what they intended to save, the man who never goes anywhere unnoticed, the preacher who combines both practical Bible teaching and church administration, and the politician who talks his state into changing its constitution so he can represent them one more time. A convincing debater, what he lacks in facts or arguments he makes up in bluff or bravado. As a teacher, he is an excellent communicator, particularly in the social sciences; rarely is he drawn to math, science, or the abstract. Whatever his professional occupation, his brain is always in motion.

The weaknesses of this man, the chief of which is hostility, are as broad as his talents. He combines the quick, explosive anger of the sanguine (without the forgiveness) and the long-burning resentment of the choleric. He is the one personality type who not only gets ulcers himself, but gives them to others. Impatient with those who do not share his motivation and energy, he prides himself on being brutally frank (some call it sarcastically frank). It is difficult for him to concentrate on one thing very long, which is why he often enlists others to finish what he has started. He is opinionated, prejudiced, impetuous, and inclined doggedly to finish a project he probably should not have started in the first place. If not controlled by God, he is apt to justify anything he does—and rarely hesitates to manipulate or walk over other people to accomplish his ends. Most ChlorSans get so engrossed in their work that they neglect wife and family, even lashing out at them if they complain. Once he comprehends the importance of giving love and approval to his family, however, he can transform his entire household.

James, the author of the biblical book that bears his name, could well have been a ChlorSan—at least his book sounds like it. The main thrust of the book declares that "faith without works is dead"—a favored concept by work-loving cholerics. He used the practical and logical reasoning of a choleric, yet was obviously a highly esteemed man of God. One human weakness he discusses—the fire of the tongue and how no man can control it (James 3)—relates directly to this temperament's most vulnerable characteristic, for we all know the ChlorSans feature a razor-sharp, active tongue. His victory and evident productiveness in the cause of Christ is a significant example to any thoughtful ChlorSan.

THE CHLORMEL

The choleric/melancholy is an extremely industrious and capable person. The optimism and practicality of the choleric overcomes the tendency toward moodiness of the melancholy, making the ChlorMel both goal-oriented and detailed. Such a person usually does well in school, possesses a quick, analytical mind, yet is decisive. He develops into a thorough leader, the kind whom one can always count on to do an extraordinary job. Never take him on in a debate unless you are assured of your facts, for he will make mincemeat of you, combining verbal aggressiveness and attendance to detail. This man is extremely competitive and forceful in all that he does. He is a dogged researcher and is usually successful, no matter what kind of business he pursues. This temperament probably makes the best natural leader. General George S. Patton, the great commander of the U.S. Third Army in World War II who drove the German forces back to Berlin, was probably a ChlorMel.

Equally as great as his strengths are his weaknesses. He is apt to be autocratic, a dictator type who inspires admiration and hate simultaneously. He is usually a quick-witted talker whose sarcasm can devastate others. He is a natural-born crusader whose work habits are irregular and long. A ChlorMel harbors considerable hostility and resentment, and unless he enjoys a good love relationship with his parents, he will find interpersonal relationships difficult, particularly with his family. No man is more apt to be an overly strict disciplinarian than the ChlorMel father. He combines the hard-to-please tendency of the choleric and the perfectionism of the melancholy. When controlled by the Holy Spirit, however, his entire emotional life is transformed and he makes an outstanding Christian.

There is little doubt in my mind that the Apostle Paul was a ChlorMel. Before his conversion he was hostile and cruel, for the Scripture teaches that he spent his time persecuting and jailing Christians. Even after his conversion, his strong-willed determination turned to unreasonable bullheadedness, as when he went up to Jerusalem against the will and warning of God. His writings and ministry demonstrate the combination of the practical-analytical reasoning and the self-sacrificing but extremely driving nature of a ChlorMel. He is a good example of God's transforming power in the life of a ChlorMel who is completely dedicated to his will.

The ChlorPhleg

The most subdued of all the extrovert temperaments is the ChlorPhleg, a happy blend of the quick, active, and hot with the calm, cool, and unexcited. He is not as apt to rush into things as quickly as the preceding extroverts because he is more deliberate and subdued. He is extremely capable in the long run, although he does not particularly impress you that way at first. He is a very organized person who combines planning and hard work.

People usually enjoy working with and for him because he knows where he is going and has charted his course, yet is not unduly severe with people. He has the ability to help others make the best use of their skills and rarely offends people or makes them feel used. The ChlorPhleg's slogan on organization states: "Anything that needs to be done can be done better if it's organized." These men are usually good husbands and fathers as well as excellent administrators in almost any field.

In spite of his obvious capabilities, the ChlorPhleg is not without a notable set of weaknesses. Although not as addicted to the quick anger of some temperaments, he is known to harbor resentment and bitterness. Some of the cutting edge of the choleric's sarcasm is here offset by the gracious spirit of the phlegmatic; so instead of uttering cutting and cruel remarks, his barbs are more apt to emerge as cleverly disguised humor. One is never quite sure whether he is kidding or ridiculing, depending on his mood. No one can be more bullheadedly stubborn than a ChlorPhleg, and it is very difficult for him to change his mind once it is committed. Repentance or the acknowledgement of a mistake is not at all easy for him. Consequently, he will be more apt to make it up to those he has wronged without really facing his mistake. The worrisome traits of the phlegmatic side of his nature may so curtail his adventurous tendencies that he never quite measures up to his capabilities.

Titus, the spiritual son of the Apostle Paul and leader of the hundred or so churches on the Isle of Crete, may well have been a ChlorPhleg. When filled with the Spirit, he was the kind of man on whom Paul could depend to faithfully teach the Word to the churches and administrate them capably for the glory of God. The book which Paul wrote to him makes ideal reading for any teacher, particularly a ChlorPhleg.

Now we turn to the predominantly introverted temperaments. Each will look somewhat similar to one we have already examined, except that the two temperaments making up their nature will be reversed in intensity. Such variation accounts for the exciting individuality in human beings.

THE MELSAN   Mr. MelSan is usually a very gifted person, fully capable of being a musician who can steal the heart of an audience. As an artist, he not only draws or paints beautifully but can sell his own work—if he's in the right mood. It is not uncommon to encounter him in the field of education, for he makes a good scholar and probably the best of all classroom teachers, particularly

on the high school and college level. The melancholy in him will ferret out little-known facts and be exacting in the use of events and detail, while the sanguine will enable him to communicate well with students.

Mr. MelSan shows an interesting combination of mood swings. Be sure of this: he is an emotional creature! When circumstances are pleasing to him, he can reflect a fantastically happy mood. But if things work out badly or he is rejected, insulted, or injured, he drops into such a mood that his lesser sanguine nature drowns in the resultant sea of self-pity. He is easily moved to tears, feels everything deeply, but can be unreasonably critical and hard on others. He tends to be rigid and usually will not cooperate unless things go his way, which is often idealistic and impractical. He is often a fearful, insecure man with a poor self-image which limits him unnecessarily.

Many of the prophets were MelSans—John the Baptist, Elijah, Jeremiah, and others. They had a tremendous capacity to commune with God, were self-sacrificing people-helpers who had enough charisma to attract a following, tended to be legalistic in their teachings and calls to repentance, exhibited a flair for the dramatic, and willingly died for their principles.

THE MELCHLOR

The mood swings of the melancholy are usually stabilized by the MelChlor's self-will and determination. There is almost nothing vocationally which this man cannot do—and do well. He is both a perfectionist and a driver. He posseses strong leadership capabilities. Almost any craft, construction, or educational level is open to him. Unlike the MelSan, he may found his own institution or business and run it capably—not with noise and color but with efficiency. Many a great orchestra leader and choral conductor is a MelChlor.

The natural weaknesses of MelChlors reveal themselves in the mind, emotions, and mouth. They are extremely difficult people to please, rarely satisfying even themselves. Once they start thinking negatively about something or someone (including themselves), they can be intolerable to live with. Their mood follows their thought process.

Although they do not retain a depressed mood as long as the other blends of the melancholy, they can lapse into it more quickly. The two basic temperaments haunted by self-persecution, hostility, and criticism are the melancholy and the choleric. It is not uncommon for him to get angry at God as well as his fellow man, and if such thoughts persist long enough he may become manic-depressive. In extreme cases, he can become sadistic. When confronted with his vile thinking pattern and angry, bitter spirit, he can be expected to explode.

His penchant for detailed analysis and perfection tends to make him a nitpicker who drives others up the wall. Unless he is filled with God's Spirit or can maintain a positive frame of mind, he is not enjoyable company for long periods of time. No one is more painfully aware of this than his wife and children. He not only "emotes" disapproval, but feels compelled to castigate them verbally for their failures and to correct their mistakes—in public as well as in private. This man, by nature, desperately needs the love of God in his heart, and his family needs him to share it with them.

Many of the great men of the Bible show signs of a MelChlor temperament. Two that come to mind are Paul's tireless traveling companion, Dr. Luke, the painstaking scholar who carefully researched the life of Christ and left the church the most detailed account of our Lord's life, as well as the only record of the spread of the early church, and Moses, the great leader of Israel. Like many MelChlors, the latter never gained victory over his hostility and bitterness. Consequently, he died before his time. Like Moses, who wasted forty years on the backside of the desert, harboring bitterness and animosity before surrendering his life to God, many a MelChlor never lives up to his amazing potential because of the spirit of anger and revenge.

THE MELPHLEG

Some of the greatest scholars the world has ever known have been MelPhlegs. They are not nearly as prone to hostility as the two previous melancholies and usually get along well with others. These gifted introverts combine the analytical perfectionism of the melancholy with the organized efficiency of the phlegmatic. They are usually good-natured humanitarians who prefer a quiet, solitary environment for study and research to the endless rounds of activities sought by the more extroverted temperaments. MelPhlegs are usually excellent spellers and good mathematicians. These gifted people have greatly benefited humanity. Most of the world's significant inventions and medical discoveries have been made by MelPhlegs.

Despite his abilities, the MelPhleg, like the rest of us, has his own potential weaknesses. Unless controlled by God, he easily becomes discouraged and develops a very negative thinking pattern. But once he realizes it is a sin to develop the spirit of criticism and learns to rejoice, his entire outlook on life can be transformed. Ordinarily a quiet person, he is capable of inner angers and hostility caused by his tendency to be vengeful.

MelPhlegs are unusually vulnerable to fear, anxiety, and a negative self-image. It has always amazed me that the people with the greatest talents and capabilities are often victimized by genuine feelings of poor self-worth. Their strong tendency to be conscientious allows them to let others pressure them into making commitments that drain their energy and creativity. When filled with God's Spirit, these people are loved and admired by their family because their personal self-discipline and dedication are exemplary in the home. But humanitarian concerns can cause them to neglect their family. Unless they learn to pace themselves and enjoy diversions that help them relax, they often become early mortality statistics.

The most likely candidate for a MelPhleg in the Bible is the beloved Apostle John. He obviously had a very sensitive nature, for as a youth he laid his head on Jesus' breast at the Lord's Supper. On one occasion he became so angry at some people that he asked the Lord Jesus to call fire from heaven down on them. Yet at the crucifixion he was the lone disciple who devotedly stood at the cross. John was the one to whom the dying Jesus entrusted his mother. Later the disciple became a great church leader and left us five books in the New Testament, two of which (the Gospel of John and the Book of Revelation) particularly glorify Jesus Christ.

THE PHLEGSAN   The easiest of the twelve temperament blends
                       to get along with over a protracted period of
time is the PhlegSan. He is congenial, happy, cooperative, thoughtful, people-oriented, diplomatic, dependable, fun-loving, and humorous. A favorite with children and adults, he never displays an abrasive personality. He is usually a good family man who enjoys a quiet life and loves his wife and children. Ordinarily he attends a church where the

pastor is a good motivator; there he probably takes an active role.

The weaknesses of a PhlegSan are as gentle as his personality—unless you have to live with him all the time. Since he inherited the lack of motivation of a phlegmatic and the lack of discipline of a sanguine, it is not uncommon for the PhlegSan to fall far short of his true capabilities. He often quits school, passes up good opportunities, and avoids anything that involves "too much effort." Fear is another problem that accentuates his unrealistic feelings of insecurity. With more faith, he could grow beyond his timidity and self-defeating anxieties. However, he prefers to build a self-protective shell around himself and selfishly avoids the kind of involvement or commitment to activity that he needs and that would be a rich blessing to his partner and children. I have tremendous respect for the potential of these happy, contented people, but they must cooperate by letting God motivate them to unselfish activity.

The man in the Scripture that reminds me most of the PhlegSan is gentle, faithful, good-natured Timothy, the favorite spiritual son of the Apostle Paul. He was dependable and steady but timid and fearful. Repeatedly, Paul had to urge him to be more aggressive and to "do the work of an evangelist" (2 Tim. 4:5).

The PhlegChlor

The most active of all phlegmatics is the PhlegChlor. But it must be remembered that since he is predominantly a phlegmatic, he will never be a ball of fire. Like his brother phlegmatics, he is easy to get along with and may become an excellent group leader. The phlegmatic has the potential to become a good counselor, for he is an excellent listener, does not interrupt the client with stories about himself, and is genuinely interested in other people. Although the PhlegChlor rarely offers his services to others, when they come to his organized office where he exercises control, he is a first-rate professional. His advice will be practical, helpful, and—if he is a Bible-taught Christian—quite trustworthy. His gentle spirit never makes people feel threatened. He always does the right thing, but rarely goes beyond the norm. If his wife can make the adjustment to his passive life-style and reluctance to take the lead in the home, particularly in the discipline of their children, they can enjoy a happy marriage.

The weaknesses of the PhlegChlor are not readily apparent but gradually come to the surface, especially in the home. In addition to the lack of motivation and the fear problems of the other phlegmatics, he can be determinedly stubborn and unyielding. He doesn't blow up at others, but simply refuses to give in or cooperate. He is not a fighter by nature, but often lets his inner anger and stubbornness reflect itself in silence. The PhlegChlor often retreats to his "workshop" alone or nightly immerses his mind in TV. The older he gets, the more he selfishly indulges his sedentary tendency and becomes increasingly passive. Although he will probably live a long and peaceful life, if he indulges these passive feelings it is a boring life—not only for him, but also for his family. He needs to give himself to the concerns and needs of his family.

No man in the Bible epitomizes the PhlegChlor better than Abraham in the Old Testament. Fear characterized everything he did in the early days. For instance, he was reluctant to leave the security of the pagan city of Ur when God first called him; he even denied his wife on two occasions and tried to palm her off as his sister because of fear. Finally, he surrendered completely to God and grew in the Spirit. Accordingly, his greatest weakness became his greatest strength. Today, instead of being known as fearful Abraham, he has the reputation of being the man who "believed in the Lord; and he counted it unto him for righteousness."

THE PHLEGMEL

Of all the temperament blends, the PhlegMel is the most gracious, gentle, and quiet. He is rarely angry or hostile and almost never says anything for which he must apologize (mainly because he rarely says much). He never embarrasses himself or others, always does the proper thing, dresses simply, is dependable and exact. He tends to have the spiritual gifts of mercy and help, and he is neat and organized in his working habits. Like any phlegmatic, he is handy around the house and as energy permits will keep his home in good repair. If he has a wife who recognizes his tendencies toward passivity (but tactfully waits for him to take the lead in their home), they will have a good family life and marriage. However, if she resents his reticence to lead and be aggressive, she may become discontented and foment marital strife. He may neglect the discipline necessary to help prepare his children for a productive, self-disciplined life and so "provoke his children to wrath" just as much as the angry tyrant whose unreasonable discipline makes them bitter.

The other weaknesses of this man revolve around fear, selfishness, negativism, criticism, and lack of self-image. Once a PhlegMel realizes that only his fears and negative feelings about himself keep him from succeeding, he is able to come out of his shell and become an effective man, husband, and father. Most PhlegMels are so afraid of overextending themselves or getting overinvolved that they automatically refuse almost any kind of affiliation.

Personally I have never seen a PhlegMel overinvolved in anything— except in keeping from getting overinvolved. He must recognize that since he is not internally motivated, he definitely needs to accept more responsibility than he thinks he can fulfill, for that external stimulation will motivate him to greater achievement. All phlegmatics work well under pressure, but it must come from outside. His greatest source of motivation, of course, will be the power of the Holy Spirit.

Barnabas, the godly saint of the first-century church who accompanied the Apostle Paul on his first missionary journey, was in all probability a PhlegMel. He was the man who gave half his goods to the early church to feed the poor, the man who contended with Paul over providing John Mark (his nephew) another chance to serve God by accompanying them on the second missionary journey. Although the contention became so sharp that Barnabas took his nephew and they proceeded on their journey alone, Paul later commended Mark, saying, "He is profitable to me for the ministry" (2 Tim. 4:11). Today we have the Gospel of Mark because faithful, dedicated, and gentle Barnabas was willing to help him over a hard place in his life. PhlegMels respond to the needs of others if they will just let themselves move out into the stream of life and work with people where they are.

ADDITIONAL   With twelve temperament blends to choose
VARIABLES TO   from, it should be easier for you to identify
CONSIDER   with one of them than it was when presented
                    with only the four basic temperaments. Don't
be discouraged, however, if you find that you don't quite fit into any one of the twelve either. No two human beings are exactly alike. Consequently, other variables could alter the picture sufficiently so that

you will not fit any model precisely. Consider the following:

1. Your percentages may be different from the 60/40 I arbitrarily chose as a basis for this section. I think you will agree that it would be nearly impossible to detail all the conceivable mixtures of temperament. I leave that to the reader. For example, a MelChlor of 60/40 will be significantly different from an 80/20 MelChlor. Or consider the disparity between a 55/45 SanPhleg and an 85/15 SanPhleg. Only detailed scientific testing can establish an accurate diagnosis.

2. Different backgrounds and childhood training alter the expressions of identical temperament blends. For example, a SanPhleg raised by loving but firm parents will be much more disciplined than one raised by permissive parents. A MelPhleg brought up by cruel, hateful parents will be drastically different from one raised by tender, understanding parents. Both will share the same strengths and talents, but one may be overcome with hostility, depression, and self-persecution, so that he will never use his strengths. Although upbringing wields a powerful influence on the child, it is all but impossible to assess a wide variety of backgrounds in such a temperament analysis as this. I can only suggest that if the reader cannot identify his temperament blend readily, he will consider this variable.

3. You may not be objective when looking at yourself. Therefore, you may wish to discuss your temperament with loved ones and friends. All of us tend to view ourselves through rose-colored glasses. To paraphrase the yearning of the poet Robert Burns: "Oh, to see ourselves as others see us."

4. Education and I.Q. will often influence the appraisal of a person's temperament. For example, a MelSan with a very high I.Q. will appear somewhat different from one who is average or lower in intelligence. An uneducated person takes longer to mature than an educated man as a rule, because it may take much longer to excel at something and thus "find himself." By "educated" I include the trades. It is not uncommon for a man who learns a skill (such as plastering, plumbing, and so on) to be more outgoing, confident, and expressive than he would be otherwise. Even so, if you carefully study the strengths and weaknesses of people of a particular temperament blend, you will find, in spite of the I.Q., educational, or experience levels, they will be basically similar in their strengths and weaknesses.

5. Health and metabolism are important. A ChlorPhleg in top physical condition will be more aggressive than one with a faulty thyroid gland or other physical ailment. A nervous PhlegMel will also be more active than one who is suffering from low blood pressure. Recently I

worked with a hyperactive SanChlor minister who is a charming, superaggressive charger who made me tired just being around him. He was too powerful even to be a SanChlor. It didn't come as a surprise to learn that he had high blood pressure, which often produces the "hyper" dimension to any temperament.

6. Three temperaments are sometimes represented in one individual. In doing the research for my temperament test, I discovered a small percentage of people who have one predominant temperament with two secondary temperaments.

7. Motivation is the name of the game! "Out of [the heart] are the issues of life" (Prov. 4:23). If a person is properly motivated, it will have a marked impact on his behavior regardless of his temperament blend. Actually, that is why I have written this book—so people who are improperly motivated at present will experience the power of God to completely transform their behavior. I have heard testimonies that this has happened to thousands as a result of reading my other books on temperament or attending my lectures on the subject. I trust God will use this book with its greater detail and suggestions to help an even greater number of people.

8. The Spirit-controlled life is a behavior modifier. Mature Christians whose temperament has been modified by the Holy Spirit often find it difficult to analyze their temperamental makeup because they make the mistake of examining the temperament theory in light of their present behavior. Temperament is based on the natural man; there is nothing spiritual about it. That is why we find it so much easier to diagnose and classify an unsaved person or a carnal Christian than a dedicated, mature Christian. Because such a person has already had many of his natural weaknesses strengthened, it is difficult to assess his temperament. He should either concentrate only on his strengths or consider his behavior before he became a Spirit-controlled believer.

TEMPERAMENT   The temperament theory is not the final
THEORY—   answer to human behavior, and for these and
A USEFUL TOOL   other reasons it may not prove satisfactory to
                     everyone. But of all behavior theories ever
devised, it has served as the most helpful explanation. Additional factors could be included to explain some of the other differences in people, but these will suffice. If you keep them in mind, you will probably find that you and those you try to help in life fall into one of the twelve blends we have studied. Now a question arises: What can be done about it?

Evaluating Your Strengths and Weaknesses

Dr. Henry Brandt, a Christian psychologist, has probably helped more people than any other person in that profession. He certainly had a profound influence on this writer's life, both personally and in my role as a family counselor. He made a profound statement that I have never forgotten in relation to maturity. He defines a mature person in relation to his attitude toward his own strengths and weaknesses: "A mature person is one who is sufficiently objective about himself to know both his strengths and his weaknesses and has created a planned program for overcoming his weaknesses."

The Bible says, ". . . we are more than conquerers through him [Jesus Christ] that loved us" (Rom. 8:37). He has given us his Holy Spirit to strengthen our weaknesses so he can use us. We will now examine both your potential weaknesses and your potential strengths. Knowing both your strengths and weaknesses is the first giant step toward that mature person you have always wanted to be.

The chart we studied earlier listed ten strengths and ten of the most prominent weaknesses for each temperament. There are more, but based on my counseling, testing of thousands of people, and many years of observations I have selected these as the most common. First let's examine the strengths of each temperament.

SPARKY SANGUINE'S STRENGTHS

Sparky is not just an extrovert, he is a super-extrovert. Everything he does is superficial and external. He laughs loudly and dominates every conversation whether he has anything meaningful to say or not.

He loves the limelight and excels at public speaking. He rarely waits for others to speak first, but usually is the first to initiate a conversation.

Mr. or Mrs. Sanguine's ability to respond to others is instantaneous. If he catches another person looking at him, he always responds with a nod, wink, or greeting. No one enjoys life more than Sparky Sanguine. He never seems to lose his childlike curiosity for the things that surround him. Even the unpleasant things of life can be forgotten by his change of environment. It is a rare occasion when he does not awaken in a lively mood, and he will often be found whistling or singing his way through life.

The natural trait of Mr. Sanguine that produces both his hearty and optimistic disposition is defined by Dr. Hallesby, a European authority on this subject: "The sanguine person has a God-given ability to live in the present." He easily forgets the past, and is seldom frustrated or fearful of future difficulties. The sanguine person is optimistic.

He is easily inspired to engage in new plans and projects, and his boundless enthusiasm often carries others along with him. If yesterday's project has failed, he is confident that the project he is working on today will definitely succeed. The outgoing, handshaking, backslapping customs of the cheerful sanguine stem basically from his genuine love for people. He enjoys being around others, sharing in their joys and sorrows, and he likes to make new friends. No one makes a better first impression.

One of the greatest assets of Mr. Sanguine is that he has a tender, compassionate heart. No one responds more genuinely to the needs of others than the sanguine. He is able to share the emotional experiences, both good and bad, of others. By nature, he finds it easy to obey

the scriptural injunction, "Rejoice with those that do rejoice, and weep with those who weep."

The sincerity of Mr. Sanguine is often misunderstood by others. They are deceived by his sudden changes of emotion, and they fail to understand that he is genuinely responding to the emotions of others. No one can love you more nor forget you faster than sanguines. The world is enriched by these cheerful, responsive people. When motivated and disciplined by God, they can be great servants of Jesus Christ.

ROCKY CHOLERIC'S STRENGTHS

Mr. Choleric is usually a self-disciplined individual with a strong tendency towards self-determination. He is very confident in his own ability and very aggressive.

Once having embarked upon a project, he has a tenacious ability that keeps him doggedly driving in one direction. His singleness of purpose often results in accomplishment.

The choleric temperament is given over almost exclusively to the practical aspects of life. Everything to him is considered in the light of its utilitarian purpose, and he is happiest when engaged in some worthwhile project. He has a keen mind for organization but finds detail work distressing. Many of his decisions are reached by intuition more than by analytical reasoning.

Mr. Choleric has strong leadership tendencies. His forceful will tends to dominate a group, he is a good judge of people, and he is quick and bold in emergencies. He not only will readily accept leadership when it is placed on him, but will often be the first to volunteer for it. If he does not become too arrogant or bossy, others respond well to his practical direction.

When Rocky sets his mind to do something,

he never gives up. Just about the time his optimism has come home to engulf him in impossibility, he doggedly burrows out another way. And if people don't agree with him, that's just too bad—he is going to do it with or without them. What other people think of him or his projects makes very little difference to him.

No one is more practical than a choleric. He seems to have a utilitarian mentality. He has strong workaholic tendencies. Mr. Choleric's outlook on life, based on his natural feeling of self-confidence, is almost always one of optimism. He has such an adventuresome spirit that he thinks nothing of leaving a secure position for the challenge of the unknown. Adversity does not discourage him. Instead, it whets his appetite and makes him even more determined to achieve his objective.

MARTIN MELANCHOLY'S STRENGTHS

Usually melancholies have the highest I.Q. of any member in their family. They may be musical, artistic, or athletic. Sometimes you will find all these traits in one individual.

Mr. Melancholy has by far the richest and most sensitive nature of all the temperaments. A higher percentage of geniuses are melancholy than any other type. He particularly excels in the fine arts, with a vast appreciation for life's cultural values. He is emotionally responsive, but unlike the sanguine is motivated to reflective thinking through his emotions. Mr. Melancholy is particularly adept at creative thinking, and during high emotional peaks will often launch into an invention or creative production that is worthwhile and wholesome.

Mr. Melancholy has strong perfectionist tendencies. His standard of excellence exceeds others', and his requirements of acceptability in

any field are often higher than either he or anyone else can maintain. The analytical abilities of the melancholy, combined with his perfectionist tendencies, make him a "hound for detail." Whenever a project is suggested, Mr. Melancholy can analyze it in a few moments and pick out every potential problem.

A melancholy person can always be depended upon to finish his job in the prescribed time or to carry his end of the load. Mr. Melancholy rarely seeks the limelight, but prefers to do the behind-the-scenes task. He often chooses a very sacrificial vocation for life, for he has an unusual desire to give himself to the betterment of his fellow men.

He is prone to be reserved and seldom volunteers his opinion or ideas. Melancholy temperaments are extremely self-disciplined individuals. They rarely eat too much or indulge their own comforts. When they engage a task, they will work around the clock to meet deadlines and their high self-imposed standards. One of the reasons they can go into a deep depression after completion of a big project is because they have so neglected themselves seeing the task to completion by going without sleep, food, and diversion that they are literally exhausted physically and emotionally.

PHIL PHLEGMATIC'S STRENGTHS

Just because they are superintroverts does not mean phlegmatics are not strong. Actually the phlegmatic's calm and unexcited nature is a vital asset. There are things he can do and vocations he can pursue that extroverts could never do. Phlegmatics rarely, if ever, leap before they look. They are thinkers and planners.

Phil is a born diplomat. Conciliatory by nature, he does not like confrontation and would rather negotiate than fight. He has a knack for defusing the hostile and excitable types and is a walking example that "a soft answer turns away wrath."

The unexcited good humor of the phlegmatic keeps him from being intensely involved with life so that he can often see humor in the most mundane experiences. He seems to have a superb inborn sense of timing in the art of humor and a stimulating imagination.

Mr. Phlegmatic is dependability itself. Not only can he be depended upon to always be his cheerful, good-natured self, but he can be depended upon to fulfill his obligations and time schedules. Like the melancholy, he is a very faithful friend, and although he does not get too involved with others he rarely proves disloyal.

Mr. Phlegmatic is also practical and efficient. Not prone to making sudden decisions, he has a tendency to find the practical way to accomplish an objective with the least amount of effort. He often does his best work under circumstances that would cause other temperaments to "crack." His work always bears the hallmark of neatness and efficiency. Although he is not a perfectionist, he does have exceptionally high standards of accuracy and precision.

The administrative or leadership capabilities of a phlegmatic are seldom discovered because he is not assertive and doesn't push himself. But when once given the responsibility, he has a real ability to get people to work together productively and in an organized manner.

SUMMARY

The variety of strengths provided by the four temperament types keeps the world functioning properly. No one temperament is more desirable than another. Each one has its vital strengths and makes its worthwhile contribution to life.

Someone facetiously pointed out this sequence of events involving the four temperaments: "The hard-driving choleric produces the inventions of the genius-prone melancholy, which are sold by the personable sanguine and enjoyed by the easygoing phlegmatic."

The strengths of the four temperaments make each of them attractive, and we can be grateful that we all possess some of these strengths. But there is more to the story! As important as are the temperament strengths, even more important, for our purposes, are their weaknesses. It is our intent to contrast the strengths of the temperaments with their weaknesses. Our purpose in so doing is to help you diagnose your own weaknesses and develop a planned program for overcoming them.

Don't be afraid to be objective about yourself or to face your weaknesses. Many people have decided what basic temperament they are at this point in the study, then changed their mind when confronted with their unpleasant weaknesses. Strengths carry corresponding weaknesses, so face them realistically, then let God do something to improve them.

Temperament Weaknesses

This will doubtless be the most painful section in this book. For no one likes to be confronted with his weaknesses. But if we think of ourselves only in terms of the strengths of our temperament, we will develop a faulty view of ourselves. Everyone has weaknesses.

THE SANGUINE WEAKNESSES

Sanguines are voted "most likely to succeed" in college, but often fail in life. Their tendency to be weak-willed and undisciplined will finally destroy them unless it is overcome. Since they are highly emotional, exude considerable natural charm, and are prone to be what one psychologist called "touchers" (they tend to touch people as they talk to them), they commonly have a great appeal for the opposite sex and consequently face sexual temptation more than others. Weakness of will and lack of discipline make it easier for them to be deceitful, dishonest, and undependable.

They tend to overeat and gain weight, finding it most difficult to remain on a diet. Someone has said, "Without self-discipline, there is no such thing as success." Lack of discipline is Mr. Sanguine's greatest weakness.

The only temperament more emotional than a sanguine is a melancholy, but he isn't anywhere near as expressive as Sparky Sanguine. Not only can Sparky cry at the drop of a hat (one pro football player's wife won't watch a sad film on TV with her husband because "his blubbering embarrasses me!"), but his spark of anger can instantly become a raging inferno.

A lack of emotional consistency usually limits him vocationally, and it certainly destroys him spiritually. When filled with the Spirit, however, he becomes a "new creature," an emotionally controlled sanguine.

Every human being is plagued with egotism, but sanguines have a double dose of the problem. That's why a Spirit-filled Sparky is easily detected; he will reflect an unnatural spirit of humility that is refreshing.

Sanguines are notoriously disorganized and always on the move. They seldom plan ahead but usually take things as they come. They rarely profit by past mistakes and seldom look ahead. As one man said, "They are a disorganized accident waiting to happen."

Wherever Sparky works or lives, things are in a disastrous state of disarray. He can never find his tools, even though they are right where he left them. Sparky's garage, bedroom, closet, and office are disaster areas unless he has an efficient wife and secretary to pick up after him. His egotism usually makes him a sharp dresser, but if his friends or customers could see the room where he dressed, they would fear that someone had been killed in the explosion. How does Sparky get by with that kind of living? The way Mr. Sanguine handles all confrontations caused by his temperament—a disarming smile, a pat on the back, a funny story, and a restless move to the next thing that sparks his interest. The sanguine will never become a perfectionist, but the Spirit of

God can bring more planning and order into his life. And when that happens, Sparky is a much happier person—not only with others but also with himself.

Behind that superextroverted personality that frequently overpowers other people, giving him a false reputation as a very self-confident person, Sparky Sanguine is really quite insecure. His insecurity is often the source of his vile profanity.

Sanguines are not usually fearful of personal injury and often resort to outlandish feats of daring and heroism. Their fears most often arise in the area of personal failure, rejection, or disapproval. That's why they often follow an obnoxious display of conversation with an equally mindless statement. Rather than face your disapproval, they are hoping to cover up the first goof with something that will gain your approval.

Perhaps the sanguine's most treacherous trait, one that really stifles his spiritual potential, is his weak or flexible conscience. He usually is able to talk others into his way of thinking, earning him the reputation of being the world's greatest con artist. When things go wrong, he has no difficulty convincing himself that whatever he did was justified. He "bends the truth" until any similarity between his story and the facts is totally coincidental; yet this rarely bothers him, for he cons himself into believing that "the end justifies the means."

Others often find it incredible that he can lie, cheat, or steal, yet seldom endure a sleepless night. That is why he frequently walks over the rights of others and rarely hesitates to take advantage of other people.

Sooner or later, Sparky Sanguine will weave a web of deceit that will produce his own destructon. The Bible says, "Be not deceived; God is not mocked: for whatsoever a man soweth, that shall he also reap" (Gal. 6:7). The only way to conquer that problem is to concentrate on truth and honesty. Every time a man lies or cheats, it becomes easier—and the next temptation is bigger.

Sparky Sanguine's penchant for exaggeration, embellishment, and plain old-fashioned deceit catches up with him most quickly in his marriage and family. While he may fool those who see him occasionally, it is impossible for him to cheat and deceive his way through life without teaching his wife and children that they cannot depend on his word. One of the nine necessary building blocks in any love relationship (according to 1 Cor. 13:4-8) is trust. Part of the reason our Lord and the Scriptures speak so frequently on the subject of truth or honesty is that it not only produces the necessary clear conscience all men need, but it creates the kind of foundation on which lasting and enjoyable interpersonal relationships are made.

THE CHOLERIC WEAKNESSES

Cholerics are extremely hostile people. Some learn to control their anger, but eruption into violence is always a possibility with them. If their strong will is not brought into control by proper parental discipline as children, they develop angry, tumultuous habits that plague them all through life. It doesn't take them long to learn that others are usually afraid of their angry outbursts and thus they may use wrath as a weapon to get what they want—which is usually their own way. The choleric can cause pain to others and enjoy it. His wife is usually afraid of him, and he tends to terrify his children.

Rocky Choleric often reminds me of a walking Mount Vesuvius, constantly gurgling until, provoked, he spills out his bitter lava all over someone or something. He is a door slammer, table pounder, and horn blower. Any person or thing that gets in his way, retards his progress, or fails to perform up to the level of his expectations will feel the eruption of his wrath.

No one utters more caustic comments than a sarcastic choleric! He is usually ready with a cutting comment that can wither the insecure and devastate the less combative. Even Sparky Sanguine is no match for him, because Sparky isn't cruel or mean. Rocky will rarely hesitate to tell a person off or chop him to bits. Consequently, he leaves a path of damaged psyches and fractured egos wherever he goes.

It is a happy choleric (and his family members) who discovers that the tongue is either a vicious weapon of destruction or a tool of healing. Once he learns the importance of his verbal approval and encouragement to others, he will seek to control his speech—until he gets angry, whereupon he discovers with the Apostle James that "the tongue can no man tame; it is an unruly evil, full of deadly poison" (James 3:8). Ready speech and an angry spirit often combine to make a choleric very profane.

The milk of human kindness has all but dried up in the veins of a choleric. He is the most unaffectionate of all the temperaments and becomes emotionally spastic at the thought of any public show of emotion. Marital affection to him means a kiss at the wedding and on every fifth anniversary thereafter. His emotional rigidity rarely permits him the expression of tears. He usually stops crying at the age of eleven or twelve and finds it difficult to understand others when they are moved to tears.

Similar to his natural lack of love is the choleric's tendency to be insensitive to others' needs and inconsiderate of their feelings. When a choleric is sensitive and considerate, he can be a great blessing to others, for, as we have seen, what he thinks of others is of vital importance to them. By nature Rocky Choleric has the hide of a rhinoceros. However, the Spirit of God will make him "kind, tenderhearted. . . ."

The choleric's natural determination is a temperament asset that stands him in good stead throughout life, but it can make him opinionated and bullheaded. Since he has an intuitive sense, he usually makes up his mind quickly (without adequate analysis and deliberation), and once made up, it is almost impossible to change. No temperament type more typifies the old cliche: "Don't confuse me with the facts; my mind is made up."

One of the undesirable characteristics of the choleric involves his inclination to be crafty if necessary to get his own way. He rarely takes

no for an answer and will often resort to any means necessary to achieve his ends. If he has to juggle his figures and bend the truth, he rarely hesitates, for to him the end justifies the means.

Since he easily comes to conclusions, he finds great delight in making decisions for other people and forcing them to conform to his will. If you work for a choleric, you rarely wonder what he wants you to do, for he tells you five times before eight-thirty in the morning—and usually at the top of his lungs.

The Rocky Cholerics of life are very effective people if their weaknesses are not indulged until they become a dominating life-style. When they are filled with the Spirit, their tendencies toward willfulness and harshness are replaced by a gentleness which verifies clearly that they are controlled by something other than their own natural temperament. From the days of the Apostle Paul until the present, both the church of Jesus Christ and society have benefited much from these active, productive people. Many of our great church institutions were founded by venturous cholerics. But to be effective in God's service, they must learn the divine principles of productivity.

THE MELANCHOLY WEAKNESSES

The admirable qualities of perfectionism and conscientiousness often carry with them the serious disadvantages of negativism, pessimism, and a spirit of criticism. Anyone who has worked with a gifted melancholy can anticipate that his first reaction to anything will be negative or pessimistic. This one trait limits a melancholy's vocational performance more than any other. The minute a new idea or project is presented, his analytical ability ignites and he begins to concoct every problem and difficulty that may be encountered in the effort. The most damaging influence upon a person's mind, in my opinion, is criticism; and melancholies have to fight that spirit constantly. I have observed that the most psychologically disturbed children come from homes of predominantly melancholy or choleric parents. Cholerics are hard to please; melancholies are impossible to satisfy. Even when the children bring home B's and Bpluses, the parent will grimace with dissatisfaction because they didn't get A's. Instead of commending their wives and encouraging them, melancholies criticize, carp, and censure. Even when they realize the importance of their approval to both wife and children, it is hard for them to offer it because they cannot endure the hypocritical taint of saying something that isn't 100 percent true.

The same high standard is usually turned inward by a melancholy, making him very dissatisfied with himself. Self-examination, of course, is a healthy thing for any Christian who wants to walk in the Spirit, for through it he gains the realization that he must confess his sins and seek the Savior's forgiveness (1 John 1:9). But the melancholy is not satisfied to examine himself; he dissects himself with a continuing barrage of introspection until he has no self-confidence or self-esteem left.

Everything in life is interpreted by the melancholy in relation to himself. He tends to compare himself with others on looks, talent, and intellect, invariably feeling deficient because it never occurs to him that he compares himself to the best of another's traits and fails to evaluate their weaknesses.

He is ever examining his spiritual life and typically coming up short in his own mind. This keeps him from enjoying confidence before God. A melancholy finds it difficult to believe he is "approved of God," basically because he can seldom approve himself.

This self-centered trait, together with his sensitive nature, makes a melancholy thin-skinned and touchy at times. Although not as expressive of his anger as the sanguine or choleric, he is very capable of long-term seething and slow-burning anger in the form of revengeful thinking patterns and self-persecution reveries. If indulged long enough, this can make him manic-depressive or at least erupt into an angry outburst that is unlike his normally gentle nature.

One of the most prominent characteristics of a melancholy's temperament concerns his mood swings. On some occasions he is so "high" that he acts like a sanguine; on others he is so "down" that he

feels like sliding under the door rather than opening it. The older he gets (unless transformed by a vital relationship to Jesus Christ), the more he is prone to experience dark moods. During such times he is gloomy, irritable, unhappy, and all but impossible to please. Such moods make him particularly vulnerable to depression.

Three years ago I read an article on depression in *Newsweek* magazine that stated: "Depression is the emotional epidemic of our times. Fifty thousand to seventy thousand depressed individuals commit suicide annually." Having counseled over one thousand depressed people by that time, I felt compelled to write a book, *How to Win Over Depression*; it became a best-seller in only three months.

Anyone with a depression problem, particularly a melancholy, should make 1 Thessalonians 5:18 a way of life: "In every thing give thanks: for this is the will of God in Christ Jesus concerning you." You cannot rejoice and give thanks over something while maintaining a state of depression.

No other temperament is so apt to be rigid, implacable, and uncompromising to the point of unreasonableness as the melancholy. He is intolerant and impatient with those who do not see things his way; consequently he finds it difficult to be a team player and is often a loner in the business world, but at home it is a different matter. A wife and children subjected to such rigid standards will often become insecure and unhappy and sometimes give up on him. Once he learns that flexibility and cooperation are the oil that makes interpersonal relationships run smoothly, he is a much happier person and so are those around him.

We have already seen that the melancholy is an idealist, a trait we list as a strength. However, on the other side of that characteristic, he is apt to be impractical and theoretical, often campaigning for an ideal that is so altruistic it will never work. A melancholy should always subject his plans to the practicality test.

God has used many melancholies who made their talents available to him. In fact, many of the characters recorded in the Bible were melancholies. However, the key to their success was not their temperament, talents, or gifts, but their commitment to the Holy Spirit.

THE PHLEGMATIC WEAKNESSES

The most obvious of Phil Phlegmatic's weaknesses and that which caused Hippocrates (who originated the idea of the four temperaments) to label him phlegm (slow or sluggish) is his apparent lack of drive and ambition. Although he always seems to do what is expected of him, he will rarely do more. Rarely does he instigate an activity, but thinks up excuses to avoid getting involved with the activities of others.

More than any other temperament, the phlegmatic is vulnerable to the law of inertia: "A body at rest tends to stay at rest." He needs to reverse that trend with premeditated activity. Both he and his family will benefit by such efforts.

No one likes to be hurt, and that is particularly true of Phil Phlegmatic. Although not as sensitive as a melancholy, he does have a thin skin and accordingly learns early in life to live like a turtle—that is, to build a hard shell of self-protection to shield him from all outside griefs or affronts. But even a turtle could give Phil a valuable piece of advice: "You can never go anywhere unless you stick your neck out." Nor will you ever help anyone else unless you risk the possibility of an emotional injury.

One of the less obvious weaknesses of the phlegmatic is his selfishness. Every temperament faces the problem of selfishness, but Phil is particularly afflicted with the disease, though he is so gracious and proper that few people who don't live with him are aware of it. Selfishness makes him self-indulgent and unconcerned about his family's need for activity.

No one can be more stubborn than a phlegmatic, but he is so diplomatic about it that he may proceed halfway through life before others catch on. He almost never openly

confronts another person or refuses to do something, but he will somehow manage to sidestep the demand. In church administration I have found this gracious, kindly, placid individual to be most exasperating at times. He will smile as I detail the program, even nod his head as if he understands, and then walk away and ignore the mandate. He simply will do it his way—quite affably and with less contention than any other temperament, but definitely his way. In a family situation, phlegmatics never yell or argue; they just drag their feet or set their legs and will not budge.

Beneath the gracious surface of a diplomatic phlegmatic beats a very fearful heart. He is a worrier by nature who erroneously seems to misinterpret Philippians 4:6 as: "Be anxious for everything, and by worry and fear let your requests be made known unto God." This fear tendency often keeps him from venturing out on his own to make full use of his potential.

Fear keeps phlegmatics from being used in the church. I'm convinced that they would like to teach, sing in the choir, or learn to share their faith, but fear stifles them. One of the strengths of the Holy Spirit is faith, which dissolves our fears. A salient result of reading and studying the Word of God is a growing faith. Most people are fearful of failure, but those who succeed in effectively serving God replace their fears with faith.

I have found it well worth the time to try motivating phlegmatics to work in the church. They make good board members and policy-makers as well as excellent Sunday school teachers and department superintendents. Once committed, they become very dependable workers for many years. The difficult task is to get them to agree to an assignment in the first place.

SUMMARY

Now you have the bad news—all temperaments have weaknesses. At least ten according to their temperament. But there is a power that can enable you to improve your temperament. Read on.

CHAPTER FOUR

Strengthening Your Weaknesses

One thing about temperament—it never changes. If your parents' genes combined to make you a ChlorSan, a MelPhleg, or a SanMelPhleg, you will never be anything else. Like your appearance, height, and I.Q., your temperament will be a part of you as long as you live. And remember, your temperament probably has more to do with your current behavior than anything else in your life. The rest is the result of your childhood training, home life, education, motivation, and other things. The following formula will put it all together for you.

BEHAVIOR FORMULA

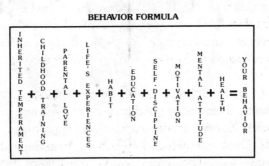

INHERITED TEMPERAMENT + CHILDHOOD TRAINING + PARENTAL LOVE + LIFE'S EXPERIENCES + HABIT + EDUCATION + SELF-DISCIPLINE + MOTIVATION + MENTAL ATTITUDE + HEALTH = YOUR BEHAVIOR

As you look over this list, you are probably struck with the realization that you have very little control over most of the ingredients in this formula. Don't be deceived! It is true that you cannot change your temperament, but there are three things in that formula that you do control and so can improve your temperament and change your life: motivation, mental attitude, and habit.

Your Motivational Potential

When God created Adam, he made him unique from all other living creatures. He gave him a "soul." This soul not only has a capacity for God but is a source of external motivation that is all but untapped by most people today. But it does account for the tremendous transformation that occurs in people when they have a "born again" experience with Jesus Christ. To understand this, you must visualize the four parts of human nature as described in the Bible.

Jesus Christ knew more about human nature than anyone who has ever lived. (He should, for he was the Creator of man in the first place.) And he said, "Thou shalt love the Lord thy God with all thy heart, and with all thy soul, and with all thy mind, and with all thy strength" (Mark 12:30). Notice carefully the four aspects of human nature: heart, soul, mind, strength. Notice these on the following chart.

THE NATURAL MAN

1) Heart: The emotional center—source of feeling and motivation. "As a man thinks in his heart so is he."

2) Soul: Source of human life and the will. God has given each person sovereignty over his own will. Your self is by nature the control mechanism of your will.

3) Mind: The most incredible organ in the body. It contains twelve billion brain cells, and how you fill those cells influences your feelings, which in turn influences everything you do.

4) Strength: This refers to the perishable part of man, or that which we see the most.

Your inherited temperament probably resides in the heart, where it influences the method of your thinking—not the content. It can be influenced by the mind, soul, and heart. It is what the Bible means when it speaks of "the flesh" or "nature" or "natural man."

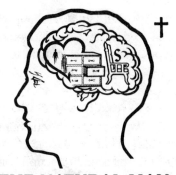

Guilt
Fear
Emptiness
Misery
Purposelessness
Confusion

THE NATURAL MAN

Christ is not in the natural man; he is outside his life. He knocks at the door of our life through the convicting of the Holy Spirit in preaching, tracts, radio, television, personal witness, etc. If God's Spirit is not *within* him, he will experience the guilt, fear, emptiness, misery, purposelessness, confusion, and other negative things pictured above. The amount of negative feelings will depend on his willfulness and sin. His greatest need is his emptiness—his unfilled "God-shaped vacuum" that Pascal said was in the heart of every man and can be filled with no one save Jesus Christ. This emptiness that plagues mankind all through life not only cheats man out of God's daily presence in his life, but His power to improve his temperament.

God never forces his way into a person's life; he leaves it to an individual to decide whether or not to receive Christ as his Savior and Lord. But if you believe Jesus Christ died for your sins and rose again the third day, you can humbly repent of your sins and submit your will to him by praying a simple but beautiful prayer like this: "O God, I know I am a sinner and have willfully disobeyed you many times. I believe Jesus died for my sins and rose again that I might have eternal life. Therefore, I invite you to come into my life to both save me from my sins and to direct my future. Today I give myself to you."

"As many as received him [Jesus], to them gave he the power to become the sons of God" (John 1:12). All who believe in him are born again and have two natures. The new one is the new man in Christ, opening up a whole new source of power. The old nature still wants to sin.

Both natures are alive. Which one is dominant depends on which one you feed the most. If you feed the old nature the food of the sin-sick culture that surrounds us, don't be surprised when the weaknesses of your temperament dominate you. If, however, you feed your new nature the spiritual food of the Word of God and things pertaining to God, your new nature will become so dominant it will overcome the natural weakness of your temperament, enabling God to make maximum use of your inherited strengths or talents.

Who's in Control?

We hear a lot in our humanistic culture about "taking control of your life." That sounds good at first, but if you look deeper into this cult of the self-actualizers, you will find the worst sin of all—selfishness.

God wants to control your life. He makes no secret of that. He challenges us, "Therefore, I urge you, brothers, in view of God's mercy, to offer your bodies as living sacrifices, holy and pleasing to God—which is your spiritual worship. Do not conform any longer to the pattern of this world, but be transformed by the renewing of your mind. Then you will be able to test and approve what God's will is—his good, pleasing, and perfect will" (Rom. 12:1-2, NIV). Who controls your life? It is not hard to tell. Ask yourself, "Do I do what Jesus Christ wants or what I want?" Jesus said, "If you love me keep my commandments." It is ridiculous to sing "Oh, How I Love Jesus" while doing as you please with your life. When Christ is in control, you will do what he tells you in his Word.

Three Modern Life-Styles

There are only three possible life-styles today. You should analyze which is yours and see if the results of that kind of life are what you really want.

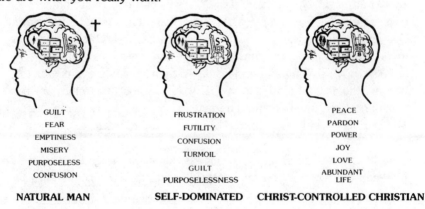

GUILT	FRUSTRATION	PEACE
FEAR	FUTILITY	PARDON
EMPTINESS	CONFUSION	POWER
MISERY	TURMOIL	JOY
PURPOSELESS	GUILT	LOVE
CONFUSION	PURPOSELESSNESS	ABUNDANT LIFE
NATURAL MAN	**SELF-DOMINATED**	**CHRIST-CONTROLLED CHRISTIAN**

Note the similarity of results in the two life-styles pictured above where self is on the throne. The only real difference between 1 and 2 is that Christ was at one time invited into the Christian's life and he will go to heaven when he dies. But he is as miserable as the individual who doesn't know Christ. In fact, some times he is more miserable because the Holy Spirit can convict him from within. Both of these individuals will be dominated by their natural temperament weaknesses.

The third drawing illustrates the individual who has surrendered the center of his life to Christ (or most of the time lives this way—no one is perfect). We all give in to the flesh on occasion, but at least this person has the capability of living up to his divine potential.

How to Strengthen Your Weaknesses

"Therefore, if anyone is in Christ, he is a new creation; the old has gone, the new has come!" (2 Cor. 5:17, NIV).

One of the fundamental premises of the Christian life is, "When a natural individual is indwelt by a supernatural power, he ought to be different!" Think about that. If God is *really* in your life, you will be different than if he were not.

But it is also true that growth takes place *slowly.* You don't see much growth in a fruit tree on a daily basis, but there is growth if the tree is alive. So it is with a Christian. The growth in us is painfully slow sometimes, but it does take place.

The Power to Change

What will be different after the Holy Spirit of God comes to reside in you? Your looks? Unfortunately not. Will you get smarter? No! What changes? Your *emotions.* The Holy Spirit of God brings emotional stability into our lives.

Paul describes it in these words, "The fruit of the Spirit is love, joy, peace, patience, kindness, goodness, faithfulness, gentleness and self-control (Gal. 5:22-23, NIV). As you study these verses, you discover nine specific strengths that God provides the Christian to enable him to overcome his emotional weaknesses. The Spirit-controlled Christian will be an emotionally controlled Christian.

The nine emotional strengths of the Spirit-filled temperament make any temperament what God originally intended. It does not matter what one's natural temperament is. Any man filled with the Holy Spirit, whether sanguine, choleric, melancholy, or phlegmatic, is going to manifest these nine spiritual characteristics. He will have his own natural strengths and maintain his individuality, but the Spirit will transform his weaknesses.

These nine characteristics represent what God wants each one of his children to be. We shall examine each in detail. There is a longing in the heart of every child of God to live this kind of a life. It is not the result of man's effort, but the supernatural result of the Holy Spirit controlling every area of a Christian.

LOVE

The first characteristic in God's catalog of Spirit-filled temperament traits is love—love for God and for our fellow men. The Lord Jesus said, "Love the Lord your God with all your heart and with all your soul and with all your mind and with all your strength. . . . Love your neighbor as yourself" (Mark 12:30, NIV).

A love for God that causes a man to be more interested in the Kingdom of God than in the material kingdom in which he lives is supernatural, for man by nature is a greedy creature.

The Christian who says he is "filled with the Spirit," but is unmoved by the suffering of others, is kidding himself. If we have the love of God flowing through us, it will benefit others around us.

I must also point out that the love God's Spirit provides makes us want to obey him. If you would like to test your love for God, try this simple method given by the Lord Jesus: "If ye love me, keep my commandments." Just ask yourself, "Am I obedient to his commandments as revealed in his Word?" If not, you are not filled with the Holy Spirit.

JOY

The second temperament characteristic of the Spirit-filled man is joy. One theologian gave this comment concerning the gracious emotion of joy: "Yes, joy is one of the cardinal Christian virtues; it deserves a place next to love. Pessimism is a grave fault. This is not fatuous joy such as the world accepts; it is the enduring joy that bubbles up from all the grace of God in our posses-

sion, from the blessedness that is ours, that is undimmed by tribulation. . . ."

The joy provided by the Holy Spirit is not limited by circumstances. No Christian can have joy if he depends upon the circumstances of life. The Spirit-filled life is characterized by a "looking unto Jesus the author and finisher of our faith," which causes us to know that "in all things God works for the good of those who love him, who have been called according to his purpose" (Rom. 8:28, NIV).

In the Scriptures, "joy" and "rejoicing" are not the result of self-effort, but are the work of the Holy Spirit in your life. "You have filled my heart with greater joy than when their grain and new wine abound" (Ps. 4:7, NIV). The Apostle Paul, writing from a prison dungeon, said, "Rejoice in the Lord always. I will say it again: Rejoice!" (Phil. 4:4, NIV). Any man that can rejoice in prison has to have a supernatural source of power!

This supernatural joy is available for any Christian regardless of his basic or natural temperament. Jesus said, "These things have I spoken unto you, that my joy might remain in you, and that your joy might be full" (John 15:11). This is only possible as we are filled with the Holy Spirit.

Martin Luther said, "God does not like doubt and dejection. He hates dreary doctrine, gloomy and melancholy thought. God likes cheerful hearts. Christ says: 'Rejoice, for your names are written in heaven.' "

PEACE

The third temperament trait of the Spirit-filled man is peace. The preceding verses in Galatians 5 describe not only the works of the natural man without the Spirit, but also his emotions. His emotional turbulence is described by " . . . hatred, variance (strivings), emulations, wrath, strife, seditions, heresies." We see that the further man gets from God, the less he knows of peace.

The "peace" spoken of here is really twofold. It is peace with God and the peace of God. The Lord Jesus said, "Peace I leave with you, my peace I give unto you" (John 14:27). The peace he leaves us is peace with God. "My peace I give unto you" is the peace of God, for in the same verse he defines it as the peace of an untroubled heart: "Let not your heart be troubled, neither let it be afraid." And the preceding verse describes the coming of the Holy Spirit. The Holy Spirit is the source of peace.

Peace with God is the result of salvation by faith. Man outside of Jesus Christ knows nothing of peace in relationship with God, because his sin is ever before him and he knows he is accountable before God at the Judgment. However, when this individual takes Jesus Christ at his word and invites him into his life as Lord and Savior, Jesus Christ not only comes in as he promised to do (Rev. 3:20), but immediately cleanses all his sin (1 John 1-7, 9). "Therefore being justified by faith, we have peace with God through our Lord Jesus Christ" (Rom. 5:1).

The peace of God, the antidote to worry, is not as automatically possessed by Christians as the peace with God. This peace, enabling one to be untroubled in the face of difficult circumstances, is illustrated by the Lord Jesus who was sound asleep in the lower part of the ship while the twelve disciples were frightened beyond rationality. Many are prone to worry, further complicating their emotional, physical, and spiritual life, while those who believe God get a good night's sleep, awaken refreshed and available for God's use the next day.

Just becoming a Christian does not spare us from the difficult circumstances of life. However, the Holy Spirit's presence in our lives can supply us with one of life's greatest treasures: the peace of God, in spite of any circumstances. The Apostle Paul had this in mind when he wrote the words, "Be careful (worried or anxious) for nothing; but in every thing by prayer and supplication with thanksgiving let your requests be made known unto God. And the peace of God, which passeth all understanding, shall keep your hearts and minds through Christ Jesus" (Phil. 4:6, 7). The Holy Spirit longs to give such peace to every believer.

LONGSUFFERING

The fourth temperament trait of the Spirit-filled man is longsuffering (also known as patience or endurance). It can be characterized by an ability to bear injuries or suffer reproof or affliction without answering in kind. As the Apostle Peter said about the Lord Jesus, ". . . who, when he was reviled, reviled not again." A longsuffering person is one who can do the menial, forgotten, and difficult tasks of life graciously—as unto the Lord—without complaining or seething. He finishes his task or suffers affronts while manifesting the loving Spirit of Christ.

GENTLENESS

The fifth characteristic of the Spirit-filled temperament is described in the King James Version as gentleness. This is a thoughtful, polite, gracious, considerate, understanding act of kindness stemming from a tender heart. The world in which we live knows little of such tenderheartedness. It is the result of the compassion of the Holy Spirit for a lost and dying humanity.

The Lord Jesus' gentle spirit contrasted sharply with the disciples' cruel attitude toward the children who had been brought by their parents to be blessed by him. The Scripture tells us that the disciples rebuked those who brought them, but Jesus said, "Suffer the little children to come unto me, and forbid them not" (Mark 10:13-14).

This gentle characteristic of the Holy Spirit never asks such questions as, "How often must I forgive my brother when he sins against me?" or, "Isn't there a limit to how much a person can stand?" The Holy Spirit is able to give gentleness in the face of all kinds of pressures.

Jesus, who possessed the Holy Spirit "without measure," pictured himself as a shepherd gently caring for injured sheep; and he, through his followers, tenderly cares today.

GOODNESS

The sixth characteristic of the Spirit-filled man is called "goodness." This is benevolence in its purest sense. It includes hospitality and all acts of goodness that flow from an unselfish heart that is more interested in giving than receiving.

Instead of bringing joy to someone else's life by an act of kindness, the self-centered person sinks deeper and deeper in the slough of despondency and gloom. D. L. Moody once stated that it was his custom, after presenting himself to the Holy Spirit and asking to be led of the Spirit, to act upon those impulses which came to his mind, provided they did not violate any known truth of Scripture. Generally speaking, that is a very good rule to follow, for it pays rich dividends in mental health in the life of the giver.

FAITH

The seventh trait of the Spirit-filled man is faith, a complete abandonment to God and an absolute dependence upon him. This is a perfect antidote to fear, which causes worry, anxiety, and pessimism. Some commentators suggest that more than faith is involved— namely, faithfulness or dependability. A man who has Spirit-inspired faith will be faithful and dependable.

Many of God's people, like the nation of Israel, waste years in the desert of life because they do not believe God. Far too many Christians have "grasshopper vision." They are like the ten faithless spies who saw the giants in the land of Canaan and came home to cry, "We are as grasshoppers in their sight."

The Bible teaches that there are two sources of faith. The first source is the Word of God in the life of the believer. Romans 10:17 states, "Faith cometh by hearing, and hearing by the word of God." The second is the Holy Spirit. Faith is a fruit of the Spirit. If you find that you have a temperament that is conducive to doubts, indecision, and fear, then as a believer you can look to the filling of the Holy Spirit to give you a heart of faith which will dispel the emotions and actions of your natural nature, including fear, doubt, and anxiety. It will take time, however; habits are binding chains, but God gives us the victory in Christ Jesus. "Wait on the Lord: be of good courage, and he shall strengthen thine heart: wait, I say, on the Lord" (Ps. 27:14).

MEEKNESS

The eighth temperament trait of the Spirit-filled man is meekness. The natural man is proud, egotistical, and self-centered; but when the Holy Spirit fills the life of an individual, he will be humble, mild, submissive, and easily entreated.

The greatest example of meekness is the Lord Jesus Christ himself. He was the Creator of the universe, and yet was willing to humble himself, take on the form of a servant, and become subject to the whims of humanity, even to the point of death, that he might purchase our

redemption by his blood. Here we see the Creator of man buffeted, ridiculed, abused, and spat upon by his own creation. Yet he left us an example of not reviling again.

Meekness is not natural for us. Only the supernatural indwelling Spirit of God could cause any of us to react to physical or emotional persecution in meekness. It is a natural tendency to assert oneself, but even the most angry temperament can be controlled by the filling of the Holy Spirit and made to manifest this admirable trait of meekness.

SELF-CONTROL

The final temperament characteristic of the Spirit-filled believer is self-control. The King James Version translates it "temperance." Someone has defined it as "self controlled by the Holy Spirit."

Self-control will solve the Christian's problem of emotional outbursts such as rage, anger, fear, and jealousy, and cause him to avoid emotional excesses of any kind. The Spirit-controlled temperament will be one that is consistent, dependable, and well-ordered.

It has occurred to me that all four of the basic temperament types have a common difficulty that will be overcome by the Spirit-filled trait of self-control. That weakness is an inconsistent or ineffective devotional life. No Christian can be mature in Christ, steadily filled with the Holy Spirit, and usable in the hand of God unless he regularly feeds on the Word of God.

Mr. Sanguine is too restless and weak-willed by nature to be consistent in anything, much less in getting up a few minutes early to have a regular time of Bible reading and prayer. Mr. Choleric is by nature such a self-confident individual that even after he is converted it takes some time for him to realize what the Lord Jesus meant when he said, "Without me, ye can do nothing." Mr. Melancholy is perhaps the most likely of the four to be regular in his devotional life, except that his analytical ability often sends him off in the quest of some abstract, theologically hair-splitting truth rather than letting God speak to him concerning his personal needs. Mr. Phlegmatic is prone to recommend a regular quiet time as a necessary part of the Christian life, but if his slow, indolent, and often indifferent inclination is not disciplined by the Holy Spirit he will never quite get around to a regular feeding on God's Word.

As you look at these nine admirable traits of the Spirit-filled man, you not only get a picture of what God wants you to be, but what he is willing to make you in spite of your natural temperament. It should, however, be borne in mind that no amount of self-improvement or self-effort can bring any of these traits into our lives without the power of the Holy Spirit. From this we conclude that the most important single thing in the life of any Christian is to be filled with the Holy Spirit.

It is my conviction that God has given us at least one strength of the Spirit for every human weakness.

The Needs of the Sanguine Temperament

Sparky Sanguine needs at least six fruits or strengths of the Spirit to be the man or woman God wants him to be. He is by nature loving or compassionate, so he doesn't need that, though the Spirit of God will direct and purify that love. He also is by nature joyful, so the Spirit doesn't have to supply joy. He also has a natural "goodness" trait; that is, he loves to do good things for other people.

Peace, however, is another matter. Sanguines are so restless by nature that they need the supernatural peace of God that only the Holy Spirit can supply. Whenever you see a combustible sanguine face pressure in an attitude of peace, you are looking at a miracle of God.

Longsuffering, which basically means endurance, is foreign to the nature of a sanguine. He usually leaves a sea of unfinished projects behind him unless filled with the Spirit.

The bull-in-the-china-shop traits of sanguines are somehow replaced by the *gentleness* of the Spirit of God. One evidence of this is in their conversation. By nature they are blunt, loud, hurtful in their humorous treatment of others, seldom aware of how they have injured those who bear the brunt of their jokes. The gentleness of the Spirit of God will soften their injurious tongue.

One of the chief problems of Sparky Sanguine is ego. To him, by nature, he is the greatest. But when the spirit of *meekness* controls his life, the sanguine ceases to think more highly of himself than he ought to, but rather has a streak of humility burning in his soul, another evidence of the supernatural power of God.

Some of the lesser traits of a sanguine personality are his secret fears and insecurities. To such individuals *faith* is a wonderful source of blessing. I have seen God's Spirit not only supply the love-starved spirit of a sanguine, but give him courage in the face of adversity.

The number one need of the sanguine is *self-control*. We have seen that his natural problem of lack of self-discipline usually proves his undoing. We all know capable, lovable, charismatic sanguines who never live up to their potential and destroy themselves by lack of discipline.

The Needs of the Choleric Temperament

If you listen to the hard-driving, activity-prone choleric you might get the feeling he doesn't have emotional needs. Don't you believe it. These insensitive, caustic people have many needs and everyone around them wishes they would get help somewhere. I have noticed that the choleric is the only one of the temperaments that has a specific need for seven of the nine "fruits" or strengths of the Holy Spirit.

We have already seen that the choleric is self-disciplined and longsuffering by nature. You will recall we said he was strong-willed, determined, goal-oriented, and persistent. These traits stand in good stead when controlled by the Holy Spirit, for he is more likely to follow Jesus fully, energetically, and consistently. But even here he is vulnerable to mistaking his self-will for the will of God.

The besetting temptation of choleric Christians is to set their minds on doing something and persistently push for it without knowing whether or not it is really the will of God. This may produce a seemingly productive Christian worker, but it does not make a happy Christian, nor does it make the best use of his talents. A Spirit-filled choleric will always outperform a carnal choleric. Like every other temperament, Mr. Choleric desperately needs the filling of the Holy Spirit.

The first and primary need of the choleric temperament is *love* and compassion. Their insensitive and underdeveloped emotional nature is a real challenge to the work of the Holy Spirit. Love is not a static emotion. That is, you cannot love without being motivated to do something to express it; and the object of our expression when that love comes from the Holy Spirit will always be other people. The choleric who manifests love to his family and associates is manifesting the supernatural strength of the Holy Spirit in control of his temperament.

Although cholerics are extremely hard to please by nature, they are not an unhappy lot as long as they're busy working toward one of their goals in life. The *joy* the Holy Spirit supplies is not related to man's effort, but will characterize the choleric even in the face of adversity.

When the Holy Spirit fills cholerics' lives, they will still be activity-bound, but there is a sense of *peace* and a loss of that frenetic force that often drives them to an early grave. Cholerics desperately need peace with God.

Whenever you find a *gentle* choleric, you find a walking illustration of the supernatural power of the Holy Spirit of God, for that is not their natural forte.

The best place to manifest that Spirit-induced gentleness is in their speech patterns. No one can be more caustic and cutting than a choleric. And when the choleric tongue is modified to gracious speech and gentle approval, you know he is controlled by the Holy Spirit.

Cholerics need *goodness.* That is, they need to be involved in the goodness of God. It is important to them to invest their lives in something so worthwhile it lifts them into a new dimension of effectiveness and productivity. The Spirit of God alone provides that for a Christian choleric.

Interestingly enough, cholerics are not fearful people; they have tons of self-confidence. However, one of the lessons they must learn early in their Christian life is, "not by might, nor by power, [nor even by their choleric spirit], but by my Spirit, saith the Lord."

I have found that the temptation to which many cholerics give vent is to rush off in their own direction instead of putting their faith in the living God and following him.

A choleric is not meek by nature. Cholerics universally equate meekness and weakness. It is a happy day for the choleric who understands that God will not tolerate a haughty, proud spirit, but will bring such individuals down and humble them. It is much better for a choleric to humble himself under the mighty hand of God and to develop meekness before the Holy Spirit has to do it for him.

The Needs of the Melancholy Temperament

God used more melancholies in the Bible than all the other temperaments put together! That should be good news to the average melancholy individual who is often plagued by feelings of inadequacy in spite of recognized talents and creativity. It has long been

a mystery to me that those melancholy individuals who are endowed by
their Creator with the greatest number of talents seem to have the least
confidence in themselves. This is probably due to their everlasting
tendency toward self-criticism and self-condemnation.

In spite of that, however, down through the years, both in the Old
and New Testaments and in the history of Christianity, God has
transformed many a self-sacrificing, gentle melancholy into a faithful,
consistent servant when once filled with the Holy Spirit. Melancholies
don't need a great deal of longsuffering and self-control, for if their
motivation is oriented by the Spirit of God and they are instructed by
the Word of God, they make extremely effective Christian workers
known not for their flamboyant style, but for their self-sacrificing
consistent spirit. It seems easier to challenge a melancholy to a lifetime
of service for Jesus than any other temperament. That, too, is probably
because of their natural tendency towards self-sacrifice. The genuineness
of making a lifetime investment in a cause greater than oneself is
probably what does it. However, I'm not blind to the fact that they
nevertheless are in need of five specific fruits from the Holy Spirit.

Nothing turns a melancholy's life around like the *love* that is
characteristic of the Spirit-filled life. By nature a melancholy is self-
centered; his tendency toward perfectionism makes him very impatient
with the idiosyncrasies and carelessness of his fellow men. But when the
Holy Spirit fills him with the love of Christ, love literally transforms his
nature.

Joy is an absolute necessity for every melancholy, to replace his
naturally morose, moody, griping spirit. It seems difficult for melancholies
to understand that they must reflect the joy of the Lord. However, once
that concept grips their heart, it can have a transforming effect on their
entire being and make them delightful individuals to be around.

The *peace* of the Holy Spirit is a welcome tonic to the melancholy,
whose inner thoughts fluctuate from criticism and condemnation, to
hostility and revenge, and back to suspicion and fear. You can well
imagine the influence of the pervading Spirit of God's peace that
strengthens this aspect of the melancholy temperament.

It is absolutely essential for the melancholy to invest his life sacrificially
in the doing of *goodness* for other people. Fortunately, once he is filled
with love that gets his eyes off himself, his next objective is to apply this
new strength or compulsion within him to acts of kindness to other souls
on behalf of the gospel and the Lord Jesus Christ. In so doing, he brings
fulfillment to himself.

There is a trace of the haughty spirit in a melancholy. The Spirit-filled life, however, injects a meekness or humility that, although foreign to his natural characteristics, brings great balance to his life and makes him less critical of others and easier to get along with.

The sixth strength of the Holy Spirit needed so desperately by the melancholy is *faith*. This will get him out of his ever-present tendency to limit himself by unbelief and will inspire him to take steps of faith in the use of his natural characteristics. Most melancholy temperaments immobilize themselves by fear (of the future, for example). What they need desperately from God is the realization that he is with them constantly to supply their every need.

One of the things I hope you have noticed about these spiritual strengths provided by the Holy Spirit is how very practical they are for everyday living. Every temperament has a besetting sin or an area of weakness that so easily besets him or causes him to stumble. The Holy Spirit fortifies this area of the person's weakness, and though he doesn't change the person's temperament from its basic root, he so strengthens it in the areas of weakness that it seems that person has been transformed by walking under the control of the Spirit.

The Needs of the Phlegmatic Temperament

Phlegmatics are nice people by nature. I have often said in public that phlegmatics act more like Christians *before* they become Christians than most of the rest of us do afterwards. They are quiet, gentle, gracious people. And yet, phlegmatics are as needy as any of the other temperaments.

Their natural tendency to be gentle should not be confused with the gentleness or kindness of the Holy Spirit of God. Phlegmatics are gentle in the treatment of other people regardless of their spiritual motivation. When filled with the Holy Spirit, however, that gentility characterizes itself in a motivated servant spirit that makes them a great asset to any family, church, or organization.

Like all other temperaments, the primary need of the phlegmatic is *love* and compassion for other people. The most underdeveloped part of a phlegmatic's nature is motivation. The love of the Holy Spirit motivates them to utilize their gracious gentle spirit in the service of Christ.

Endurance is one of the great needs of the phlegmatic. He finds it only in the power of the Holy Spirit. Not only are phlegmatics good procrastinators, but they are also respectable quitters. The Holy Spirit will prompt them to keep on. Every church has more than its share of nice, kind, gentle people who warm the pews, but never get involved in the work of the Lord.

The antidote to that is the fruit of *goodness*—that is, good acts of service for Jesus Christ. Once they have committed themselves to a Sunday school class, a department superintendentship, Monday night church visitation, or some other form of Christian service, they do an excellent job, if they will accept the assignment in the first place.

One of the principal needs of the phlegmatic is *faith* to overcome his fears and worry. No one can be a more professional worrier than the phlegmatic; but when filled with the Holy Spirit he will have faith to trust God to do the impossible, even for him.

Phlegmatics without the Holy Spirit tend toward an increasing life-style of passivity, until they are motivated by the self-control of the Holy Spirit and recognize their self-indulgent attitude. The self-control of the Spirit of God will tend to cure their tendency toward procrastination. Our fulfillment in life comes in direct relationship to our being filled with the Holy Spirit of God.

How to Be Filled
with the Holy Spirit

One of the things I have tried to communicate in all of my books on temperament is that far more important than what is your personal temperament is the question, "Are you filled with the Holy Spirit?" It is almost impossible to exaggerate how dependent we are on the Holy Spirit. We are dependent on him for convicting us of sin before and after our salvation, for giving us understanding of the gospel, causing us to be born again, empowering us to witness, guiding us in our prayer life—in fact, for everything. It is no wonder that evil spirits have tried to counterfeit the work of the Holy Spirit and confuse his work.

There is probably no subject in the Bible upon which there is more confusion than that of being filled with the Holy Spirit. There are many fine Christian people who seem to equate the filling of the Holy Spirit with external signs. There are other Christians who because of excesses observed or heard of in this direction have all but eliminated the teaching of the filling of the Holy Spirit from their experience. They do not recognize his importance in their lives.

Satan places two obstacles before men: he tries to keep them from receiving Christ as Savior; and if he fails in this, he then tries to keep men from understanding the importance and work of the Holy Spirit.

One of the false impressions gained from people and not from the Word of God is that there is some special "feeling" when one is filled with the Holy Spirit. Before we examine how to be filled with the Holy Spirit, let us examine what the Bible teaches we can expect when we are filled with the Holy Spirit.

FOUR MAJOR RESULTS OF BEING FILLED WITH THE HOLY SPIRIT   There are four specific results of the Spirit-filled life—all guaranteed by the Bible. Consider them carefully, for they are the true marks of being a Spirit-controlled Christian.

1. *The nine temperament strengths of the Spirit-filled life (Gal. 5:22, 23).* We have already examined these traits in detail and have seen that they provide a strength for every natural weakness. Any individual who is filled with the Holy Spirit is going to manifest the characteristics of love, joy, peace, longsuffering, gentleness, goodness, meekness, faith, and self-control. He does not have to act out a role; he will be this way when the Spirit has control of his nature— regardless of his original temperament.

When the Holy Spirit fills your life, you will still be yourself minus the domination of your weaknesses. When filled with the Spirit, we all are able to be used of God in the areas of our natural talents or strengths as given to us by him.

2. *A joyful, thankful heart and a submissive spirit (Eph. 5:18-21).* When the Holy Spirit fills the life of a believer, the Bible tells us he will cause that believer to have a singing, thankful heart and a submissive spirit.

> And be not drunk with wine, wherein is excess; but be filled with the Spirit; speaking to yourselves in psalms and hymns and spiritual songs, singing and making melody in your heart to the Lord; giving thanks always for all things unto God and the Father in the name of our Lord Jesus Christ; submitting yourselves one to another in the fear of God.

A singing, grateful heart and a submissive spirit, independent of circumstances, are so unnatural that they can only be ours through the filling of the Holy Spirit. The Spirit of God is able to change the gloomy or griping heart into a song-filled thankful heart. He is also able to solve man's natural rebellion problem by increasing his faith to the point that he really believes the best way to live is in submission to the will of God, God's Word, and God's Spirit.

The same three results of the Spirit-filled life are also the results of the Word-filled life, as found in Colossians 3:16-18:

> Let the word of Christ dwell in you richly in all wisdom; teaching and admonishing one another in psalms and hymns and spiritual songs, singing with grace in your hearts to the Lord. And whatsoever ye do in word or deed, do all in the name of the Lord Jesus, giving thanks to God and the Father by him. Wives, submit yourselves unto your own husbands, as it is fit in the Lord.

It is no accident that we find the results of the Spirit-filled life and those of the Word-filled life to be one and the same. The Lord Jesus said that the Holy Spirit is "the Spirit of Truth." He also said of the Word of God, "Thy word is Truth." It is easily understood why the Word-filled life causes the same results as the Spirit-filled life, for the Holy Spirit is the author of the Word of God. The Christian who is Spirit-filled will be Word-filled, and the Word-filled Christian who obeys the Spirit will be Spirit-filled.

3. *Power for our witness about Jesus Christ (Acts 1:8).* The Lord Jesus told his disciples that "It is expedient [necessary] for you that I go away: for if I go not away, the Comforter [Holy Spirit] will not come unto you" (John 16:7). That explains why the last thing Jesus did before he ascended into heaven was to tell his disciples, "But ye shall receive power, after that the Holy Ghost is come upon you: and ye shall be witnesses unto me . . ." (Acts 1:8).

Even though the disciples had spent three years with Jesus, had heard his messages several times, and were the best trained witnesses he had, he still instructed them "not [to] depart from Jerusalem, but wait for the promise of the Father" (Acts 1:4). All of their training obviously was incapable of producing fruit without the power of the Holy Spirit. And when the Holy Spirit came on the day of Pentecost, they witnessed in his power and three thousand persons were saved.

Power to witness in the Holy Spirit is not always discernible, but must be accepted by faith. When we have met the conditions for the filling of the Holy Spirit, we should be careful to believe we have witnessed in the power of the Spirit whether or not we see the results. It is possible to witness in the power of the Holy Spirit and still not see an individual

come to a saving knowledge of Christ. For in the sovereign plan of God
he has chosen never to violate the right of man's free choice. We cannot
always equate success in witnessing with the power to witness!

4. *The Holy Spirit will glorify Jesus Christ (John 16:13, 14).*

> Howbeit when he, the Spirit of truth, is come, he will
> guide you into all truth: for he shall not speak of himself;
> but whatsoever he shall hear, that shall he speak: and he
> will shew you things to come. He shall glorify me: for he
> shall receive of mine, and shall shew it unto you.

A fundamental principle should always be kept in mind regarding the
work of the Holy Spirit: he does not glorify himself, but the Lord Jesus
Christ.

The late F. B. Meyer told the story of a missionary who came to him
at a Bible conference after he had spoken on the subject on how to be
filled with the Holy Spirit. She confessed that she was never consciously
filled with the Holy Spirit and was going to go up to the prayer chapel
and spend the day in soul-searching to see if she could receive his filling.

Late that evening she came back just as Meyer was leaving the
auditorium. He asked, "How was it, sister?"

"I'm not quite sure," she responded, explaining her day's activities of
reading the Word, praying, confessing her sins, and asking for the filling
of the Holy Spirit. She then stated, "I do not feel particularly filled with
the Holy Spirit, but never have I been so conscious of the presence of
the Lord Jesus in my life." To which Meyer replied, "Sister, that *is* the
Holy Spirit. He glorifies Jesus."

Let us summarize what we can expect when filled with the Holy
Spirit. Very simply, the nine temperament characteristics of the Spirit; a
singing, thankful heart that gives us a submissive attitude; and the
power to witness. These characteristics will glorify the Lord Jesus
Christ. What about certain feelings or ecstatic experiences? The Bible
does not tell us to expect these things when we are filled with the Holy
Spirit, and we should not expect what the Bible does not promise.

The Infilling of the Holy Spirit

The filling of the Holy Spirit is not optional
equipment in the Christian life, but a command of God! Ephesians 5:18
tells us, "And be not drunk with wine, wherein is excess; but be filled

with the Spirit." Since God commands us to be filled with the Holy
Spirit, it must be possible for us to be filled with his Spirit. I would like
to give five simple steps for being filled with the Holy Spirit.

1. *Self-examination (Acts 20:28; 1 Cor. 11:28).*

The Christian interested in the filling of the Holy Spirit must regularly
"take heed" to "examine himself," not to see if he measures up to the
standards of other people or the traditions and requirements of his
church, but to the previously mentioned results of being filled with the
Holy Spirit. If he does not find he is glorifying Jesus, if he does not have
power to witness, or if he lacks a joyful, submissive spirit or the nine
temperament traits of the Holy Spirit, then his self-examination will
reveal those areas in which he is deficient and will uncover the sin that
causes them.

2. *Confession of all known sin (1 John 1:9).*

> If we confess our sins, he is faithful and just to forgive us
> our sins, and to cleanse us from all unrighteousness.

After examining ourselves in the light of the Word of God, we should
confess all sin brought to mind by the Holy Spirit, including those
characteristics of the Spirit-filled life that we lack. Until we acknowledge
as sin our lack of compassion, our lack of self-control, our lack of
humility, our anger instead of gentleness, our bitterness instead of
kindness, and our unbelief instead of faith, we will never have the filling
of the Holy Spirit. However, the moment we recognize these deficiencies
as sin and confess them to God, he will "cleanse us from all
unrighteousness." Until we have done this, we cannot have the filling of
the Holy Spirit, for he fills only clean vessels (2 Tim. 2:21).

3. *Submit yourself completely to God (Rom. 6:11-13).*

> Likewise reckon ye also yourselves to be dead indeed
> unto sin, but alive unto God through Jesus Christ our
> Lord. Let not sin therefore reign in your mortal body,
> that ye should obey it in the lusts thereof. Neither yield
> ye your members as instruments of unrighteousness unto
> sin: but yield yourselves unto God, as those that are alive
> from the dead, and your members as instruments of
> righteousness unto God.

Do not make the mistake of being afraid to give yourself to God!
Romans 8:32 tells us, "He that spared not his own Son, but delivered

him up for us all, how shall he not with him also freely give us all things?" If God loved us so much as to give his Son to die for us, certainly he is interested in nothing but our good; therefore, we can trust him with our lives. You will never find a miserable Christian in the center of the will of God.

Ephesians 5:18 says, "Be not drunk with wine . . . but be filled with the Spirit." When a man is drunk, he is dominated by alcohol. So with the filling of the Holy Spirit, man's actions must be dominated by and dictated by the Holy Spirit. For consecrated Christians this is often the most difficult thing to do, for we can always find some worthy purpose for our lives, not realizing that we are often filled with ourselves rather than with the Holy Spirit as we seek to serve the Lord.

When you give your life to God, do not attach any strings or conditions to it. He is such a God of love that you can safely give yourself without reservation, knowing that his plan and use of your life is far better than yours. And remember, the attitude of yieldedness is absolutely necessary for the filling of God's Spirit. Your will is the will of the flesh, and the Bible says that "the flesh profiteth nothing."

Someone has suggested that being yielded to the Spirit is being available to the Spirit. Peter and John in Acts 3 make a good example of that. They were on their way to the temple to pray when they saw the lame man begging alms. Because they were sensitive to the Holy Spirit, they healed him "in the name of Jesus Christ of Nazareth." The man began leaping about and praising God until a crowd gathered. Peter, still sensitive to the Holy Spirit, began preaching; "many of them which heard the Word believed; and the number of the men was about five thousand" (Acts 4:4).

Many times I fear we are so engrossed in some good Christian activity that we are not available when the Spirit leads. When a Christian yields himself unto God "as those that are alive from the dead," he takes time to do what the Spirit directs him to do.

4. *Ask to be filled with the Holy Spirit (Luke 11:13).*

> If ye then, being evil, know how to give good gifts unto your children: how much more shall your heavenly Father give the Holy Spirit to them that ask him?

When a Christian has examined himself, confessed all known sin, and yielded himself without reservation to God, he is then ready to do the one thing he must do to receive the Spirit—very simply, to ask to be filled with the Holy Spirit.

The Lord Jesus compares this to our treatment of our earthly children. Certainly a good father would not make his children beg for something he commanded them to have. How much less does God make us beg to be filled with the Holy Spirit. But don't forget Step 5.

5. *Believe you are filled with the Holy Spirit! And thank him for his filling.*

> And he that doubteth is damned if he eat, because he eateth not of faith: for whatsoever is not of faith is sin. (Rom. 14:23)
> In every thing give thanks: for this is the will of God in Christ Jesus concerning you. (1 Thess. 5:18)

For many Christians the battle is won or lost right here. After examining themselves, confessing all known sin, yielding themselves to God, and asking for his filling, they are faced with a decision: to believe they are filled, or to go away in unbelief, in which case they have sinned, for "whatsoever is not of faith is sin."

The same Christian who tells the new convert to "take God at his Word concerning salvation" finds it difficult to heed his own advice concerning the filling of the Holy Spirit. If you have fulfilled the first four steps, then by faith thank God for his filling. Don't wait for feelings or for physical signs; fasten your faith to the Word of God, which is independent of feeling. Believing we are filled with the Spirit is merely taking God at his Word, and that is the only absolute this world has (Matt. 24:35).

A COMMON   The most common question I am asked after
QUESTION   my lectures on the Spirit-filled life for
                  overcoming temperament weaknesses is, "How often should I ask to be filled with the Holy Spirit?"

My answer is: every time you think you are not! Some Bible teachers think the Spirit's filling is automatic whenever we ask forgiveness for our sins (1 John 1:7-9). Personally I am not convinced. I like to make sure by asking. In fact, I ask for his filling when I awaken in the morning and many times through the day. The Greek in Ephesians 5:18 literally means, "Keep on being filled with the Spirit."

Occasionally someone protests, "But that is all too simple; being filled with the Spirit must be much more complex!" Why? As an eight-year-old boy I asked the Lord Jesus to come into my heart. He instantly answered my request. Why should he not answer when I ask to be filled

with the Holy Spirit? A. B. Simpson used to say, "Being filled with the
Spirit is as easy as breathing; you can simply breathe out and breathe
in."

One of the reasons some Christians are reluctant to think they are
filled with the Spirit is that they don't see an immediate change in their
lives, or the change is of short duration. Two factors have an important
bearing on this: temperament and habit, and they work together. The
weaknesses of our temperament have created strong habits that
involuntarily recur.

For illustration, let us consider a fear-prone melancholy or phlegmatic
Christian. These people have a deeply ingrained habit of doubt,
negativism, worry, and anxiety. I can predict the thinking pattern of such
a person after he follows the five steps of being filled with the Spirit.
Before long his negative thinking habit will stir doubts: "Am I filled with
the Spirit? I don't feel any different. I'm still afraid." This mental attitude
is sin, and the Spirit's filling and control ends.

What such people need to realize is that our feelings are the result of
thought patterns. We need to learn that feelings are reliable only when
they are based on truth and righteousness. God's people need to fill their
minds with the Word of God so their feelings will correspond to God's.

The feelings of the perennial doubter who is filled with the Spirit will
gradually change, but it will take time. If he looks to the Lord for mercy
and forgiveness each time he feels doubtful or unbelieving, he will
gradually be assured by the Lord. But if he continues to think negatively
or doubtfully and justifies it by saying, "I've always been this way," he
will remain that way. Or he may get worse, because he is quenching the
Holy Spirit by indulging in this sin and etching the habit deeper on his
mind.

Mr. Sanguine and Mr. Choleric have a similar problem with their pet
sin of anger. It isn't long after they are filled with the Holy Spirit that
their ingrained anger feelings rise up to grieve the Holy Spirit. Unless
they immediately confess this sin, they will no longer be filled with the
Spirit and the old feelings will control them. Each time they think self-
righteously of how they have been offended or insulted or cheated, they
cultivate feelings of hostility. These easily-triggered feelings are the result
of years of hostile thoughts that can be overcome only as the Spirit of
God is given access to and control of the conscious and subconscious
mind. He replaces these hostile thoughts with love, kindness, and
gentleness, but it will take time for a permanent change to be
accomplished.

How to Walk in the Spirit

"Since we live by the Spirit, let us keep in step with the Spirit" (Gal. 5:25, NIV).

Walking in the Spirit and being filled by the Holy Spirit are not one and the same thing, though they are very closely related. Having followed the five simple rules for the filling of the Holy Spirit, it is then essential to learn how to walk daily in the Spirit.

Being filled with the Spirit is just the beginning of Christian victory. We must "walk in the Spirit" to be effective (Gal. 5:16). It is one thing to start out in the Spirit-filled life and quite another to walk day by day in the control of the Spirit. The following procedure for walking in the Spirit can be a practical tool for victorious daily living.

1. *Make the filling of the Holy Spirit a daily priority.* You cannot walk in the Spirit unless you sincerely want to and unless you have his filling. As we have already seen, old habit patterns sneak back to haunt us. If we enjoy them more than the peace of God, we will indulge the sins of the flesh. Let's be honest—lust, worry, self-pity, and anger are fun, temporarily. Only when we want the filling of the Holy Spirit more than anything else in the world are we willing to give up lesser emotional satisfactions of lust, worry, self-pity, and anger.

2. *Develop a keen sensitivity to sin.* Sin short-circuits the power of the Holy Spirit in us. The moment we are conscious of any sin, we should confess it immediately, so the time between grieving, or quenching, the Spirit and reinstatement is minimal. The main advantage to the study of temperaments is that we can diagnose our most common weakness. Consequently we are on our guard for "the sin that doth so easily beset us." When it rears its ugly head, confess it, forget it (God does, so you might as well), and press on toward the fulfillment of the will of God for your life. The main secret to victorious living among those I have counseled has been the practice of instant confession.

3. *Daily read and study God's Word.* It is my conviction after a good deal of observation that it is impossible for a Christian to "walk in the Spirit" unless he develops the habit of regularly feeding his mind and heart upon the Word of God. One of the reasons Christians do not "feel" as God does about life issues is that they do not know God's way from his Word.

Since our feelings are produced by our thought processes, we will feel as carnal worldlings do if we feed our minds on the "wisdom of the world." If we feed our minds on the Word of God, we will feel as the Spirit does about life issues. (Remember that it takes some time to reorient our minds from human wisdom to divine wisdom. So regular reading is essential.)

Sometimes Christians object that this will make them legalists. Yet they don't seem to view coming to the table three times a day as legalistic. We do it because we sense a need and enjoy eating. In the same way we can feed spiritually on God's Word from a sense of need, but it takes time to build our spiritual appetite. Many Christians feel something is very wrong if they miss reading the Word of God, but they didn't start out that way.

A consistent feeding of one's mind upon the Word of God produces some interesting results. Consider the following revolutionary benefits.

Joshua 1:8	It makes your way prosperous and gives success.
Psalm 1:3	It produces fruitfulness.
Psalm 119:11	It keeps us from sin.
John 14:21	God reveals himself increasingly to keepers of his Word.
John 15:3	The Word cleanses us.
John 15:7	The Word produces power in prayer.
John 15:11	The Word brings joy to our hearts.
1 John 2:13, 14	The Word gives victory over "the wicked one."

With these transforming results from filling our minds with God's Word, it is a tragedy that so many Christians live a second-rate life with feelings of insecurity, uncleanness, discontent, anxiety, and impotence. The character of our feelings depends on the character of our thoughts, and the sincere Christian should ask himself, "What is shaping and filling my thoughts?"

A careful comparison of the Spirit-filled life (Eph. 5:18-21) with the Word-filled life (Col. 3:15-17) is revealing. Both passages promise a song in your heart, a thanksgiving attitude, and a submissive spirit. A mind that is filled with and yielded to the Word of God will produce the same effects on the emotions as the mind filled with and yielded to the Holy Spirit. We may legitimately conclude from this that the filling of the Spirit and walking in the Spirit depend upon our being filled with the Word of God!

Reading the Bible at night is especially helpful. The mind digests the events and thoughts of the day, particularly the last things we think about before going to sleep. For that reason it is very profitable to read

God's Word just before retiring—that way you can go to sleep thinking about the things just read. It is amazing how this helps us awaken with a positive outlook for the day. Get into the habit of reading the Word just before sleeping, and your subconscious mind will mold your feelings in God's patterns.

Another valuable habit is meditation. The mind is always working, and our will determines whether our mind works for or against us. To work for good, the mind must meditate on the truths and insights of God's Word. There is one catch: you must memorize in order to meditate profitably, because you can't meditate on what you don't know intimately. Whether it is a phrase, concept, or whole verse of Scripture, you must memorize it in order to meditate on it.

A simple method I use to inspire meditation is to write down special verses that bless my soul, then put the sheet of paper in my Bible or notebook. I learn at least one of these verses every week. It is hard work, but I don't know any mentally lazy Christians who walk in the Spirit.

4. *Guard against grieving the Holy Spirit.* The next step for walking in the Spirit is an extension of step two—developing a sensitivity to sin. Ephesians 4:30-32 makes it clear that all forms of hostility, including anger, bitterness, and enmity, grieve the Holy Spirit. All anger-prone believers should memorize those three verses and develop a particular sensitivity to hostility. In addition to making instant confession, they should resolve to be loving, kind, tenderhearted, and forgiving toward others. This grace is markedly unnatural for a sanguine or a choleric, but the Holy Spirit will develop in the believer a new capacity for thoughtfulness and love.

The importance of our will becomes apparent at this point of walking in the Spirit. When we feel the bludgeon of injustice or someone's wrath, we can hate the offender or forgive and pray for him. Our overall feelings as well as our walk in the Spirit depend upon our decision. Don't be surprised if you fail repeatedly at first. But be sure to confess the sin as soon as you are aware of grieving the Spirit, and let him reestablish your walk. As you choose to forgive and to let the Holy Spirit react through you with patience and love, you will find your temperament weakness changing into a strength.

5. *Avoid quenching the Spirit through fear and worry.* According to 1 Thessalonians 5:16-19, we quench the Holy Spirit when we doubt and resist his dealings in our lives. When a Christian says, "I don't understand why God let this awful thing happen to me," he has already

quenched the Spirit through fear. The Christian who is trusting God could face the same circumstances and say, "I thank God he is in control of my life! I don't understand his dealings with me right now, but I trust his promise that he will never leave me and he will supply my every need."

We have seen that melancholy and phlegmatic people have a predisposition toward fear, just as the more extrovertive temperaments have a predisposition toward anger. Some people possess both introvertive and extrovertive temperaments, and consequently may have deep problems with both fear and anger. God's grace is sufficient to cure both problems through his Holy Spirit. But if you have these tendencies, you need to watch carefully your reaction to seemingly unfavorable events. If you groan or complain inwardly, you have already quenched the Holy Spirit. This can be remedied immediately if you are willing to call your doubt-induced complaining exactly what it is—sin—and ask God to transform this habit pattern and fill you with his Spirit.

God is not nearly so interested in changing circumstances as he is in changing people. It is no victory to live without worry when there is nothing to worry about, and becoming a Christian did not exempt you from trouble. Job said, "Yet man is born unto trouble, as the sparks fly upward" (Job 5:7). Jesus warned us we would face tribulation in this world, and the Bible tells us God sends testings to strengthen us. Many Christians flunk the tests by seeking their removal rather than rendering obedience in the Spirit.

It is impossible for a fear-prone Christian to walk in the Spirit any length of time without strong infusions of God's Word to encourage his faith. The more God's Word fills his mind, the more his feelings will abound in faith. But worriers usually enjoy wallowing in their misery, especially with God watching the piteous scene. All worriers should memorize Philippians 4:6, 7: "Do not be anxious about anything, but in everything, by prayer and petition, with thanksgiving, present your requests to God. And the peace of God, which transcends all understanding, will guard your hearts and your minds in Christ Jesus" (NIV).

These verses direct prayer to be made "with thanksgiving." You cannot genuinely pray with thanksgiving and finish with the same burdens you started with. Consider the following two prayers—and the emotions they create—offered by Christian parents with a sick child.

"Dear Lord, we come to you on behalf of our little girl so near death. The doctor tells us there is no hope for her. Please, dear Lord, heal her.

You know how much she means to us. If this sickness is caused by sin in our lives, forgive and cleanse us that she may live. After all the other tragedies in our lives, we do not think we can bear another. In Jesus' name. Amen."

"Dear Heavenly Father, we thank you that we are your children and can look to you at this time of need. You know the report of the doctors, and you have promised that all things work together for good to folks like us. We don't understand our dear child's sickness, but we know you love us and are more than able to heal her. We commit her little body to you, Father, asking for her healing according to your perfect will. We dedicated her to you before she was born, and we thank you that you are able to supply all her needs right now, as well as ours. In Jesus' name. Amen."

It is obvious which set of parents will feel the "peace of God" and which couple will wring their hands in anguish during this time of deep need. The difference comes in learning the attitude of thanksgiving from the Word of God. Lest you think the above prayer is hypothetical or idealistic, let me share a personal experience. The blonde, blue-eyed cutie named Lori that God sent to us is the apple of my heart. Several years ago I stood at her bedside in Children's Hospital and prayed that prayer. Frankly, I don't know how people without Jesus Christ go through such trials. My wife and I can testify that in spite of Lori's raging fever and delirium, and no known hope, God imparted peace to our troubled hearts. However, not until we prayed with thanksgiving beside her oxygen tent did we receive that peace.

If you tend to worry or grumble, you will find that you are not a very thankful person. You may be a fine person in many other respects, but unless you learn to be thankful you can never walk far in the Spirit, nor will you be consistently happy. The secret to a thankful attitude is in coming to know God intimately as he reveals himself in his Word. This will require consistent Bible reading, studying, and meditation. When your faith is established through the Word, it is easier to give thanks, but it is still an act of the will. If you have not accepted his full leading for your life, you will complain because you doubt things will turn out all right. And doubt quenches the Spirit and sidetracks your real progress.

One last practical suggestion for walking in the Spirit is in order. Although mental attitude is important at all times, prayer is of paramount importance twice during each day: when we go to bed and when we arise. It is very important to pray "with thanksgiving," as well as to read the Scriptures, at night. Though it may be hard, the other strategic time to give thanks is the first thing in the morning. The psalmist helps us: "This is the day which the Lord hath made; we will rejoice and be glad in it" (Ps. 118:24).

After beginning your day with thanksgiving, yield yourself anew to God according to Romans 6:11-13. Tell him you are available to share your faith with the needy one he sends to you. Yield your lips to the Holy Spirit and let him open the conversation. Walk in the Spirit, and you will bear fruit for God. As soon as you sense you have grieved or quenched the Spirit, confess your sin and again ask for his filling. If you follow these steps, your spirit will improve regardless of your temperament. And when you improve your spirit, you permit God to make the most out of your life.

Give Yourself a Temperament Test

One day an industrial psychologist from the Midwest was visiting San Diego and attended our Sunday morning church service. Afterwards he invited me to lunch with his family and, since my wife was out of town speaking at a women's conference, I accepted. We had barely returned from the buffet with our food when he said, "I have used your temperament theory in vocational counseling for ten years and find it the most helpful tool for vocational guidance I have every seen."

Here was a man with a Ph.D. in psychology who served as a consultant to the major aircraft companies of the nation and recognized that the four-temperament theory is the best single theory of human behavior yet devised. It isn't perfect, and it is not accepted universally, but it is an excellent aid to many things, particularly vocational guidance.

My psychologist friend then asked, "Have you developed a temperament test? If so, I'd like to see it." At that time I had to respond, "Not yet. I'm working on one, but I'm not satisfied with it." That was seven years ago and five temperament tests back. I am very satisfied with the one I now use—The LaHaye Temperament Analysis—which is extremely thorough. But I also developed a simple test you can give yourself or have some of your friends give you.

Through the years I have received at least a dozen tests worked out by some of the enthusiasts of my other temperament books. Some were extremely complex and others worthless. All were sincere attempts to help people. Two professors at Andrews University in Berrien Springs, Michigan, contacted me about collaborating with them on such a test.

One was a statistician and the other a computer science and testing professor. Together we worked up a test they were extremely enthused about. I administered it to several people I knew well and was not satisfied with the results. I found too many phlegmatics coming out like cholerics. These good men refined their test and later marketed it.

I went on to develop my own tests which I administered to volunteers in my congregation, among my acquaintances, and to over one thousand missionaries encountered on a world missions tour. Finally, I came up with the LaHaye Temperament Analysis which I believe is over 92 percent accurate. We have given it to almost 20,000 people and have received very few complaints. In fact, those who have taken the test are quite amazed at its thoroughness and professionalism.

One of the tests I did not use in my analysis is the simple test enclosed in this chapter. I do not claim 92% accuracy for it because it is a simple, one-celled test. The LaHaye Temperament Analysis consists of four tests in one to allow for comparison and both a lie scale and mood scale. For, interestingly enough, any subjective test like this will be influenced heavily by both your mood and how honest you are when looking at yourself (or should I say, how objective you are). In any case, to get a good handle on your primary and perhaps your secondary temperament you will enjoy the tests on the following pages.

A DOUBLE CHECK   Five temperament charts are given for your personal use. Chart 1 is to determine how you see yourself. Charts 2-4 are to give your best friends to do on you. Chart 5 is for you to average the scores of your friends. Then you can compare the average of your friends' charts with your own temperament blob chart to see if your perception of you is similar to the way your friends see you. If not, then you need to ask yourself if you really are objective about yourself or if you project a face to others so they see you as you want them to rather than as you really are.

The following test should not take more than twenty-five minutes.

C H A R T I

Your Personal Profile Blob Chart

Instructions:
1. Relax, get in a quiet place, and read the entire chart before making any markings.
2. After each word on the circle below, place a dot on the number that best describes you, 5 being *most* like you and 1 being *least* like you. Try to be objective!
3. Turn to page 97 for instructions on scoring this test *only* after completing the blob chart.

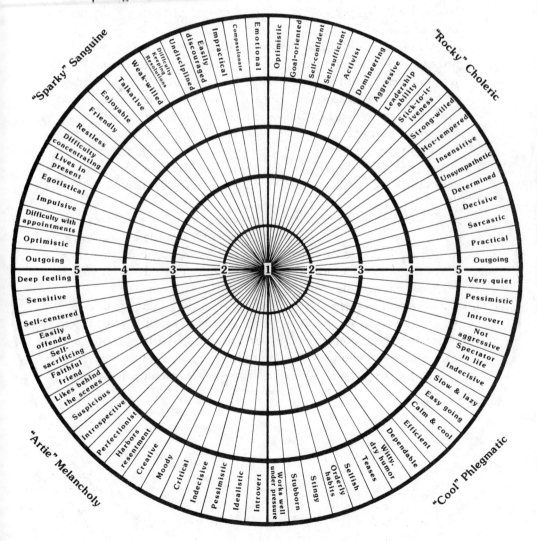

CHARTS 2-4

Your Friends Analyze You

The following blob charts are for three of your best friends to use in "analyzing" you. Ask each friend to fill out one blob chart with *your* characteristics, strengths, and weaknesses. Have each friend read the following instructions:

1. Read all the adjectives below before making a mark.
2. After each word on the chart, place a dot on the number that best describes your friend—1 being *least* like him and 5 being *most* like him.
3. Try to be objective, indicating what he is like most of the time.

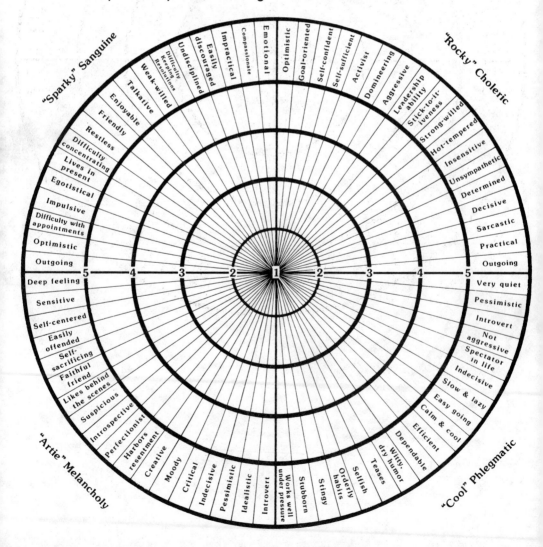

GIVE YOURSELF A
TEMPERAMENT TEST

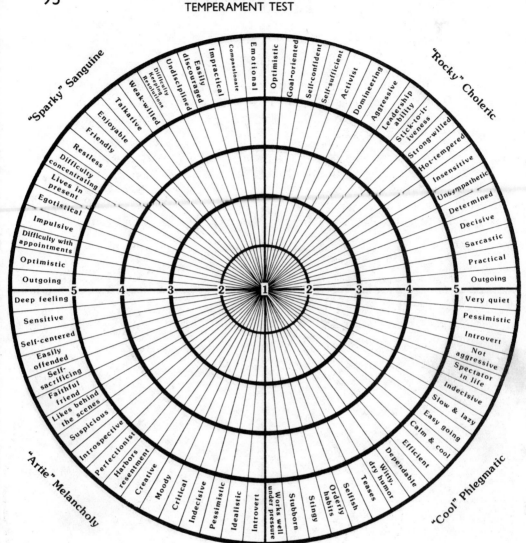

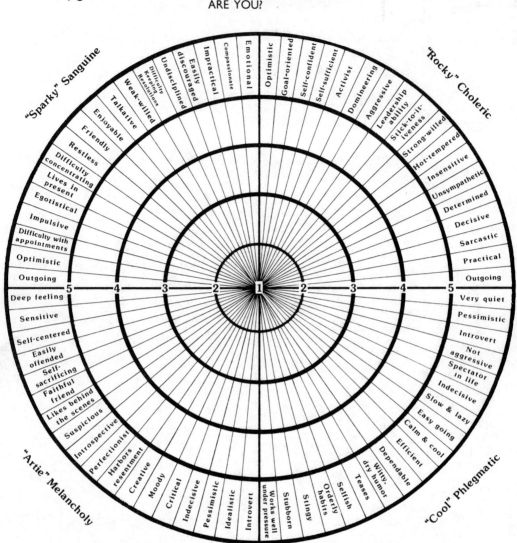

CHART 5

Scoring Your Temperament Blob

Instructions:

1. Average only the 3-5 dots listed in Charts 2-4 (omit the 1's and 2's—they are of such low intensity that they do not influence this test).
2. Place the average totals from Charts 2, 3, and 4 on the circle below.
3. Connect the dots by drawing curved lines paralleling the basic circles from dot to dot except when nothing appears in a temperament quadrant. Follow the outer edge of the quadrant to the center, then return to the next dot.
4. Now with *a different color pencil* transfer all 3-5 dots from your test in Chart 1.
5. Connect your dots as in Step 3.

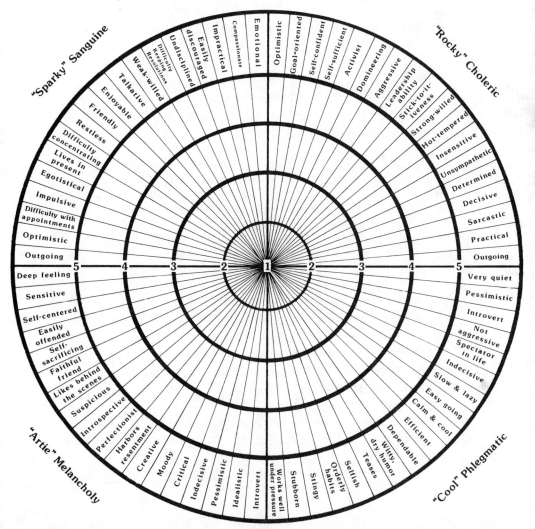

ASSESSING   Chart 5 now contains two blobs of different
THE RESULTS   colors. Ideally the blobs will be identical. In
                   most cases there will be some variation.
However, your primary temperament should stand out as the larger
blob. Hopefully, both large blobs will be in the same temperament zone.
If they are not, something for you to think about is, "Do my friends see
me as I see myself, or is there a great difference?" If two of your friends'
scores were quite similar to your own, then disregard the third chart
altogether. Some people read too much into a simple test like this.
Consequently, their excessive scores will completely alter the averages of
your other friends.

On the other hand, if your score and that of your friends is in marked
contrast, then it may mean you are trying to make yourself something
God never intended you to be—in which case you need to realistically
face yourself as you really are and be yourself as controlled by the Holy
Spirit.

FURTHER TESTS   If you are not satisfied with the accuracy of the
TO GIVE YOURSELF   above temperament blob, here are some
                   questions to ask yourself to at least identify
your primary temperament.

1. Are you an extrovert or an introvert?
2. Are you a spontaneous quick-talker?
3. Do you have to apologize frequently?
4. Do you have high emotional responses?
5. Are you quiet and slow of speech?
6. Are you a good speller?
7. Do you do well at math and detail?
8. Do you get depressed easily?

If your answer to question 1 is extrovert and you answered yes to 2-
4, your primary temperament is probably sanguine. If only one of 2-4,
you are probably a choleric temperament.

If you answered 1 that you're an introvert and yes to 6-8, your
primary temperament is probably melancholy. But if you said yes to 5
and you do not get depressed very often, your predominant
temperament is probably phlegmatic.

Obviously the above is a very casual analysis, but it can serve as an
interesting check on the accuracy of the predominant temperament in
your blob chart.

TAKE THIS TEST   One exercise you will find very interesting is to
IN TWO YEARS   concentrate on walking in the Spirit on a daily
                         basis as outlined earlier. Then retake the above
test and see how God has modified your temperament. You will find
lower scores in the weakness areas of your temperament.

   If you wish a new set of these testing charts, just send one dollar to:
Family Life Seminars, P.O. Box 16000, San Diego, CA 92116.

   Unfortunately, all that the above test will do for you is reveal your
primary and secondary temperaments. It does not provide specific
vocational aptitudes and the other information found in the more
complete testing instrument—The LaHaye Temperament Analysis. You
may wish to send for that. If you do, be sure and use the discount
certificate on page 351. (However, once you have determined your
primary and secondary temperaments you will be prepared to evaluate
whether or not you are presently pursuing the right vocation. The next
chapters will be helpful in that determination.)

PART Three

TEMPERAMENT AND YOUR VOCATION

CHAPTER SIX

Discovering Your Vocational Aptitudes

Human beings were designed by God with a special capacity for productivity. It is one of those inherited traits unique to human beings that separates mankind from animals.

Even in the Garden of Eden, God gave man responsibility and duties. Note these words: "The Lord God took the man and put him in the Garden of Eden to work it and take care of it . . ." (Gen. 2:15, NIV). It should be remembered that this whole scene took place *before* sin occurred and before the fall. Work, a command from God, has nothing to do with the fall—though that made it more difficult. Evidently weeds did not grow in the Garden of Eden until the curse came, but man still had to work. Now man's work is compounded by thorns, weeds, disease, bugs, etc.

After the fall, man was also told by God that work was his lot in life.

> To Adam he said, "Because you listened to your wife and ate from the tree about which I commanded you, 'You must not eat of it,' cursed is the ground because of you; through painful toil you will eat of it all the days of your life. It will produce both thorns and thistles for you, and you will eat the plants of the field. By the sweat of your brow you will eat your food until you return to the ground, since from it you were taken; for dust you are and to dust you will return. (Gen. 3:17-19, NIV)

All through the Bible the work ethic is exalted. Many references are given in the book of Proverbs calling the lazy "sluggards" and challenging both men and women to be workers. This concept is also fostered in the New Testament, which proclaims that "If a man will not work, he shall not eat" (2 Thess. 3:10).

All the commands of God work for the good of man. By that I mean that no one is left psychologically unfulfilled or warped by obeying the commands of God. Quite the opposite, mankind is fulfilled in the obeying of God's instructions.

We need to work because it is good for us. There is something self-enriching in a job well done. The unemployed are miserable not just because they are out of money, but because they do not have the opportunity to work productively. We have all known hard-working individuals who quit working at sixty-five and died before their sixty-seventh birthday. The real reason, not the one that appears on their death certificate, is that they could not handle the emotional vacuum that results from lack of productivity.

VOCATIONAL FRUSTRATION

Next to lack of employment, the worst thing that can happen to a person is to have the wrong job. It is incredible how many people despise their work. No wonder it becomes such drudgery to them. And as technology advances, increasing numbers of people will discover they are ill-fitted for the vocation in which they find themselves. This is particularly true of the unskilled or those whose area of skill is automated out of existence. All vocational experts warn that this will be an increasing problem in the years ahead.

One of the ways to avoid vocational frustration, or feeling like a round peg in a square hole, is to know your temperament and its natural vocational possibilities, then find work or a profession that allows you to express your natural temperament characteristics. Examine this brief exposure to the four temperaments' vocational aptitudes and see if they sound familiar.

SPARKY SANGUINE'S VOCATIONAL APTITUDES

The world is enriched by sanguines with their cheeriness and natural charisma. They usually make excellent salesmen and more than any other seem attracted to that profession. Sparky is so convincing that he could sell rubber crutches to people who aren't even crippled. If you ever want to watch Mr. Sanguine in action, just visit your local used-car dealer. Two-thirds of his salesmen are probably sanguines.

In addition to being good salesmen, sanguines make excellent actors, entertainers, and preachers (particularly evangelists). They are outstanding masters of ceremonies, auctioneers, and sometimes leaders (if properly blended with another temperament). Because of our mass media today, they are increasingly in demand within the political arena, where natural charisma has proven advantageous (sanguines have charisma to burn).

In the area of helping people, sanguines excel as hospital workers. Doctor Sanguine always has the best bedside manner. You may be on the verge of death, as white as the sheet you are lying on when he bubbles into the room, but before he leaves, he will lift your spirits by his natural charm. His obvious compassion in response to your tale of woe will almost make paying his exorbitant bill easy. (Sanguines are never moderate about anything.) Nurse Sanguine is equally enthusiastic about helping sick folk, and her radiant smile as she enters the room always gives you a pickup. In fact, most sick people respond to the sanguine's question of "How are you today?" by saying, "Fine," whereas Nurse Melancholy asking the same question would probably receive the self-pitying lament of "Miserable."

No matter what work the sanguine enters, it should always give him extensive exposure to people. I think his chief contribution to life lies in making other people happy. Certainly someone should be assigned that task in these uncertain times.

It is well known that sanguines are not too swift on detail. One of their biggest frustrations is the sales manager that wants them to use "purchase orders" or "fill in all the blanks on contracts." Most sanguines can't even remember where they put the contracts, much less fill them out. They would much rather be out on the golf course with a client than strategizing, analyzing, or filling out forms. Most sanguines lament, "Paperwork is the bane of my life."

While it is true sanguines are not *natural* detail hounds, they can do better. It is all a matter of self-discipline. That seems to be the most self-limiting thing a sanguine does: indulge his weaknesses and refuse to discipline himself. It is sad to have to say it, but sanguines usually limit their ultimate potential by their failure to discipline themselves. Every job has something undesirable about it, and changing jobs won't change that. Sooner or later you will find something in your new job that you don't like to do.

When my wife and I launched a national television program, we thought it would be an exciting way to serve our Lord. We thoroughly enjoyed the filming of the programs, the meeting of new people, the exciting experience of learning a new field, and, of course, helping millions of people instead of thousands. But I had not counted on the 224 fund-raising meetings all over the country during a recessionary year. I hated them! I love to teach and preach the Bible, but asking people for money to finance even this effective ministry? It was the hardest thing I have ever done in the work of God. In fact, I was tempted to quit 223 times.

Now that such meetings are behind us, I'm glad we didn't quit under fire. A long time ago I learned that God is interested in *finishers,* not starters. Sanguines are so capable they look for instant success, but are not used to putting their head down and ploughing on in the face of difficulty, opposition, or frustration.

Once they learn that lesson, there is no limit to what God can do with them vocationally.

ROCKY CHOLERIC'S VOCATIONAL POTENTIAL

Any profession that requires leadership, motivation, and productivity is open to a choleric, provided it does not require too much attention to details and analytical planning. Committee meetings and long-range planning bore him, for he is a doer. Although he is not usually a craftsman (which requires a degree of perfection and efficiency usually beyond his capability), he often serves as a supervisor for craftsmen. He usually enjoys construction because he is so productive and will frequently end up as a foreman or project supervisor.

Rocky is a developer by nature. When he and his wife drive through the countryside, he cannot share her enjoyment of the "beautiful rolling hillsides," for he envisions road graders carving out streets and builders constructing homes, schools, and shopping centers. Most of today's cities and suburbs were first envisioned by a choleric. You can be sure, however, that he hired a melancholy as the architect with the analytical and creative ability to draw the plans he has outlined, for he could never do that himself. He still can't understand why a few lines on the back of an envelope aren't sufficient to gain the city planning department's approval. No one fights City Hall harder than a choleric, who bitterly laments, "Why all this business of detailed plans, anyway? I've built enough projects to know that the best plans have to be modified during construction; so why not make up your mind as you go along on the little issues? I know what I want to accomplish!" It is a wise choleric who hires a melancholy as his assistant or goes into business partnership with a melancholy. Together they make an unbeatable team. Of course, since everyone has both a primary and secondary termperament, occasionally one meets a person with both traits.

Most entrepreneurs are cholerics. They formulate the ideas and are venturesome enough to launch out in new directions. They don't limit themselves to their own ideas either, but sometimes overhear a creative idea from someone who is not sufficiently adventurous to initiate a new business or project. Once Rocky has started a new business, however, it is not unlike him to get bored soon after it is successful. There are two reasons for this. First, as the business grows under his dynamic leadership, of necessity it creates more detail work. But since cholerics are not by nature good delegators of responsibility (although with proper training they can learn) and tend to prefer the fruits of their own productive and capable industry, the efforts of others are evaluated as somewhat inadequate. Consequently, they end up trying to do everything themselves. Second, when visionary Rocky finds himself so inundated with the mass of details this successful venture has spawned, he looks for a buyer to assume those responsibilities in order to free his own time to launch something new. Thus, the average choleric can be expected to start four to ten businesses or organizations in a lifetime.

Once a choleric learns to delegate responsibility to others and discovers that he is able to accomplish more through other people, he can complete an amazing amount of work. Other people cannot believe that he can be involved in so many things and keep his sanity, but to Rocky Choleric it is really very simple. Since he is completely performance-conscious and has no perfectionist hang-ups, he will reason, "I'd rather get a number of things finished 70 to 80 percent than a few things 100 percent." As Charley "Tremendous" Jones says in his talks to businessmen, "Your motto should be: From production to perfection." Cholerics love that philosophy; perfectionist melancholies reject it vigorously.

Rocky Choleric is a natural motivator of other people. He oozes self-confidence, is extremely goal-conscious, and can inspire others to envision his goals. Consequently, his associates may find themselves more productive by following his lead. His primary weakness as a leader is that he is hard to please and tends to run roughshod over other people. If he only knew how others look to him for approval and encouragement, he would spend more time patting them on the back and acknowledging their accomplishments, which would generate even greater dedication from his colleagues. The problem is, however, the choleric subconsciously thinks that approval and encouragement will lead to complacency, and he assumes that an employee's productivity will fall off if he is too complimentary. Thus he will resort to criticism and fault-finding, in the hope that this will inspire greater effort. Unfortunately, he must learn that criticism is a demotivator. Once Rocky discovers that people require reassurance and stimulation in order to perform at the height of their potential, his role as leader radically improves.

Learn a lesson from football's middle linebackers just before a crucial play. They walk up and down the line patting their teammates encouragingly. That touch silently urges, "I'm counting on you to do your best; don't let me down." As one lineman said of his defensive captain, "I'd lay down my life for that man!" Interestingly enough, the captain was a perennial back-patter.

In the early days of American industry, when business production and manufacturing were not so technical, our industrial complexes were largely built by cholerics. In these days as technology demands greater sophistication and creativity, it is gradually turning for leadership to melancholies or at least choleric/melancholies or melancholy/cholerics. Today cholerics are more apt to build the factory buildings or the streets and highways which furnish the supply routes used by industry, whereas complex organization increasingly requires a more analytical leader.

Don't feel sorry for the choleric of the future; he will figure out something worthy of his talents. He always lands on his feet. Cholerics have a built-in promotional ability and do well in sales, teaching (but always practical subjects), politics, military service, sports, and many other endeavors. Like the sanguine, Rocky Choleric makes a good preacher in the pulpit. Not only is he a dynamic Bible teacher, but his organization and promotional ability together with his strong leadership gifts make it hard for the average fearful congregation to slow him down. According to an old saying, "Fools rush in where angels fear to tread." No one ever accused a choleric of being an angel. He launches into many projects and, with proper motivation and the blessing of God, usually enjoys a successful ministry.

Western civilization has benefited much from its Rocky Cholerics (Nordic, Teutonic, Germanic, Gallic, or Frankish people often had a high degree of choleric temperament). But it has suffered much from them also. The world's greatest generals, dictators, and gangsters have been mainly cholerics. What made the difference? Their moral values and motivations. If there is such a thing as a "success tendency," cholerics have it. That doesn't mean they are smarter than other people, as is often assumed, but that their strong will and determination drive them to succeed where other more gifted people are prone to give up in the midst of their superior projects. If a job requires industry, hard work, and activity, Rocky Choleric will usually outperform the other temperaments. If it demands analysis, long-range planning, meticulous skills, or creativity, that's a different ballgame. Rarely will you find a predominant choleric as a surgeon, dentist, philosopher, inventor, or watchmaker. Rocky's interests thrive upon activity, bigness, violence, and production. He is so optimistic, rarely anticipating failure, that he seldom fails—except at home.

VOCATIONAL POSSIBILITIES OF MARTIN MELANCHOLY

As a general rule, no other temperament has a higher I.Q., creativity, or imagination than a melancholy, and no one else is as capable of perfectionism. Most of the world's great composers, artists, musicians, inventors, philosophers, theoreticians, theologians, scientists, and dedicated educators have been predominantly melancholies. Name a famous artist, composer, or orchestra leader and you have identified another genius and an often eccentric melancholy. Consider Rembrandt, Van Gogh, Beethoven, Mozart, Wagner, and a host of others. Usually the greater the degree of genius, the greater will be the predominance of a melancholy temperament.

Any vocation that requires perfection, self-sacrifice, and creativity is open to a Martin Melancholy. However, he tends to place self-imposed limitations on his potential by underestimating himself and exaggerating obstacles. Almost any humanitarian vocation will attract melancholies to its staff. For years I have watched doctors, and although there are bound to be exceptions, almost every doctor I know is either predominantly or at least secondarily a melancholy. It would almost require a melancholy's mind to get through the rigors of medical school, for a doctor has to be a perfectionist, an analytical specialist, and a humanitarian propelled by a heart that yearns to help other people.

The analytical ability required to design buildings, lay out a landscape, or look at acreage and envision a cohesive development usually requires a melancholy temperament. In the building trades the melancholy may want to supervise construction. However, he would be better off hiring a project supervisor who works better with people and then spend his own time on the drawing board. He becomes frustrated by the usual personnel problems and, with his unrealistic perfectionist demands, adds to them.

Almost every true musician has some melancholy temperament, whether he be a composer, choral conductor, performing artist, or soloist. This often accounts for the melancholy's lament that seems to find its way into so much of our music—both in and out of the church. Just yesterday my wife and I were driving to the airport when a country-western tune was crooned (or warbled, depending on your point of view) over the radio. We looked at each other and laughed as the wail of the obvious melancholy became so apparent—and that song is one of today's top tunes.

The influence of temperament on a person's musical ability was apparent several years ago as our church evaluated a very gifted minister of music and his piano-playing wife, obviously a choleric. On the way home I reflected to my wife that I couldn't understand how a choleric could be such a good pianist. Beverly replied, "She is a mechanical musician. By strong willpower she forced herself to play the piano well, but she doesn't feel her music." As it turned out, the fantastic arrangement she used that night had been written by her husband, a melancholy. Although he was not a pianist, he could feel music.

Not all melancholies, of course, enter the professions or arts. Many become craftsmen of a high quality—finish carpenters, bricklayers, plumbers, plasterers, scientists, nurserymen, playwrights, authors, mechanics, engineers, and members of almost every profession that provides a meaningful service to humanity. One vocation that seems to attract the melancholy, surprisingly enough, is acting, though we tend to identify this profession with an extrovert. On stage, the melancholy can become another person and even adopt that personality, no matter how much extroversion it requires; but as soon as the play is over and he comes down from his emotional high, he reverts back to his own more introverted personality.

VOCATIONAL APTITUDES OF THE PHLEGMATIC

The world has benefited greatly from the gracious nature of Phil Phlegmatic. In his quiet way he has proved to be a fulfiller of the dreams of others. He is a master at anything that requires meticulous patience and daily routine.

Most elementary school teachers are phlegmatics. Who but a phlegmatic could have the patience necessary to teach a group of first-graders to read? A sanguine would spend the entire class period telling stories to the children. A melancholy would so criticize them that they would be afraid to read aloud. And I can't even imagine a choleric as a first-grade teacher—the students would leap out the windows! The gentle nature of the phlegmatic assures the ideal atmosphere for such learning. This is not only true on the elementary level but in both high school and college, particularly in math, physics, grammar, literature, language classes, and others. It is not uncommon to find phlegmatics as school administrators, librarians, counselors, and college department heads. Phlegmatics seem drawn to the field of education.

Another field that appeals to phlegmatics is engineering. Attracted to planning and calculation, they make good structural engineers, sanitation experts, chemical enginers, draftsmen, mechanical and civil engineers, and statisticians. Most phlegmatics have excellent mechanical aptitude and thus become good mechanics, tool-and-die specialists, craftsmen, carpenters, electricians, plasterers, glassblowers, watch and camera repairmen.

The biggest problem faced by industry pertains to personnel. With wages for many jobs skyrocketing, disharmony in a department can so demotivate employees that the employer may lose millions of dollars in productivity. In recent years, management has begun to discover that experienced phlegmatics in their employ often make excellent foremen, supervisors, and managers of people. Because they are diplomatic and unabrasive, people work well with them. When given positions of leadership, they seem to bring order out of chaos and produce a working harmony that is conducive to increased productivity. They are well organized, never come to a meeting unprepared or late, tend to work well under pressure, and are extremely dependable. Phlegmatics often stay with one company for their entire working career.

An interesting aspect of their leadership ability is that they almost never volunteer for authoritative responsibilities, which is why I labeled them "reluctant leaders." Secretly a phlegmatic may aspire for a promotion, but it would be against his nature to volunteer. Instead, he may patiently wait until more discordant and inept personalities make a mess out of things and then assume the responsibility only after it is forced upon him. Unfortunately, in many instances phlegmatics wait their lives away and opportunity never knocks—because although employers appreciate their capabilities, they don't envision them as leaders. Consequently, both the company and the employees lose. Rarely does a phlegmatic either live up to his full capabilities or fail in life.

Phlegmatics may take a job with retirement or security benefits in mind. Therefore, civil service, the military, local government or some other "good security risk" will attract them. Rarely will they launch out on a business venture of their own, although they are eminently qualified to do so. Instead they usually enhance the earning power of someone else and are quite content with a simple life-style.

TEMPERAMENT TEST   You will find the self-scoring temperament test on page 93 very interesting now that you realize your temperament is the key to your vocational aptitude. You may even be more interested in the more professional temperament test which I developed over a fifteen-year period to help Christians find the right vocation and the best place in their own local church to serve the Lord. In the personalized analysis, which gives a thorough appraisal of your primary and secondary temperament, I included fifty vocational aptitudes which would fit your unique combination of temperaments. You also will find helpful the thirty possible places of service in your local church to which you would be best suited, based on your temperament combination. The $10 gift certificate in the back of this book entitles you to a discount off the current cost of this test. For details see page 351.

HOW TO FIND THE RIGHT JOB   Next to salvation, marriage, and your family, your vocation is the most important thing in your life. For that reason I would like to give you some of the practical suggestions I have personally shared with hundreds of men and women about how to change jobs, find one, or evaluate a new one.

Finding a lifetime vocation is really not too difficult *if* you're a Christian and *if* you're committed to seeking the Lord's will for your life. But don't expect it to be the dramatic thing it is for some people. I find that the narration of a dynamic experience of finding God's will to be very inspirational in a church service, but with most of us it is a slow, step-by-step process. While it is still true that God speaks to us today, it is rarely in the audible voice with which he spoke to Abraham, Isaac, and Moses. Most of us hear God by the gentle urging of our heart, or a "burden" that he puts into our hearts to do something. As we walk by faith, moving in the direction of that burden, we gradually find ourselves doing that will. For most of us, finding the will of God is not the electrifying experience of a moment, but a continuing process over a long period of time. We climb the mountain at hand only to find it leads to the next mountain. Then when we get to a central point we can look back and say, "Thank you, God, for your faithful leading."

God is interested in directing your life into the most productive and effective place where you can serve him. But he is first and foremost interested in you as a person. Most Christians have the attitude about finding God's will that was reflected by one man's honest but somewhat irreverent prayer. "Dear Lord, please write out on paper your plan for my life during the next ten years and if I like it, I'll do it!" Naturally we would never say such a thing, but often Christians act that way. Instead, God wants us to walk in unbroken fellowship with him so he can lead us in the making of the thousands of decisions in life that ultimately lead us to fulfill the perfect will of God.

The problem with most of us is that we are always in a hurry. God never rushes. He is more interested in our daily dependence on him than in all of the specifics. The reason he seldom gives us much advance warning or leading about his will is because he knows that even if we saw a ten-year blueprint, we would be off trying to do it and seldom check in at headquarters until we completed it or ran into a problem. Finding God's will for your life is not only the best possible way to live; it should also bring you closer to him in the process. My favorite verses in the Bible on this subject are:

> Trust in the Lord and do good; dwell in the land and enjoy safe pasture. *Delight yourself in the Lord,* and he will give you the desires of your heart. *Commit your way to the Lord; trust in him* and he will do this: He will make your righteousness shine like the dawn, the justice of your cause like the noonday sun. *Be still before the Lord and wait patiently for him;* do not fret when men succeed in their ways, when they carry out their wicked schemes. (Ps. 37:3-7, NIV)

> Trust in the Lord with all your heart and lean not on your own understanding; in all your ways acknowledge him, and he will make your paths straight. (Prov. 3:5, 6, NIV)

Once you have committed yourself to live the kind of life described above, you cannot go wrong. That doesn't mean you won't have problems or face obstacles. I have never known anyone who accomplished anything for God, great or small, who didn't find obstacles in his path. But it is end-results with which we are concerned. The following steps will guide you to finding the Lord's direction in your vocation.

SEVEN STEPS TO FINDING THE RIGHT VOCATION

1. Establish your *primary* purpose in life according to Matthew 6:33.

What is your *real* purpose in changing jobs or finding a new vocation? It should be the same as your life's motivation which Jesus outlined for every Christian— "But seek first his kingdom and his righteousness, and all these things will be given to you as well" (Matt. 6:33, NIV). Once you have determined that your *primary purpose* is to seek first the kingdom of God, then and only then are you ready to find a different position.

"More money," "better opportunity for advancement," or "more enjoyable work" are not good answers in themselves. Settle the matter of who is first in your life, whose servant you are (see 1 Cor. 6:19, 20); then you can get on with what is second. You may need more money, better opportunity, etc., and God knows that. But you need to know that your primary desire is to seek *first* the advancement of the kingdom.

That principle alone will save you many headaches. For example, all through the years of my counseling I have said, privately and publicly, that "anyone who has a job that requires they work every Sunday so they can rarely, if ever, attend church has the wrong job." God's will on Sunday is that we attend church; there is no question on that. If your job will not permit you to obey God, then you have the wrong job.

Twenty years ago a personable supermarket manager with a wife and three small girls told me, "I can't come to church because I work on Sundays; that way I get double-time pay." I told him that was wrong motivation for working on Sunday. Once in a while is understandable. Even in the Old Testament, when the ox got into the ditch on the Sabbath day, it had to be pulled out. Jesus also endorsed that plan. Obviously, someone is going to have to work on the Sabbath and get dirty. But God said OK because it was only occasional or an emergency. But every Sabbath day was different. So it is with the Lord's day. I watched that man lose his wife and three girls to a carnal, Southern California life-style. His double-time pay cost him far more than it gained him. And now that it is too late, he has realized it.

This same principle will help guide you in the kind of employment you seek. If it involves illegal or harmful products, that is not seeking the kingdom of God. A woman told me she turned down "$20,000 a year

and perks" as an executive secretary because it involved all-night
entertaining of some of the firm's out-of-town customers. There are
some things more important in life than money—Matthew 6:33 makes
that clear.

2. Analyze your temperament.

The simple temperament test on page 93 will help you determine
your temperament, which is a key to your vocational aptitude. We have
already gone into detail on the vocational capabilities of each of the four
temperaments. The following rule of thumb will give you general
guidance, although you would really benefit from taking the
temperament test described in the back of this book.

Sanguines	are people-oriented salesman types who excel in public relations, people-helping, or anything that requires charisma.
Cholerics	are strong natural leaders that are goal- or project-oriented individuals who like to manage people.
Melancholies	are creative, analytical individuals with strong perfectionist tendencies who often have aesthetic traits.
Phlegmatics	are cool, detailed individuals who tend to limit themselves. They can do statistical, microscopic work that would drive others berserk.

With that brief overview you can tell generally what kind of vocation
best suits your needs. If you are discontent in your present employment,
your temperament test may reveal you are in the wrong type of work.

3. Pray.

The introductory verse at the beginning of this section covered the
key words, "pray," "trust," "commit," and "acknowledge" God. That
is what prayer is. It is what asking God is based upon. If you are
unemployed or dissatisfied where you are employed, then pray about it.
God will either remove your discontentment or open the door to a new
opportunity—if you give him time and draw closer to him during the
waiting period.

4. Share your concern with others you can trust.

Regardless of your temperament, you will find it helpful to share your burden with a friend. That's what friends are for. As the Scripture says, "bear one another's burdens and fulfill the law of Christ." How can a friend share a burden unless you let him? Usually it is helpful just to verbalize to another person your innermost thoughts. And those who find that kind of talk the most difficult are the very ones who need it most.

Be sure the friend with whom you seek counsel shares your spiritual values. Psalm 1:1 says, "Blessed [happy] is the man who does not walk in the counsel of the wicked" (NIV). That is so important! Many a Christian has sought counsel from a professional counselor or vocational counselor and failed to filter that counsel in the light of the fact that the individual did not share his eternal perspective in relation to God, life, death, or eternity. As a pastor, I saw many individuals heed the advice of non-Christians at their peril.

Talking out your burden or sharing it with your friends does more than just help you clarify your thinking. It puts others on the alert for opportunities. I have been amazed at the way God opens doors through other people.

5. Investigate.

Don't plan to sit back after you have prayed about it and expect God to send down a job on a white cloud. Prayer usually motivates us to do something, like look in the want ads. I have a friend who while praying about her need felt the urge to read the want ads and found a local Christian doctor looking for help. He had prayed for guidance three days before and felt led to call the newspaper. His ad was only in the paper three days. She caught it the first day, and now two Christians who wanted to work with a Christian both got the answer to their prayer.

Oftentimes the biblical directive, "you have not because you ask not" seriously limits our lives vocationally.

Some reading this may be entirely unskilled. You may have married young thinking "it will all work out" and now find yourself unemployable. You may well need to go back to school. An industrial arts program or some other specialized training plan may be your need.

Make a list of the kind of jobs you think you would enjoy doing and that pay what you feel you will need for your family to live on. Then prioritize those on the top of your list and start contacting them. If you need to take night school or specialized training, do it. It is becoming increasingly necessary that everyone going out into the work force be trained in some area. Even the Bible says a "workman" is one who "studies" (2 Tim. 2:15). There are very few positions that do not require "study." If that's what it takes, do it!

When I was forty-eight years old, I enrolled in graduate school at Western Conservative Bible Seminary, through their San Diego satellite program. It took four long years and lots of hard work to meet their rigorous demands, but finally I earned my degree. I found it a very stimulating influence on my whole ministry to go back to school. (Even after being a college president for six years, you're never too old to learn.) Many people have found a whole new stimulating vocational life open to them by paying the price to get some advanced training either in their chosen field or in another.

God has given you certain basic skills. You will never get more than he gave you, but through training, discipline, and practice you can improve and refine those skills. Personally, I don't believe God will do anything for us vocationally that we can do for ourselves.

6. Be faithful and watch for the open door.

Our Lord said, "These are the words of him who is holy and true, who holds the key of David. What he opens, no one can shut; and what he shuts, no one can open. I know your deeds. See, I have placed before you an open door that no one can shut" (Rev. 3:7, 8, NIV).

I have found that our Lord is the master of the "open door." That is, he leads us to an open door of opportunity to serve him. The best advice I have ever heard is that we do not need a lifetime roadmap or masterplan for our lives. We just need to stay in close fellowship with the Master, who does have a plan for our lives. So we should busy ourselves cleaning up the room we are now in and God will, in his own time, open another door for us. Once inside, we will find it too needs a lot of hard work, so we should busy ourselves cleaning up the second room. About the time we get that room cleaned up, there will be a third door open to us, then a fourth and so on. Finally we will look back and say, "Hasn't God been faithful to lead us into so many places of opportunity to serve him?" But in the meantime we need to be found "faithful," cleaning up the room we are in.

I shall never forget my first church. We were building a sign in front of the church, and I was in my study when the truck delivering bricks arrived. I signed for the delivery and the driver said, "Who do you have to unload these bricks?" I said, "We're paying you to deliver them." To which he replied, "I am a truck driver, not a laborer. Unless you find someone to unload these bricks, I will return them to the plant!" So I jumped up in the truck and proceeded to unload the bricks. That was thirty years ago. I have never wanted for work. In fact, my only frustration is that I can't do all the things I would like to. I've often wondered how long that truck driver kept his job—with that attitude, probably not very long.

God doesn't ask us all to be successful or to hit a home run every time at bat. He does, however, ask that we be "faithful." That is something everyone should be. Right where we are. Don't let your interest in a new job keep you from being faithful where you are.

7. Anticipate the future with peace and confidence.

God holds the key to your future, so don't worry about it. Our Lord spoke about that many times in words like these:

> Therefore I tell you, do not worry about your life, what you will eat or drink; or about your body, what you will wear. Is not life more important than food, and the body more important than clothes? Look at the birds of the air; they do not sow or reap or store away in barns, and yet your heavenly Father feeds them. Are you not much more valuable than they? Who of you by worrying can add a single hour to his life? And why do you worry about clothes? See how the lilies of the field grow. They do not labor or spin. Yet I tell you that not even Solomon in all his splendor was dressed like one of these. If that is how God clothes the grass of the field, which is here today and tomorrow is thrown into the fire, will he not much more clothe you, O you of little faith? So do not worry, saying, 'What shall we eat?' or 'What shall we drink?' or 'What shall we wear?' For the pagans run after all these things, and your heavenly Father knows that you need them. But seek first his kingdom and his righteousness, and all these things will be given to you as well. Therefore do not worry about tomorrow, for tomorrow will worry about itself. Each day has enough trouble of its own. (Matt. 6:25-34, NIV)

It is one thing to be concerned about the future; it is quite another to worry about it. When you commit your way to God, you don't have to worry about the future. I have to remind myself of that fact every now and then. It helps to have many Bible verses hidden in your heart for instant recall. When you're in a ministry like mine, where you're dependent on the response to monthly mailings to carry on the Lord's work, you are very vulnerable to the erratic responses of people.

Summer is a disaster, December is almost as bad, and January and February are slow starters. That leaves six good months out of the year. Recession, inflation, late mailings, foul-ups at the printers, the mailing house or some other vendor can even lose one of those months. Such ministries are well labeled "faith ministries"—you live week by week by faith. But then, who doesn't? Insurance companies and even banks can fail, and only God knows if Social Security will last. In the final analysis you're in good hands only when you trust the living God.

The one thing you have going for you is that your God is the God of the future. I have often comforted myself with this thought: "God has never failed anyone, Tim; so why should he make an exception of you? You're just not that important." God gets more glory for himself by being faithful.

He won't let you down! Remember Noah, Abraham, Moses, Job, David, Peter, John, Paul, and millions of others!

CHAPTER
SEVEN

Uses of Temperament in the Workplace

As a student of psychology for over thirty years, I long ago made the observation that the business community had a much more effective model of human behavior than did the academic. The colleges seemed obsessed with humanistic psychology that started out on so many false premises we shouldn't be surprised that it changes every few years. We have seen Freudian psychology, once the shrine before which the university crowd gladly bowed, replaced by Rogerianism, behaviorism, Gestalt theory, reality therapy, transactional analysis, and much frustration—particularly by the patients whose only consistent observation was the exorbitant bill that came to their home each month.

What are the false premises of humanistic psychology? Very simply that: (1) man is an evolved animal; (2) man has no inherited conscience; (3) there is no Creator God; (4) there is no absolute standard for behavior given by that God; (5) man, like the animals, has no soul—so when you're dead you're dead; and (6) man's ultimate end is self-actualization.

Given those basic assumptions, it is no wonder modern psychology has wrought such havoc in our society. We have more schizophrenic, mentally ill, depressed, suicidal, hostile, and upset people today than before we had psychologists. The reason is very simple. A basic axiom of all logic is: If you start out on a wrong premise, you will end up with a wrong conclusion. I've counseled enough psychologists and their wives to know that their solutions, without God, are impractical. They just don't work! Much of the advice given by secular humanist psychologists is not only wrong, but harmful.

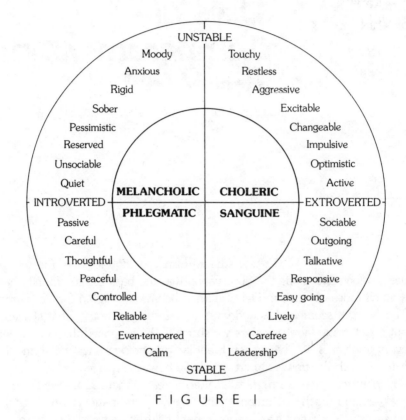

F I G U R E I

Business is quite a different matter. Industrial psychology may not be given much schrift in the halls of academia, but it helps far more people than clinical psychology. And interestingly enough, it is based on the theory of the four temperaments.

For some reason, American psychologists have been heavily influenced by Sigmund Freud, although they have discounted many of his obsolete theories and developed a godless modern version of their own. But few American professors have embraced the scholarly works of Dr. H. J. Eysenck of England. He is highly respected in Europe and in the industrial, sales, and management fields of psychology in this country. In fact, most of the popular programs used in business management, sales, and personal development are based on his exhaustive research. And Dr. Eysenck is an advocate of the four-temperament theory, which he ascribes to Hippocrates.

The Educational and Industrial Testing Service is a San Diego-based

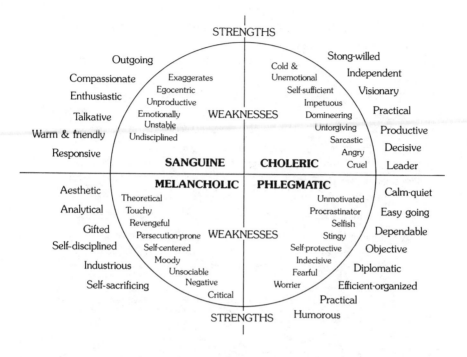

F I G U R E 2

company that produces the E.P.I.—Eysenck Personality Inventory. The following diagram (Fig.1) is an Eysenck trademark of both his books and this test. Note how similar it is to the basic chart (Fig.2) which I have refined from many other sources plus my own observations. The similarities are such that both are obviously based on the ancient theory of the four temperaments.

Through the years I have received hundreds of letters from people who have read my books on temperament or have heard my lectures on the subject. Many of those letters are about personality testing they have gone through, sales management training, or vocational training programs they have taken. In all the materials I have received, there is a consistent similarity to the four temperament theory. I have studied these materials, whether produced in Denver, Minneapolis, Chicago, or Dallas; I find they are based on the careful research of Dr. Eysenck or the theory of the four temperaments or both.

HARVARD BUSINESS
REVIEW

For example, in the Harvard Business Review, published by the graduate schools of business administration of Harvard University, Dr. Theodore Levitt wrote an interesting article entitled "The Managerial Merry-go-round," in which he points out: "People have different cognitive styles—that is, ways of gathering and evaluating information. Some are systematic thinkers, others intuitive thinkers, some are receptive thinkers and others perceptive thinkers. These styles seem to be inherent and are fairly fixed by the time people reach maturity. What is even more instructive is that the research found that these styles greatly affect the way people perform the jobs they choose, and can even determine the industries they enter" (*Fact and Fiction in Psychology*, Penguin Books, 1965, p. 55).

You will notice that this article is divergent from humanistic psychology's claim that all people are born neutral and that environment molds one's behavior. The business community recognizes that it is worthwhile to train management personnel at every level, but it also recognizes that there are inborn characteristics in people that are irreversible.

"Each of us marches to a different drummer; the secret of good teamwork is blending contrasting executive styles," argue Stuart Atkins and Allan Katcher, president and vice-president respectively of Atkins-Katcher Associates, Inc., management consultants in Beverly Hills, California. The following excerpts appeared in *Nation's Business* (March 1975):

> To get the best performance from your executive team, you have to orchestrate them, getting each to give his best and helping them to blend their strengths for peak performance as a group. To achieve this, you must analyze their different styles of operating. Everyone is a mixture of four basic behavior patterns, usually with one dominating. The others, less used, come into play when the situation calls for them. There are, however, no "good" or "bad" styles.

> A person whose dominant style is Supporting-Giving tends to be trusting, responsive, idealistic and loyal. He tries to do the very best he can whenever you assign him a task, and he sets high standards for himself and his people. Highly receptive to others' ideas, he cooperates and is helpful, a natural team player.

PERSONALITY
PROFILE TESTING

In recent years the business community has begun using a series of tests which they administer to screen employees for major industries. The individual takes a test consisting of 150 adjectives (mostly worked out by Dr. Eysenck). One firm sends a test to five of the prospect's friends to determine how the individual is seen by other people.

The test results do not use the terms sanguine, choleric, phlegmatic, melancholy; but anyone familiar with their meaning will recognize their parallel with "expressive," "driver," "analytical," and "amiable." Call it what you may, the final results are much the same.

One testing group calls them "four social styles" and points out that most people are a combination of at least two social styles. As you examine their instrument in Fig. 3, you will find a basic similarity to what we have studied as the four basic temperaments. The test results locate a person's primary and secondary social style.

FOUR BASIC SOCIAL STYLES

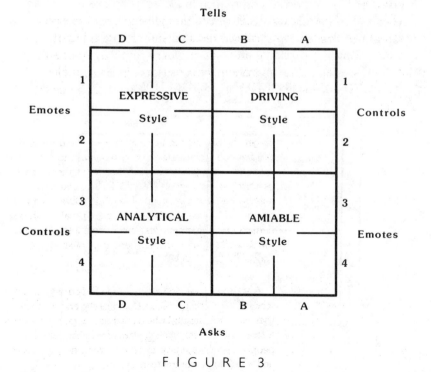

FIGURE 3

A verbal description of each social style as pictured in Fig. 4 shows a marked similarity to our four temperament theory.

In the September 1979 issue of *Dallas* I found a very interesting article on the variety of Chief Executive Officers (CEO's) in the dynamic world of Metro Dallas. I've been to that city several times and even as I write this am standing in the Registry Hotel located in the heart of the boom growth of North Dallas.

Bill Sloan, author of *Life at the Top,* had noticed four styles of CEO's in the plush offices of the mirrored towers in Dallas. He called them "initiator, thinker, feeler, and sensor," titles used by many management consultants, but they are just different names for melancholy, phlegmatic, sanguine, and choleric. He used Mary Kay, the famous head of a gigantic cosmetic industry, as an example of a "feeler," which he describes as "sentimental, loyal and true blue," "thrives on personal relationships." He then explains she is heavy into the world of people and is an excellent motivator.

To him, Ross Perot, the genius who started out renting time on computers to sell to clients and today owns banks of computers and heads a multimillion dollar corporation in Dallas, is an example of an intuitor or melancholy whose creativity and penchant for innovation together with his workaholic drive have taken him to the top.

**SHORTHAND DESCRIPTIONS
OF THE BASIC SOCIAL STYLES**

	Asks / Controls		Asks / Emotes	
ANALYTICAL	Critical Indecisive Stuffy Picky Moralistic	Industrious Persistent Serious Exacting Orderly	Manipulative Excitable Undisciplined Reacting Egotistical	Ambitious Stimulating Enthusiastic Dramatic Friendly	**AMIABLE**
EXPRESSIVE	Conforming Unsure Ingratiating Dependent Awkward	Supportive Respectful Willing Dependable Agreeable	Pushy Severe Tough Dominating Harsh	Strong-willed Independent Practical Decisive Efficient	**DRIVING**
	Tells / Emotes		Tells / Controls	

FIGURE 4

Not only did this personnel expert point out the four types of managers in parallel to the four temperament theory, but he confirms what I have long suspected. That all four types can make successful CEO's, but in different fields and with different styles. "Feelers" (or sanguines) make good sales managers, personnel directors, and goodwill ambassadors. "Intuitors" (melancholies) make excellent advertising executives, public relations directors, heads of research, or anything that demands creativity. "Thinkers" (phlegmatics) are best suited as finance directors, heads of engineering groups, executive vice presidents, etc. The sensor (choleric) is in charge and can run any kind of corporation if given the right personnel.

Whether you call them "thinkers" or phlegmatics, "intuitors" or melancholies, they are the same. You are talking about inherited temperament that can be improved, educated, and refined, but does not change. Mary Kay was a "feeler" at four years of age, and as a supersuccessful sanguine she is still a "feeler," "toucher," or people-person. No doubt she has learned discipline, organization, and management, but she was a born motivator with charisma to burn.

We all inherited a temperament that produces our "style." No one style is better than another, but each fits different kinds of work better than others. Management would be advised to spend more time discovering an employee's temperament so he can train him for the work for which he is best fitted.

FOUR TYPES—THE
DOMINANT MODEL
During the past fifty years many theories of behavior have been proposed. The most effective and long lasting are based to some degree at least on a model of four types or styles of behavior. People are different. They act different, respond different, and react different.

One government training specialist pointed out that the November 1982 issue of *Training* magazine listed fifteen of the most common theories. Some of the most common are listed below. Admittedly, they are abbreviated drastically, but notice how each fits under one of the four temperament theory categories. Although the authors may not wish to admit to such similarity to the world's most ancient theory of behavior which we have been studying, when put on this chart (Fig. 5) it would seem such similarities exist.

THE FOUR-BEHAVIOR-STYLE THEORIES

	HIGH ASSERTIVENESS HIGH RESPONSIVENESS	HIGH ASSERTIVENESS LOW RESPONSIVENESS	LOW ASSERTIVENESS HIGH RESPONSIVENESS	LOW ASSERTIVENESS LOW RESPONSIVENESS
1. BASIC SYSTEMS Stuart Atkins, LIFO® (Life Orientations)	Adapting-Dealing	Controlling-Taking	Supporting-Giving	Conserving-Holding
William M. Marston, *"Emotions of Normal People"*	Inducement of Others	Dominance	Steadiness	Compliance
Medieval Four Temperaments	Sanguine	Choleric	Melancholy	Phlegmatic
David W. Merrill– Roger H. Reid, *"Personal Styles and Effective Performance"*	Expressive	Driver	Analytical	Amiable
2. CONFLICT RESOLUTION Jay Hall Conflict Management Survey	Synergistic	Win-Lose	Yield-Lose	Lose-Leave
Donald T. Simpson, *"Conflict Styles: Organizational Decision Making"*	Integration	Power	Suppression	Denial
Thomas-Kilmann Conflict Mode Instrument	Collaborating	Competing	Accommodating	Avoiding
3. PERFORMANCE APPRAISAL Robert E. Lefton et al., *"Effective Motivation Through Performance Appraisal"*	Dominant-Warm	Dominant-Hostile	Submissive-Hostile	Submissive-Warm

F I G U R E 5

This chart (Fig. 5) could only have been produced by a thorough student of both the four temperaments and the modern attempts to explain or test man's behavior based on Eysenck's research. I reproduce it here for students of both fields so they can see how the modern trends are taking us back to the days of Hippocrates and even to Agur in the book of Proverbs.

The business community for the past twenty years has been increasingly aware of the practicality of the temperament theory. They may call him expressive instead of Sparky Sanguine, but they mean the same temperament. They may call him driver-analytical, but they still mean the choleric-melancholy temperament.

I predict that whatever they call it, the business community because of its commitment to practicality, cost effectiveness, and personnel development will lead us away from the unrealistic idealism of humanistic psychology to the more relevant four-temperament theory of behavior to explain why man acts the way he does and what he can do about it. The reason is very simple—it works.

The most obvious use of the four behavioral styles of business or the four-temperament theory comes in helping people to understand why they act the way they do and in helping them learn to modify their communication styles. The four-temperament theory of the ancients or the four-behavior styles of modern industry are an excellent way to present training programs. It is a handy aid in not only improving communication skills, but time management, leadership styles, performance appraisals, team building, conflict resolution, and improved productivity.

Recently I sent the department heads of Family Life Seminars to a management conference conducted by Arthur F. Miller of People Management, Incorporated. This man, who has spent a lifetime in management training and consultation said that one out of two persons in the United States is in the wrong job. This increases job-related conflicts and stress in both the work place and in the employee's home or family life.

Now you see why I say our nation has ignored the four-temperament theory at its peril for many years. If the psychology departments of our major universities would once again return to the ancient theory of human temperament, update it, and use it on our thirteen million college students and/or twenty million high school students, it would have a positive affect in both the workplace and family life.

Mr. Miller says that he is familiar with the inside personnel procedures of some of the largest companies in America, but unfortunately "no one has a plan to match an employee's job with his strengths and weaknesses." That would explain why so many people spend their life doing a job they dislike and then go home to take out the frustrations on the people they love most, or ease their stress (temporarily) by drug or alcohol.

Hopefully the last decade and a half of this century will find more emphasis on job fitness or helping people select the vocation in life for which they are best fitted. The temperament theory can really help this field.

As modern research continues to produce new and better ways of testing, training, and developing people's natural traits, work habits, and social styles, we will find a continuing use of the four-temperament theory. You, as a reader of this book, will be ahead of the pack because you understand the basic theory. And if you have experienced the powerful work of the Spirit of God as outlined earlier, you will already have a handle on overcoming your weaknesses and maximizing your potential.

CHAPTER
EIGHT

Other Ways to Use the Four-Temperament Theory

The four-temperament theory is not a cure-all for everything, but it certainly is a good tool to use in helping us get along with other people. I have always presented it with two primary uses in mind: self-improvement, and improving your interpersonal relationships. But there are many other ways which you will find helpful. I shall suggest a dozen or so, then you can add some of your own.

I have found the temperament theory to be most helpful, and there is no end to the uses or applications you can make for it. However, the first and best use is on yourself. Once you have learned the theory and how to strengthen your own weaknesses, you will find it helpful in the following ways:

1. *Counseling others.* I mention counseling to begin with because that is one place I have personally used it in helping thousands of people. It is a wonderful tool for diagnosing people's problems. You cannot help anyone unless you know what their root problem is. Many times the things they say are not the real cause of their difficulties. To me, counseling is helping people apply biblical principles to their lives where they cannot apply them alone. Most counselees don't know why they are so miserable. Consequently, the first thing any counselor does is listen and try to diagnose the individual's major difficulty. If you understand the four temperaments, it streamlines the diagnostic process.

By watching the counselee carefully for giveaway signs through body language, speech, attitudes, and the general flow of their conversation, it is usually easy to diagnose an upset person's primary temperament. Once I have done this, I look for problems associated with their temperament. If he is a sanguine, I look for anger, insecurity, lack of discipline, and sometimes immorality. If he is choleric, I look for anger, bitterness, and other forms of hostility, self-justification, coldness, or eruptions and a tendency to run roughshod over others. If I am working with a melancholy person, I expect self-condemnation, depression, self-limitation, criticism, a negative and critical spirit, or ingratitude toward God and others. In a melancholy man I sometimes anticipate male impotence or in a woman the frustration of frigidity. Phlegmatics tend to clutter their lives with worry, fear, procrastination, and lack of motivation. I rarely have discovered immorality among phlegmatic men; but occasionally a phlegmatic woman, due to her tendency to "go along and keep the peace," may give in to the temptation.

All of these problems and others for the various temperaments need to be considered and addressed in the counseling room. Unless an individual is confronted with biblical standards of behavior, he will not be lastingly helped. Once you diagnose and confront the individual with the problem, she needs a spiritual prescription to build the cure on. But the administration of the prescription should be given with her temperament in view. Sanguines and phlegmatics need a midweek call just to check up on their faithfulness. They need that extra prod to get going. The choleric needs to be assured that the formula will work, and the melancholy needs to keep from making a three-hour production out of a twenty-minute a day assignment.

Counseling people can be an enjoyable experience if you see progress in most of them. Knowing and using the temperament theory is a tool for improving the counselor's success ratio.

2. *Using the temperament theory in selling.* The salesman who approaches people according to their temperaments will be more successful than the one who approaches everyone alike. People differ, and good salesmen know it and approach them accordingly.

Sanguines are impulse buyers and are notorious for having no sales resistance. They aren't interested in details, but enjoy success stories. They love being entertained, and usually they enact their biggest deals on the golf course or in the restaurant. Be sure to stress feelings, ego, and "everyone has one" and usually you will make a sale (80 percent of the time). Get a good down payment though, for he changes his mind easily.

Cholerics are tougher to sell. Being practical, they respond to need. Why do they need it? How will they use it? What real value does it have? How much will it be worth five years from now? Ask his opinion and listen as if to an expert. He loves bargains; so give him a discount. He is opinionated; so get the kind and color he wants. Don't try to con him, but be sure and show him how he can pay for it. If you have been convincing, he may buy. Don't clutter your presentation with too much detail. Give one or two success stories, but don't waste his "valuable time" talking too much. If he really wants what you have, he is a 70 percent sales prospect and not usually given to shopping around. Let him see it and handle it; then back off. He will sell himself.

Melancholies need facts, statistics, charts, and detail. Don't try to bluff them! If you don't know your product, don't even bother to call on them. They can ask more questions about your product than both the inventor and manufacturer ever thought of. When he asks a question, find the answer. But always tell the truth; he has a memory like an elephant. Leave a good brochure, go find the answer, and then return. He has thousands of honest doubts and questions. Treat all his doubts and criticisms as requests for more information. He only buys the best he can afford; so convince him your product is the best on the market for the price. (If it isn't, go work for the best or don't try to sell him.) He doesn't want to hear a lot of success stories. He wants to know what your product will do for him, his home, or his company. Don't try to entertain him. He prides himself on the fact that he can't be bought. Send him something at Christmas time or after your first sale. Build a relationship of reliability and see that your firm services his account, and he will become a customer for years. Sales prospects are 50-50, but he gets terrible buyer's remorse the day after signing a contract. A follow-up call and enthusiastic report do wonders. And be sure to instruct him or his people on the use of your product. Remember, you're building a lifetime client. He has that potential.

Phlegmatics love to be "sold," but cannot be pressured. They like a combination of detail and success stories. They buy for many reasons, including prestige and practicality. Rarely do they buy the top of the line. Remember, they are not flamboyant. They prefer the stripped-down version. Give them plenty of latitude in choosing a price range ($20,000 or $50,000). Let them guide you to their needs. They beg to be entertained and love to be persuaded. Invite their wives along; it makes them feel important. They ask intelligent questions and must have all their fears assuaged or it's "no sale." Help them to see that your product will save money in the long run. Treat them with respect; don't fawn over them, but answer their questions and go back until they buy. The more attention you give them, the more obligated they feel. But

after the sale, if you drop them like a hot potato they may never buy
from you again. Like the melancholy, they can develop "buyer's
remorse." They need assurance after the sale that they did the right
thing—another success story or news about another company that just
bought your product will do it. They usually use their old equipment one
or two years longer than others.

I heard an interesting thing in a Chicago airport as I was writing the
above. A businessman who identified himself as a "salesman for a major
household product" and I began talking, and he asked what I was
writing. When I described the four-temperament approach to selling, his
eyes opened wide and I asked if he agreed. His response was
interesting: "I can name people and describe examples of these four
types. We deal with them every day."

3. *Using temperaments in managing people.* Good management
involves selection, training, motivating, and controlling people as they
work harmoniously toward a united goal. The first and most important
thing in good management is to put the right people in the right place.
We have already seen how understanding the four temperaments and
applying this to people is helpful. But it is also a good tool for managers
to use in getting the most out of people once they are on the payroll.

Sanguines are predictably unpredictable. Their natural lack of
discipline makes them late and unprepared when they come to work
each day. Either they must be trained to do detail or provided with a
secretary who can do it for them. Their greatest asset is production and
sales. Don't expect them to conform to all company policy. The biggest
task a manager has is guiding them to spend 90 percent of their time in
their most productive area. If they cannot conform, they will become
liabilities. I know a salesman who could not resist the temptation to
throw in extra goodies to his customers and make extra promises that
were not company policy in order to make sales. The company
president told me, "He made so many sales his commissions were more
than my salary. And when we fired him for giving away the company
store, we discovered that his expenses, commissions, shipping charges,
etc., cost us $800,000 more than our profits." Obviously, such
individuals need close supervision, but they don't like it.

Cholerics are self-starters and quick-learners. Don't be afraid to
delegate responsibility to them. But make sure they fully understand the
guidelines, objectives, and limits. Expect confrontation. They will
challenge your authority. Don't flunk their test. If you give them an inch,
they will take three miles. And don't let them run roughshod over

people. They need management training but are worth it because they can accomplish a ton of work. Just remember—he is after your job.

Melancholies are temperamental people. Make sure they are in the right field. They need constant encouragement that they have worth and are capable, and they usually are. Try not to give them too many things to do at the same time or they will explode, quit, or collapse. He is the one person who may foul up his homelife working too late or taking work home. Help him see that his brand of perfectionism is not necessary to the production of a top-quality product. With proper encouragement and reward he may be with you for life.

Phlegmatics are nuts-and-bolts, quiet people who can be depended on if you keep their eyes on the goals. But you must set their goals. By nature they would accept 55 percent of their capability. They work best under pressure but balk at high pressure; so keep it gentle, reasonable, and encouraging. They also need plenty of approval. Sometimes time-study training will be needed to help them make better use of their time. They may never defy you, but don't be surprised if they ignore you. They need constant reminders of productivity.

The thing all managers need to keep in mind is, don't expect other people to do things like you would. They are individuals. They have distinct talents and abilities. Help them function within those capabilities. I have found that most people, particularly Christians, will rise to a challenge if they are treated with love and respect.

4. *Use it in educating others.* The four-temperament theory is an invaluable tool in educating individuals. One of my criticisms of the monstrous business of education today is that they have ignored the temperaments of children in their teaching process. Educators have made a shambles out of our once great school system with their untested theories that have set the learning process back instead of forward. The gifted melancholy student is a fast-learner who may not need rote learning. But to scrap the rote method for all students is to disregard their temperaments. The sanguine, choleric, or phlegmatic child needs rote learning and disciplined drills to become proficient. Gradually, as the basic principles of math, reading, or history begin to fall into place, he can become a self-starter thinker. Sanguines are restless, temperamental flitters; phlegmatics are daydreamers; and cholerics spin-off on their own tangents. A wise teacher will try to diagnose her pupils' tendencies and motivate them according to need. Sanguines and phlegmatics need prodding; cholerics need goals and knowledge as to why something is relevant; melancholies need exposure to the subject

and encouragement. And as we have seen in a previous chapter, each temperament has subject strengths they enjoy and subject weaknesses. If you know his temperament, you can give him the encouragement he needs accordingly.

5. *Use the temperament theory to resolve personality conflicts.* Some people are so difficult, the Lord himself couldn't get along with them. During his day he clashed with the legalists who refused to believe in him and finally called them "whited sepulchres filled with dead men's bones." But most people with whom we clash are different temperaments; that's why we clash. For example, the melancholy-perfectionist is orderly and precise. As such he is destined to clash with the free-spirited casual carelessness of the sanguine. They will irritate each other. The sanguine can get irritated by what he considers the fastidiousness of the melancholy. One great cause of conflict between the two is exactness of language. The sanguine guestimates on figures, mileage, and details, while the melancholy feels it his duty to "correct" the sanguine. No wonder they irritate each other, whether in marriage, business, or church. The melancholy destroys the sanguine's ego by such corrections, so the sanguine lashes out in retaliation with his best weapon—his tongue.

Cholerics have a similar problem. They walk faster, talk faster, and think faster than the laid-back phlegmatic. The relationship of the phlegmatic is both a source of irritation to the choleric and a challenge. The more the choleric tries to motivate the phlegmatic, the more the phlegmatic digs in his heels and stubbornly refuses to move. The hostility such interpersonal contacts can generate is incredible. However, sanguines can irritate cholerics also, but not for the same reasons that irritate the melancholy. But if you want to see an explosion, just watch a sanguine and choleric locked in personality conflict. The two temperaments that seem to have the least conflict are the sanguine and the phlegmatic.

There are two main reasons for personality clashes: (1) temperament conflicts—that is, two individuals that are so different they spontaneously act and react entirely opposite in almost every situation; or (2) we see our weaknesses in someone we love and tend to overreact. This often happens to a parent who clashes with a child who picks up the parent's weaknesses. The first is easier to resolve than the second.

Once you recognize that your conflict with another person is because your temperaments are so opposite, it is easier to accept that difference; you recognize it is not personal but natural. This is the old "equal but different" idea. You can respect the other person's right to be different from yourself without superiority or inferiority being involved. The problem is, many people tend to look down on another's differences.

That is where the Spirit-filled life is of great value. When we are filled with love, joy, peace, etc., including "meekness," we will find it easier to accept the erratic or different reactions of others. That is just one step to anticipating them. For example, I have a sanguine friend who used to drive me up the wall with his gross exaggerations. (He calls them embellishments.) I could never count on his facts, estimates, or schedules. Instead of getting irritated all the time, I just began dividing everything he said by four, and then I could realistically anticipate his cost estimates and projections. For my pessimistic friends, I just anticipate their gloom, doom, and despair mentality and work around it. For example, my dentist wanted to tear out my bridge and rework the whole thing. I challenged him to "patch it" and even suggested how. It took a lot of persuasion, but he finally did it against his better judgment saying, "It won't last!" I am now on my third year with that repair job, and he still can't believe it will hold. If you take no for an answer from some people, you will both be the losers for it.

The temperament theory won't solve all personality conflicts, but it can reduce them down to size and make them livable.

6. *Use the theory to understand the other members of your church boards and committees.* One of the proofs that the local church is divinely inspired and empowered of God is that even democracy, demanded by most church leaders, still hasn't killed it. This is a day when everyone wants to be a part of the decision-making process. If the pastor is a dictator, the people complain that the church is dominated by one man. If it is a deacon-led church with seventy elders or deacons, there will be people who complain it entrusts too much power in the board. I have come to the conclusion that most people complain about any leader if he makes a decision they don't like.

I have worked with church boards for thirty-two years, and I can vouch for the fact that all four temperaments get on any board of seven or more people and usually react according to temperament. I'll never forget the time we were $56,000 in the red during a recession, and the melancholies on the eleven-member Board of Trustees wanted to cut salaries and lay off several staff members. It took all the optimistic persuasion I could muster to talk them into giving me more time, but they finally did—only to find that in seven months we had a small bank balance and had laid off no one. Before I heard about temperaments, I would have to fight harboring a bitter attitude toward such dooms-dayers. Once I recognized their natural tendency, I wrote it off as their temperament and refused to take it personally—or to give in without a fight.

Sanguine board members are talkers, not doers or listeners. They need to be given something to do and held accountable. Their talk at board meetings should be limited to their production.

Cholerics tend to take over if you give them a chance. But if you have a project of importance you want passed by a board you serve on, I suggest you talk to the cholerics in advance and get them on your team. When the meeting comes, they will carry the ball for you and will intimidate all the dooms-dayers into agreement.

Melancholies can be exasperating with their inexhaustible supply of questions. No matter what you bring up, they can think of objections, difficulties, and problems that will be encountered. It has always mystified me that they can always remember illustrations of those who failed trying to do what you suggest, but they can never remember those who succeeded.

Phlegmatics are easy to get along with on boards, particularly if you don't expect them to be anything. But if your proposal is going to cost them money, don't count on their support. Always present the cost of a project along with a reasonable plan for repayment, and your phlegmatic friends will go along with you.

Since no board or committee is made up of just one kind of temperament, but usually will have all four represented, you will find life as a leader, pastor, or chairman easier if you plan your presentation with all temperaments in mind. Preparation is the name of the game. But don't forget to pray. That's where the real power comes from.

7. *Use the temperament theory in parenting.* Every child is different not only in size, shape, looks, and intelligence, but in temperament blend. For that reason, you will find the temperament theory a helpful tool in parenting, particularly in the way you discipline. We have one child that I only gave two spankings during her entire childhood, and yet she is an unspoiled young woman today. The other three children? I won't estimate the times we went to the woodshed. What made the difference? Their temperaments.

Sanguine children are the easiest to love. They are born charmers, and if you aren't careful they will charm you out of obedience. Such children grow up to lie, cheat, and in some cases steal. Sanguines need love, but even more they need discipline. And don't let them *sass* you or they will learn to be disrespectful toward all adults.

Choleric children usually take more spankings to raise than any other type. And they can be willful! You must break their will, but be careful you don't break their spirit. How do you keep from breaking their spirit while you mold their will? By being loving and cultivating a close relationship while at the same time you demand obedience. They will test you—don't fail their test.

Melancholy children need love and security, while at the same time they need to learn self-sufficiency. They usually don't require a great deal of physical discipline, but will respond to a soft word of displeasure. One trait you must watch is criticism and a negative spirit, particularly if their secondary temperament is choleric. A MelChlor can be both negative and willful. Melancholy children need lots of parental reassurance that they do have worth and value—and that is what parents are for.

Phlegmatic children are easy to raise, particularly if you don't care if they never amount to anything in life. They don't cause trouble and rarely sass you back; they just live in their fantasy world of daydreams and function up to 60 percent of their potential—unless you prod them along. It is important to cultivate their curiosity level when they are very young. This is the one child that should rarely be kept in a playpen, for it is those early years, according to the experts, that ignite or stifle a child's curiosity, depending on whether he is free to inquire or confide. Like all children, they thrive on affection and do their best when gently but consistently pressured.

Child-training is almost a full-time vocation in the early years when a child needs what psychiatrist Harold Voth calls "mother constancy." That is why God gave children two parents—so one can be with them in those most formative years of life. Today's emphasis on working mothers (whether it is necessary or not) is destined to create a whole generation of rebellious or insecure young people. You don't have to be perfect or an expert parent to be a good parent, but parenting *must* be high on your priority list when your children are under ten. Ideally they will have one parent at home until they start working or playing sports after school.

For additional insight into good child-raising, see my wife's book *How to Develop Your Child's Temperament.*

THE USE AND ABUSE OF TEMPERAMENTS

Like any good book, the temperament theory can be abused. It is not a cure-all for everything. And sometimes a person doesn't even fit into a temperament blend because his

two temperaments are so evenly matched, or he may even have three
temperaments. In addition, his childhood or lifetime experiences may
have overemphasized or overdominated one temperament at the
exclusion of the other. However, this theory is still the best tool for
helping the largest number of people that has ever been devised.

Unfortunately, some people abuse this tool, which causes some to
turn against it before giving it careful consideration. Here are the three
most common ways of abusing the theory.

1. As a psychological club to bludgeon their friends. One of the things
that has turned more people against this theory than anything else is the
thoughtless individuals who publicly humiliate their friends by analyzing
them, with special emphasis on the negative characteristics. Parents can
do this with devastating harm to their children.

I rarely tell a person what temperament I think he is even when he
asks—and never do I tell him in public. Not that any temperament is a
shame or should be, but no one likes to be stripped psychologically bare
in public. Use it for self-help and understanding or to improve your
relations with others, but never use it like a club. You may evoke
laughter, but whether you know it or not, you will also evoke pain.

2. As an excuse to indulge your weaknesses. Improvement is what
this book is all about—self-improvement, that is. But if you condone
your temperament-induced weaknesses by saying "it's because of my
temperament," you're hopeless. It may be that your temperament
makes you a twenty-four-hour-a-day nonstop talker. But you can
improve—*if* you face that weakness and summon God's help to gain a
quiet spirit. You may be a dominant compulsive, but don't say, "I'm a
choleric melancholy and can't change." You're right—you can't because
you *won't.* God can induce you though, with a hefty dose of
compassion, much to the relief of your friends. But you must let him.

And don't think that because you're a melancholy, you have to go
through life nitpicking everyone else, criticizing others, and making
yourself depressed by indulging in self-pity. God can give you joy, peace,
love, and a gracious spirit—if you want it.

Or if you happen to be a phlegmatic, don't sit around and let your life
slip by because it takes too much effort to get out of your easychair.
And don't excuse your passivity by saying, "That's the way I am." You
have many positive traits; concentrate on those, and force yourself to be
available to God to help other people. You will like the results better.

3. To categorize everyone you meet. While it is true, we all have a
temperament combination, it is no service to you or other people to

always think of them in the light of their temperament. In the first place, snap decisions can be wrong; and in the second place, you may forget the person while concentrating on his temperament. One thing we all need to develop is a sincere interest in and love for other people. Just as we learn to love and accept people regardless of their looks or physical characteristics, we need to learn to get acquainted with people regardless of their temperaments.

Our Lord looked into the *heart* of Nicodemus, Andrew, and others, not just their outer shell. While we do not have his divine ability to see the heart as it really is, we can learn to see the real person that is often shrouded by physical characteristics and temperament. The Bible speaks of "the hidden man of the heart." That is the real person—get to know him.

THE PROPER USE OF THE TEMPERAMENT THEORY

There are many good uses for the temperament theory that far outweigh any dangers or misuse the tool can be put to. We have already spent a whole chapter on these, but let me summarize this book by listing the three I think are the most important.

1. *Self-acceptance.* This theory helps you come to grips with who you are in the framework that exposes the fact that everyone has strengths and weaknesses.

2. *Self-improvement.* Once you have examined your weaknesses and understand why you act the way you do, you are better able to call upon God for his resources to improve your temperament by strengthening your weaknesses.

3. *Understanding and accepting others.* As long as you live, you will be confronted by people. When you understand why they do what they do, it is easier to accept and love them.

It is my sincere desire and prayer that reading this book is helping you in all three of the above uses of this theory. If it has, we will both be pleased.

In the event you are a teacher of these principles and would like to order a set of the overhead transparencies that go with it as a handy aid to communication, just write my office. Of if you have a specific question on temperament that is not answered in this book, please send it to me and I will include it in my next book on this subject.

In the meantime, I recommend taking the LaHaye Temperament Analysis as a very valuable help in further improving your temperament.

PART *Four*

TEMPERAMENT AND YOUR EMOTIONS

CHAPTER NINE

How to Deal with Fear and Anger

"What you are emotionally is what you are!" may be too strong a statement to be true, but it's close. We are all such emotional creatures that our emotions can influence every area of our lives—for good or bad. I have noticed that whenever our emotions conflict for a length of time with any other area of our being, they eventually triumph.

Consider the power of emotion to influence the other three most important areas of life—mind, will, and body. No matter how intelligent a person is, when he gets emotionally upset he cannot think in an orderly fashion. Emotions can break his concentration and stifle his creativity. Some people's minds are totally dominated by their emotions. I well recall a professional scholar who had achieved world recognition at the age of twenty-seven. But his bad marriage kept him so distraught, fluctuating between anger and depression, that he squandered his potential and retired with less prestige and position than he had at twenty-seven.

Everyone has had the experience of letting their emotions impair their judgment. How often have you asked, "Why did I buy that car, house, dress, etc.?" You knew better, but you did it anyway. You made an emotional decision. I wish I had a dollar for all the people who asked, "Why did I marry him? We have nothing in common." Now you can see why I say all emotionally made decisions are bad decisions. The good life is one in which your mind controls your emotions, never vice versa.

The same, however, is true of your will. I don't care how strong-willed you are, if conflict between your will and your emotions lasts long enough, your emotions will win. That's why the Bible tells us to "flee youthful lusts" and sins. Our emotions are particularly powerful between the ages of fourteen and twenty-four. That is why the devil uses society, education, drugs, friends, and amusements on our young people during those years. He knows how vulnerable they are to making bad lifetime decisions when they are most emotionally combustible.

Physically it is the same. Doctors tell us that 65-80 percent of all illnesses are emotionally induced. What do they mean by that? Very simply, most people in our country ruin or break down their health long before necessary by indulging bad emotions for long periods of time. Good emotions seem to have a healthful effect on us; bad emotions destroy us. The Bible says, "A cheerful heart is good medicine, but a crushed spirit dries up the bones" (Prov. 17:22, NIV).

TWO EMOTIONAL CULPRITS

All of us experience many emotions during our lifetime. But in my opinion they all stem from two basic roots—anger and fear. Fear was the first emotion to surface in the Bible after the fall. Adam said, "I was afraid" because he had disobeyed God. Since then billions have known guilt-induced fears, plus many other forms it takes. Anger caused the first family quarrel, which resulted in murder as you may recall, when Cain became "wroth" (a heart filled with anger) at his brother Abel and killed him.

Throughout the Bible there are literally hundreds of illustrations of the harmful effects of fear and anger. And there are hundreds of biblical admonitions to "fear not," "let not your heart be troubled," and "cease from anger." God knew that fear and anger feed on all mankind, working relentlessly toward our destruction or limiting our potential. Additionally, the Bible offers many antidotes to these two emotional cripplers.

These emotions and actions stem from the basic problem of fear. Some counselors spend too much time dealing with these symptoms rather than the basic cause. I am convinced that if we can help a person overcome his tendency to fear, he will automatically solve these other problems.

Perceptive questioners after my seminars have asked, "Why do you associate the emotions of anger and fear with your teachings on both the four temperaments and marriage and the family?" The answer is, anger and fear in their many forms are the most significant causes of limiting the strengths of a person's temperament and also are the principle causes of breakdown in marriage and the family.

In addition, I teach that the way to overcome your temperament weaknesses is to be filled with the Spirit. The Bible warns us against quenching the work of the Holy Spirit in our lives through "fear" (1 Thess. 5:16-19) and against "grieving the Spirit " through "anger" (Eph. 4:30-32). Anyone who doesn't quench the Spirit through fear or grieve the Spirit through anger walks in the Spirit as God commands us all to live (Gal. 5:16-18). For that reason we should examine carefully the relation between our inherited temperament and the emotional sin that so easily besets us.

THE EMOTIONAL PREDISPOSITIONS OF THE TEMPERAMENTS

There is a sense in which all human beings experience fear and anger. But I have found that most people have a "besetting sin" tendency or what I call a temperament predisposition. That is, certain temperaments have a predisposition toward one emotional sin more than another. Its influence on their lives, of course, will depend on their second temperaments, their background, training, and of course their motivation. (To me, motivation means whether they do or do not have the Holy Spirit in their life to motivate them.)

As a pastor-counselor for many years, I specialized in helping fearful, angry and depressed people. It wasn't until later, when marital breakdown became so prevalent, even in that church, that I began to specialize in marriage counseling. Anyway, long before I learned anything about the four temperaments, I realized that the two cripplers of my counselees were fear and anger. It got so that before I opened my counseling room door and found a man or woman to be counseled, I knew in advance they were either fearful or angry. The only exceptions to that rule were those few people I met who had both problems.

When I read *Temperament and the Christian Faith* by the Norwegian theologian O. Hallesby, it fell open to me like an overripe melon. I saw that two of the temperaments had a predisposition for fear and two leaned toward anger. In the twenty years since then, I have researched everything I could find on the subject of temperament. I have tested over 6,000 people and studied thousands of counselees. And nothing has occurred to change that first impression. All melancholies and phlegmatics have a fear tendency, and all cholerics and sanguines have an anger tendency. Consider the following chart and the other emotional problems that stem from these basic emotions.

Sanguine   Choleric   Melancholy   Phlegmatic

ANGER   **FEAR**

Bitterness	Intolerance	Jealousy
Malice	Criticism	Attack
Clamor	Revenge	Gossip
Envy	Wrath	Sarcasm
Resentment	Hatred	Unforgiveness
	Seditions	

Worry	Withdrawal	Suspicion
Anxiety	Loneliness	Depression
Timidity	Overaggression	Hesitancy
Indecision	Doubts	Haughtiness
Superstition	Inferiority	Shyness
	Cowardice	

Fear is the paralyzing emotion that inhibits or restricts normal feelings of love, confidence, and well-being. It triggers negative thought patterns, breeding anxiety, worry, and the other emotions listed, which can multiply like a giant snowball and consume a person's entire life.

The following chart is used by permission of Dr. Jay Adams, from his excellent book *Competent to Counsel*. It shows the entire cycle of life activities. Now notice the next diagram which shows fear, worry, and anxiety at the core of a person's thinking. You can see how it reaches into every area of a person's life. Fear is not related only to one area of your life, like your vocation or profession. Fear is to your emotions what cancer of the blood is to your body; it invades the total person.

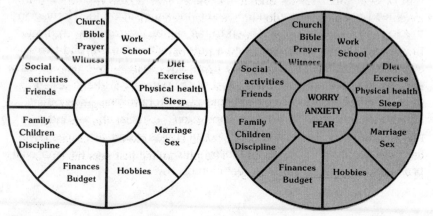

Everyone will face fear the first time he does anything dangerous in life; there is nothing new about that. Everyone is nervous or afraid when facing the trauma of driving a car, motorcycle, or airplane, or diving off a high diving platform, etc., That is normal fear. But those who let their fears inhibit them from attempting whatever they would like to do or should do have crossed the line from normal fears to destructive fears. The key as to which kind of fear it is seems to be whether we let our fears keep us from doing God's will.

Sanguine   ANGER   Choleric   Melancholy   FEAR   Phlegmatic

Having acknowledged that everyone experiences fear, worry, and anxiety, it should be pointed out that some people have a greater problem with it than others. And the differences can be detected in early childhood. Watch the children in your next Sunday school program. That can be the most terrifying experience your child will have all year, if he has a predisposition toward fear or if the prospect of getting up before a group terrifies him. If singing and giving a speech petrify him, that is fear. Some children, the sanguines and cholerics, love it or at least are not afraid of what others see them do or what others think of them. Not so with the melancholy and the phlegmatic. Those temperaments, as are afraid to leave their mothers, as children they're afraid of getting hurt or being abandoned, and as teens they fear rejection by their peers much more acutely than do cholerics and sanguines.

I have pondered a great deal about the difference between the fears of the melancholy and those of the phlegmatic without coming to much of a conclusion. In many ways they are the same fears and have the same ill effects, except that the fears of the melancholy seem more intense and have a more inhibiting influence on him. Phlegmatics let fear inhibit their activities, but they don't get so upset over the incident. Melancholies who fear flying break out in a cold sweat, can't eat, and can't sleep even thinking about it. The phlegmatic just sets his stubborn jaw and says, "I don't want to go."

Vocationally, the phlegmatic is extremely security conscious. Whenever an opportunity comes up offering a choice between high pay and security, the phlegmatic will choose security. The melancholy can hardly make the choice. Both are driven by fear. Melancholies rarely change professions—it's too scary. Phlegmatics are easier to persuade to do something new than melancholies, but the new venture must offer more security than the present position. I suspect that one reason so many melancholies spend their lifetime in academic pursuits is because they feel secure there, having spent eighteen or so of their first twenty-three years of life there. (Admittedly, they are highly intelligent also.)

The fears of the melancholy that make him insecure about himself are also more intense than those of a phlegmatic. Somehow, even though the mild-mannered phlegmatic has a difficult time feeling capable enough to aggressively pursue something he wants or needs, his fear is not as intense as the melancholy who rejects himself and his abilities. Melancholies seem more self-centered than phlegmatics, so that compounds their fears. A self-centered person worries about everything, even his worry. One melancholy woman told me, "I suppose you noticed that I didn't take communion today. It was because I confessed all my sins, but I'm afraid there must be one or two sins I forgot." While we may admire her spiritual consciousness, we are appalled at her fears of displeasing God. No wonder these people are so sad. "An anxious heart weighs a man down" (Prov. 12:25, NIV).

Even the "fear of the Lord" becomes a pathetic fear—to such an extent that it can interfere with love for God. The Bible mentions hundreds of times that the righteous should "fear the Lord." That is not the same fear as worry, anxiety, and dread. You can't love someone you feel that way about. The word for "fear" as an attitude toward God means "revere, reverence, and special honor." The only people that should "fear" (dread) God are those who disobey him. If we love him, we obey him; and if we obey him, it is because we "revere" or "honor" him. These are not the same thing. Melancholies and some phlegmatics have a difficult time telling the difference, and it tends to cripple their spiritual lives.

The major difference that I can detect between the fears of the melancholy and those of the phlegmatic is that the melancholies' fears are more intense, last longer, occupy more of their thinking, and inhibit their life more. While the phlegmatic is a worrier and prone to limit himself by his fears, he has a relatively happy outlook on life and can forget his fears as soon as he returns to a more familiar place in life.

**THE RESULTS
OF FEAR**

Fear is a cruel taskmaster which inhibits every area of one's life. To those in its grip, fear becomes the most powerful force in their life and it affects everything they do. The following are only part of the expensive toll it extracts.

1. *The emotional results of fear.* Every year countless thousands of individuals fall into mental and emotional collapse because of fear. Electric shock treatments and insulin shock treatments are becoming more and more common as forms of treatment to patients suffering from the tyrannical force of fear. Many a tearful person draws into a shell and lets life pass him by, never experiencing the rich things that God has in store for him, simply because he is afraid. The tragedy of it all is that most of the things he fears never happen. A young businessman addressing a sales company somehow came up with the figure that 92 percent of the things people fear will occur never take place. I cannot attest to the accuracy of his figure, but it is obvious in looking at anyone's life that the overwhelming majority of the things that cause our fear do not take place or are not nearly as severe as we thought they would be.

I counseled a woman who ten years before drove her husband from her because she was so emotionally upset due to fear. She became obsessed with the idea that another woman was going to take her husband away from her, and her emotionally upset mind caused such erratic and abnormal behavior in the home that she herself drove her husband away from her, though the "other woman" never existed.

The emotional cost of fear is very clearly seen in this statement by the late Christian physician Dr. S. I. McMillen: "About nine million Americans suffer from emotional and mental illness. As many hospital beds are filled by the mentally deranged as are occupied by all the medical and surgical patients combined. In fact, one out of every twenty Americans will have a psychotic disturbance severe enough to confine him in a hospital for the insane. Mental disease is indeed the nation's No. 1 health problem. What does it cost to take care of the patients in our mental hospitals? The annual cost is about one billion dollars. Besides, outside the asylums there are a vast number who do not need confinement but who are incapable of supporting themselves. They work little or not at all and constitute a great burden on the taxpayer." This cost does not include the heartache and confusion in the families from which these patients are admitted to sanitariums and asylums. Mothers and fathers are left to raise children singlehandedly, and children often go untrained or uncared for as a result of emotional illness of one parent or the other.

2. *The social results of fear*. The social results of fear are perhaps the easiest to bear, but it is difficult nonetheless. Fear-dominated individuals do not make enjoyable company. Their pessimistic and complaining spirit causes them to be shunned and avoided, thus further deepening their emotional disturbances. Many otherwise likeable and happy people are scratched off social lists and cause their companions to be equally limited simply because of ungrounded fears.

3. *The physical results of fear*. It is almost impossible to overestimate the harmful affects fear can have on one's physical body. In recent years doctors have called this dangerous cause for many of our physical maladies to our attention. The book that helped put this in perspective for me is *None of These Diseases* by S. I. McMillen. His thrust was essentially that Christians do not have the same incidence of disease that non-Christians do because their emotions are better. I agree if we mean Spirit-controlled Christians. Obviously, a Christian whose emotions are love, joy, and peace is going to be much better off physically than one whose emotions battle fear, worry, and anxiety. The following diagram, reproduced from Dr. McMillen's book, shows the importance of the emotions to one's physical condition.

Notice how the emotion center (which the Bible calls "the heart") is neurologically tied in with all the vital organs of the body. Although the body can sustain an enormous amount of abuse, tension over a long period of time will eventually cause it to break down. Everyone seems to have his own tolerance level. In fact, some think every human being has his own point of least resistance—that is, a point which is most vulnerable to protracted stress. For some, an emotional upset will cause a breakdown in the kidneys, to others it might be their gallbladder, to others their colon or any of the fifty-one diseases listed by Dr. McMillen. Wherever it is, protracted stress caused by fear, worry, or anxiety will find it and the person will experience anything from high blood pressure to heart attacks, from gallstones to arthritis.

The sex drive is a good example of emotional effects on a person's physical body. Few things are more powerful than the sex drive; yet both men and women can be rendered inoperative sexually by fear. Fear of pregnancy, injury, or discovery can render a normal woman frigid. Fear of rejection or feared inability to perform can make a normal man impotent. Fear feeds on itself and causes physical maladies, which in turn increase one's fears. It is a vicious circle.

EMOTIONAL CONTROL
OF PHYSICAL ORGANS

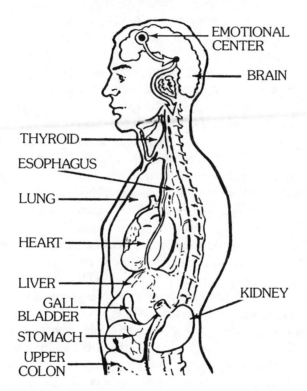

ULCERS OF STOMACH AND INTESTINE	KIDNEY DISEASE
COLITIS	HEADACHES
HIGH BLOOD PRESSURE	MENTAL DISTURBANCES
HEART TROUBLE	GOITER
STROKES	DIABETES
ARTERIOSCLEROSIS	ARTHRITIS

Other diseases mentioned by Dr. McMillen are high blood pressure, heart trouble, kidney disease, goiter, arthritis, headaches, strokes, and most of the same fifty-one illnesses which he listed as caused by anger. In illustrating the effect of fear upon the human heart, he quotes Dr. Roy R. Grinker, one of the medical directors of Michael Reese Hospital in Chicago: "This doctor states that anxiety places more stress on the heart than any other stimulus, including physical exercise and fatigue."

Dr. McMillen points out that fear causes a chemical reaction to take place in the human body, as when the saliva seems to be drained from our mouth as we stand up in a speech class to speak. Such a reaction does not harm a person, because it is short-lived, but that type of experience indulged in hour after hour because of fear can cause physical damage to the body.

A doctor friend explained it to me in this way. We have an automatic alarm bell system that rings whenever we are confronted with an emergency. If the doorbell rings at 2 a.m., you are awakened suddenly and in complete control of your faculties, no matter how sound a sleeper you happen to be. This is God's natural gift to the human being. What has happened is that your adrenal gland has been triggered by the fright of the emergency and has secreted adrenalin into your bloodstream, causing you to be immediately in control of all your faculties. In fact, you will probably be stronger and more mentally alert than normally so that you might adequately cope with the problem.

When I pastored a country church in South Carolina, one of the men of the congregation was speeding his expectant wife to the hospital. As they came down the muddy mountain road, the front of the car slipped into the ditch. In the face of the emergency his adrenal gland pumped adrenalin into his system; he leaped around in front of the car and literally slid it back up onto the road, got back into the car, and drove his wife to the hospital. The next day in the parking lot of the hospital he tried to prove to incredulous friends that he had lifted the front of his car, but to his amazement he could not budge it one inch. He used every ounce of energy and strength at his command, but the car would not move. What he didn't understand was that he had possessed supernormal strength because of his God-given emergency alarm system the night before that was not available for the parking lot demonstration.

My doctor friend explained that this does not cause any damage to the human body because after the emergency is over, the adrenal gland settles down to its normal function and the bloodstream throws off the excessive adrenalin chemical with no ill effects. That is not the case, however, for the man who sits down at one o'clock in the afternoon to pay his bills and suddenly is overcome with fear because he does not have enough money in his checking account to pay for everything he owes. Hour after hour, as long as he worries, his adrenal gland is pumping adrenalin into his bloodstream, a process which can ultimately create much physical damage. This is sometimes the cause of excessive calcium deposits and sometimes produces the pain-racked bodies of arthritis sufferers.

I know a lovely Christian lady who has been afflicted with arthritis and was finally restricted by the disease to a wheelchair. She had had every medical treatment known to science and was finally told by her third arthritis specialist, "I'm sorry, Mrs. _____, but we can find nothing organically wrong with you. The cause of your arthritis is emotional." When I heard that analysis, my mind went back to my childhood when she was in perfect health. Even though we enjoyed going to her house for the delicious cookies that she baked, we referred to her as "the professional worrier." She worried about everything. She fretted over her husband's employment, yet he worked thirty years for the same company and never knew a day without pay. She was apprehensive about the future of a daughter who today has a lovely home and six children. She was anxious about her weak, sickly son who grew up to be a six foot, four inch, 225-pound tackle for a Big Ten football team. I can hardly think of anything she didn't worry about, and all to no avail.

No wonder the Lord Jesus said in his Sermon on the Mount, "Take no thought for your life, what ye shall eat, or what ye shall drink; nor yet for your body, what ye shall put on . . ." (Matthew 6:25). Literally, he said, "Take no anxious thought." The Holy Spirit also tells us, "Be careful [anxious] for nothing" (Phil. 4:6). Anxiety and worry which stem from fear cause untold physical suffering, limitations, and premature death not only to non-Christians, but also to Christians who disobey the admonition to "commit thy way unto the Lord; trust also in him" (Ps. 37:5).

One day I called upon what I thought was an older woman who was bedridden. I was amazed to find that she was fifteen to twenty years younger that I had estimated. She made herself old before her time by being a professional worrier. As gently and yet as truthfully as I could, I tried to show her that she should learn to trust the Lord and not worry about everything. Her reaction was so typical it bears repeating. With fire in her eye and a flash of anger in her voice she asked, "Well, someone has to worry about things, don't they?"

"Not if you have a Heavenly Father who loves you and is interested in every detail of your life," I replied. But that dear sister didn't get the point. I hope you do!

Thank God we are not orphans! We live in a society that accepts the concept that we are the products of a biological accident and a long unguided process of evolution. That popular theory, which is rapidly falling into scientific disrepute, is not only incorrect but is enslaving mankind in a prisonhouse of physical torture due to fear. If you are a Christian, memorize Philippians 4:6, 7. Then, every time you find yourself worrying or becoming anxious, pray. Thank God that you have a Heavenly Father who is interested in your problems, and turn them over to him. Your little shoulders are not broad enough to carry the weight of the world or even your own family problems, but the Lord Jesus "is able to do exceeding abundantly above all that we ask or think" (Eph. 3:20).

How thrilled I was recently when a little girl in our Beginners Department quoted her memory verse for me. She said, "I learned in Sunday school today what God wants me to do with my problems. For he said, 'Casting all your care upon him; for he careth for you,' 1 Peter 5:7." Much of the physical suffering and consequent heartache, including financial difficulties, that occur in the average Christian home would be avoided if believers really acted upon that verse.

4. *The results of fear.* As already mentioned, fear quenches or stifles the Holy Spirit, and so keeps us from being effective in this life and steals many of our rewards in the life to come. Fear keeps us from being joyful, happy, radiant Christians, and instead makes us thankless, complaining, defeated Christians who are unfaithful. A fearful person is not going to manifest the kind of life that encourages a sinner to come to him and say, "Sir, what must I do to be saved?" If Paul and Silas had let their fears predominate, the Philippian jailer would never have been converted and we would not have the great salvation verse, Acts 16:31.

Fear keeps the Christian from pleasing God. The Bible tells us, "Without faith it is impossible to please God" (Heb. 11:6). The eleventh chapter of Hebrews, called the "Faith Chapter," names men whose biographies are given in sufficient detail throughout the Scriptures to establish that they represent all four of the basic temperament types. The thing that made these men acceptable in the sight of God is that they were not overcome by their natural weakness of either fear or anger, but walked with God by faith. Consider these four men, representative of the four temperament types: Peter the Sanguine, Paul the Choleric, Moses the Melancholy, and Abraham the Phlegmatic. It is difficult to find more dynamic illustrations of the power of God working in the lives of men than these four. "God is no respecter of persons." What he did to strengthen their weaknesses, he will do through his Holy Spirit for you!

You may be surprised to know that God used more fear-prone people than anger-prone in Bible times to serve him. That may be because the undisciplined or willful Christian has a harder time overcoming his rebellion than fear-prone people have in overcoming their fear. But be sure of this—all of those he used had to overcome their fears before they were usable by him. What he did for them, he will do for you. Remember, God is no respecter of persons. But before we consider how to overcome fear, we should examine what causes it.

WHAT CAUSES FEAR? Because fear is such a universal experience of man and because most of the readers of this book will be parents who can help their children avoid this tendency, I would like to answer this question simply in layman's terms. There are at least eight causes of fear.

Temperament predisposition. The most significant reason people have a problem with fear is because of their inherited temperament. By this time you know which temperaments have the greatest problem with it. In a sense, all people have a predisposition to fear, due to sin in the human race and its subsequent guilt, and also due to the individual's temperament combination. Depending on the combination, of course, you will have either a strong or weak predisposition toward it. We have seen that MelPhlegs or PhlegMels will have the greatest problem with it. However, even the choleric will have *some* tendency toward fear by virtue of his identification with the human race, and also his secondary temperament can introduce an element of fear into him. Obviously ChlorSans would not be as fear-prone as ChlorMels or ChlorPhlegs, but all temperaments are going to have a tendency toward fear. It's just that some people have it more than others.

Childhood experiences may induce fear. Psychologists and psychiatrists agree that the basic needs of man are love, understanding, and acceptance. The most significant human thing that parents can do for their children, short of leading them to a saving knowledge of Jesus Christ, is to give them the warmth and security of parental love. This does not exclude discipline or the teaching of submission to standards and principles. In fact, it is far better for a child to learn to adjust to rules and standards in the loving atmosphere of his home than in the cruel world outside. There are, however, two specific parental habits I suggest you diligently avoid:

(1) Overprotection. An overprotective parent makes a child self-centered and fearful of the very things happening to him that his parent is afraid will happen. Children quickly learn to read our emotions. Their bodies can far more easily absorb the falls, burns, and shocks of life than

their emotions can absorb our becoming tense, upset, or hysterical over these minor experiences. The fearful mother that forbids her son to play football probably does far more harm to his emotional development by her repeated suggestions of fear than the damage done to Junior if his front teeth were knocked out or his leg broken. Legs heal and teeth can be replaced, but it takes a miracle of God to remove the scar tissues of fear from our emotions.

(2) Domination. Angry, explosive parents who dominate the lives of their children or who critically pounce upon every failure in their lives often create hesitancy, insecurity, and fear in them. Children need correction, but they need it done in the proper spirit. Whenever we have to point out our children's mistakes, we should also make it a practice to note their strengths and good points, or at least criticize them in such a way as to let them know that they are still every bit as much the object of our love as they were before.

The more I counsel with people, the more convinced I am that the most devasting blow one human being can inflict upon another is disapproval. The more a person loves us, the more important it is for us to seek some area in his life where we can show our approval. A six foot, two inch husband in the midst of marriage counseling said rather proudly, "Pastor, I have never laid a hand on my wife in anger!" As I looked at his timid, cowering, 110-pound wife, I knew by the look in her eye what she was thinking: "Well, I would a thousand times rather that you beat me physically than constantly run me down and club me with disapproval."

The Spirit-filled parent is inspired through his loving compassionate nature to build others up and to show approval whenever possible. Even in the times of correction he will convey his love. To do otherwise with our children is to leave lasting fear scars on their emotions.

A traumatic experience. Child assault or molesting leaves a lasting emotional scar that often carries into adulthood, causing fear concerning the act of marriage. Other tragic experiences in childhood frequently set fear patterns into motion that last throughout life.

During the past few years our family has enjoyed some wonderful occasions waterskiing. The only member of the family that has not tried it is my wife, and she is deathly afraid of the water. I have begged her, encouraged her, and done everything I could to entice her to get over this fear of the water, but to no avail. Finally one summer I gave up. She made a Herculean attempt to overcome this fear by donning a wetsuit that could easily sustain her body in water. She then put on a life jacket, which also by itself could sustain her in water, and very hesitantly lowered herself over the side of the boat. The moment her hand left the security of the boat and she was floating freely in the water, I noted a look of terror in her eyes. For the first time I really understood how frightened she was of the water. Upon questioning her, I found that it all went back to a childhood experience in Missouri when she came within an eyelash of drowning. These experiences leave hidden marks on a person's emotions that often follow him through life. However, the Holy Spirit is able to overcome the effects of such an experience, as I shall point out a little further on.

A negative thinking pattern. A negative thinking pattern or defeatist complex will cause a person to be fearful of attempting any new thing. The moment we start suggesting to ourselves "I can't, I can't, I can't," we are almost certain of failure. Our mental attitude makes even ordinary tasks difficult to perform when we approach them with a negative thought. Repeated failures or refusal to do what our contemporaries are able to accomplish often causes further breakdown in self-confidence and increases fear. A Christian need never be dominated by this negative habit. By memorizing Philippians 4:13 and seeking the Spirit's power in applying it, one can gain a positive attitude toward life.

Anger. Anger can produce fear. I have counseled with individuals who had indulged bitterness and anger until they erupted in such explosive tirades that they afterward admitted, "I'm afraid of what I might do to my own child."

Sin produces fear. "If our heart condemn us not, then have we confidence toward God" (1 John 3:21) is a principle that cannot be violated without producing fear. Every time we sin, our conscience reminds us of our relationship to God. This has often been misconstrued by psychiatrists who blame religion for creating guilt complexes in people which, they say, in turn produces fear. A few years ago our family doctor, who at that time was not a Christian, made the following statement to me: "You ministers, including my saintly old father, do irreparable damage to the emotional life of men by preaching the gospel." I questioned his reason for such a statement and he said, "I took my internship in a mental institution, and the overwhelming majority of those people had a religious background and were there because of fear induced by guilt complexes."

The next day I attended a ministers' meeting where Dr. Clyde Narramore, a Christian psychologist from Los Angeles, gave a lecture on pastoral counseling. During the question period I told him of the previous day's conversation and asked his opinion. Dr. Narramore instantly replied: "That is not true. People have guilt complexes because they are guilty!" The result of sin is a consciousness of guilt, and guilt causes fear in modern man just as it did to Adam and Eve in the Garden of Eden. A simple remedy for this is to walk in the way of the Lord.

Lack of faith. Lack of faith, even in a Christian's life, can produce fear. I have noticed in counseling that fear caused by lack of faith is basically confined to two common areas.

The first is fear concerning the sins of the past. Because the Christian does not know what the Bible teaches in relationship to confessed sin, he has not come to really believe that God has cleansed him from all sin (1 John 1:9). Some time ago I counseled with a lady who was in such a protracted period of fear that she had sunk into a deep depression. We found that one of her basic problems was that she was still haunted by a sin committed eleven years before. All during this time she had been a Christian, but had gone through a complete emotional collapse, haunted by the fear of that past sin.

When I asked if she had confessed that sin in the name of Jesus Christ, she replied, "Oh, yes, many times." I then gave her a spiritual prescription: to make a Bible study of all Scriptures verses that deal with the forgiveness of sins. When she came back into my office two weeks later, she was not the same woman. For the first time in her life she really understood how God regarded her past sin, and when she began to agree with him that it was "remembered no more," she got over that fear.

A man I counseled who had a similar problem gave me a slightly different answer when I asked, "Have you confessed that sin to Christ?" "Over a thousand times," was his interesting reply. I told him that was 999 times too many. He should have confessed it once and thanked God 999 times that he had forgiven him for that awful sin. The Word of God is the cure for this problem, because "Faith cometh by hearing, and hearing by the word of God" (Rom. 10:17).

The second area in which people are prone to be fearful because of lack of faith concerns the future. If the devil can't get them to worry about their past sins, he will seek to get them to worry about God's provision in the future, and thus keep them from enjoying the riches of

God's blessing today. The psalmist has said, "This is the day which the Lord hath made; we will rejoice and be glad in it" (Ps. 118:24). People who enjoy life are not dreading tomorrow or worrying about the past; they are living today.

Anyone who thinks about the potential problems and difficulties he might encounter tomorrow will naturally become fearful, unless he has a deep, abiding faith in God's ability to supply all his need. My wife shared with me a very beautiful saying she heard which bears repeating: "Satan tries to crush our spirit by getting us to bear tomorrow's problems with only today's grace."

If you are worrying about tomorrow, you can't possibly enjoy today. The interesting thing is that you can't give God tomorrow; you can only give him what you have, and you have today. Dr. Cramer quoted a comment by Mr. John Watson in the *Houston Times* which read: "What does your anxiety do? It does not empty tomorrow of its sorrow, but it empties today of its strength. It does not make you escape the evil; it makes you unfit to cope with it if it comes."

Habit can intensify fear. Never underestimate the power of habit to intensify any negative force, particulary an emotion such as fear. Anything you do frequently becomes easier to do the next time. A fearful person creates a deeply ingrained habit of responding to every difficult or different circumstance in life with fear. It becomes what psychologists call "a conditioned response." Each time a certain condition occurs, he becomes fearful. Such conditioning can make people lifetime servants of fear unless the Lord is allowed to come into their lives and empower them so that fear does not rule them for life.

Once a link in this fear chain is broken, it is easier to break it again, and so on until the "conditioned response" is broken completely and a new habit is begun, the facing of that same condition with faith instead of fear. Victory over one fear increases one's faith to try overcoming others, and a new life cycle based on faith can begin. As we shall see, faith is built one step at a time.

Now I think you are about ready to face the primary cause of fear. The above eight causes of fear are only contributing factors. The basic cause of fear is . . .

Selfishness. As much as we don't like to face this ugly word, it is a fact nonetheless. We are fearful because we are selfish. Why am I afraid? Because I am interested in self. Why am I embarrassed when I stand before an audience? Because I don't wish to make a fool of myself. Why am I afraid I will lose my job? Because I am afraid of being

a failure in the eyes of my family or not being able to provide my family
and myself with the necessities of life. Excuse it if you will, but all fear
can be traced basically to the sin of selfishness.

**DON'T BE
A TURTLE**
A Christian woman went to a Christian
psychologist and asked, "Why am I so
fearful?" He asked several questions. "When
you enter a room, do you feel that everyone is looking at you?" "Yes,"
she said. "Do you often have the feeling your slip is showing?" "Yes."
When he discovered she played the piano he asked, "Do you hesitate to
volunteer to play the piano at church for fear someone else can do so
much better?" "How did you know?" was her reply. "Do you hesitate to
entertain others in your home?" Again she said, "Yes." Then he
proceeded to tell her kindly that she was a very selfish young woman.
"You are like a turtle," he said. "You pull into your shell and peek out
only as far as necessary. If anyone gets too close, you pop your head
back inside your shell for protection. That shell is selfishness. Throw it
away, and start thinking more about others and less about yourself."

The young lady went back to her room in tears. She never thought of
herself as selfish, and it crushed her when she was confronted with the
awful truth. Fortunately she went to God, and he has gradually cured
her of that vicious sin. Today she is truly a "new creature." She
entertains with abandon, has completely thrown off the old "shell," and
consequently enjoys a rich and abundant life.

**WHO WANTS TO
BE AN OYSTER?**
A similar statement is made by Dr. Maltz in his
book *Psycho-Cybernetics*: "One final word
about preventing and removing emotional
hurts. To live creatively, we must be willing to be a little vulnerable. We
must be willing to be hurt a little, if necessary, in creative living. A lot of
people need a thicker and tougher emotional skin than they have. But
they need only a tough emotional hide or epidermis, not a shell. To
trust, to love, to open ourselves to emotional communication with other
people is to run the risk of being hurt. If we are hurt once, we can do
one of two things. We can build a thick protective shell, or scar tissue, to
prevent being hurt again, live like an oyster, and not be hurt. Or we can
'turn the other cheek,' remain vulnerable and go on living creatively.

"An oyster is never 'hurt.' He has a thick shell which protects him
from everything. He is isolated. An oyster is secure but not creative. He
cannot 'go after' what he wants, he must wait for it to come to him. An
oyster knows none of the 'hurts' of emotional communication with his

environment, but neither can an oyster know the joys."

HOW TO OVERCOME FEAR

You can learn to live without fear, worry, and anxiety. The key is to learn to live by faith. We will now illustrate how replacing fear with faith will change your whole life and set you free. Instead of being uptight and negative when faced with a challenge, you can appraise all life situations with confidence. This is a blessing which God has offered all of his children. Unfortunately, many have not taken advantage of it.

Through the years as a counselor I have developed a simple but very workable step by step procedure for overcoming worry and fear. We know it's possible, for our Lord said, "Do not be anxious about anything" (Phil. 4:6, NIV; cf. Matt. 6). If you have a problem with fear, memorize these steps and follow them *daily.*

Face your fear reactions as sin (Rom. 14:23). "Everything that does not come from faith is sin" (NIV). Remember, it is not unusual to feel fear or apprehension when you do a scary thing, particularly for the first time. But if your fear keeps you from doing what you should, or if the fear absorbs your thoughts for a period of time, it is wrong.

Don't justify fear! As one woman said, "If you had my background you would be afraid, too." To which I said, "You may be right, but all that would prove is that we are both wrong." Those who will not face fear as a sin but try to excuse or justify it are incurable. Instead, look objectively at your fear; admit it is sin and that God does not want you to be dominated by it.

Confess your fear as a sin (1 John 1:9). God is in the sin removal business. That is why he sent his Son to die on the cross for us, that his Son might "cleanse us from all sin" (1 John 1:7). After you have confessed it, thank him for his cleansing and go on your way rejoicing.

Ask God to take away the habit of fear (1 John 5:14, 15). "This is the assurance we have in approaching God: that if we ask anything according to his will, he hears us. And if we know that he hears us—whatever we ask—we know that we have what we asked of him" (NIV).

We have already seen that fear is a habit that God does not want to rule over you. This verse promises not only victory over that sin, which is contrary to his will, but also promises to give you the "assurance." He will give victory.

Ask for the filling of the Holy Spirit (Luke 11:23). "He who is not with me is against me, and he who does not gather with me, scatters."

Some Bible scholars tell us that step four is not necessary. That the minute we confess our sins in Jesus' name we are refilled by his Spirit. And they may be right (though I have not seen any Scripture to justify that claim). But personally I like to make sure. God won't be upset at us if we ask unnecessarily. Since Jesus told his disciples to ask for the Holy Spirit, I see no problem asking for his filling even though he is already inside me. Frankly, I ask several times a day.

Thank him by faith for victory over fear (1 Thess. 5:18). "Give thanks in all circumstances, for this is God's will for you in Christ Jesus."

Thank God verbally as an act of faith which appropriates the experience and makes it real.

Repeat! Repeat! Repeat! Repeat that formula every time you become fearful and *gradually* it will no longer dominate you. One of the greatest misconceptions of the Spirit-controlled life is that it is an experience we have that lasts for life. That is neither biblical nor possible! If you are a fearful person, you may be excited to read the above formula for conquering fear. (I hope you are.) The problem is, you try it once and have deliverance for two or three hours and then get discouraged because your fears return.

Don't forget the habit factor. How old are you? That is how long you have had a temperament-induced tendency to be fearful and turn it into a lifetime habit. That habit won't vanish immediately; with God's help you *can* have victory, but it will come *gradually.* Each time you become fearful, face your sin, ask forgiveness, ask to be refilled, and thank him by faith that you are. You have broken one more strand of the rope of habit that has bound you in its grip. Gradually you will see your former fears lose their power over you.

A CLASSIC ILLUSTRATION

Fear was not my personal problem, as I will confess in a later chapter. Anger was my "thing." But typical of "opposites attract in marriage," the woman I love was a very fearful minister's wife until God filled her life by his Holy Spirit and she tried this formula. Since then, I have watched that sweet fearful lady, too afraid to speak to a handful of women in our church, blossom into a full-blown rose of personality that still amazes me. If you had told me she would learn to speak to large audiences, head the largest women's organization in America, take an aggressive stand against secular humanists, feminists, and liberals, I would not have believed it—but I've seen it. Her life in these past seventeen years is a testimony to the power of God to give a person victory over an emotional tyrant.

In her book *Spirit-Controlled Woman*, Bev has told her story. Here is how she said it. And remember, I saw it and testify that these things are true:

"Unlike many couples, my husband and I were filled with the Spirit in the same week and began the process of change. Previous to being filled with the Spirit, I had limited my ministry to working with children under the sixth grade. Gradually I began accepting speaking opportunities with women's groups and even mixed audiences in our Family Life Seminars. Today I am speaking to large women's groups all the time with my organization Concerned Women for America.

"After making so much progress in conquering this fear of speaking, the director of a mission board wrote to my husband to thank him for writing *Spirit-Controlled Temperament*, which he said was 'required reading for all our missionary trainees. There is just one problem with it. You tell how God delivered your wife from her fear of public speaking, but later admit she couldn't join you and the rest of the family in water skiing because she was afraid of the water. The problem is that our nonswimming missionary candidates readily identify with her and use her as an excuse for not learning to swim, which could prove fatal to some of them.' He went on to graciously ask, 'Isn't the fear of water just as much a sin as the fear of anything else?'

"Tim had to get me the Kleenex box after hearing that one. Finally I decided he was right and decided to take action. I lined up a heated swimming pool and a phlegmatic instructor. Then, dressed in Tim's rubber wetsuit I strapped on a lifebelt and armed myself with the New Testament. Going into the water I would quote: 'I will never leave you nor forsake you,' and other verses on assurance of God's provision. Eventually I was able to discard the unnecessary paraphernalia and learned to swim. I will never be a U.S. Olympic candidate, but with God's help I conquered my terrible fear of water."

What God has done for Bev, he will do for you. If you have a problem with fear, anxiety, or worry, then follow these six steps to a transformed life.

Facing Pressure

> "Man is born to trouble (pressure) as surely as sparks fly
> upward." (Job 5:7, NIV)

Pressure is a part of life; no one escapes it. We are more conscious of it in this day of jet travel, computers, and frenetic activity than those who lived in farming communities fifty years ago. But no matter where you live or what you do in life you will experience pressure; it is inescapable.

The thing you need to know about pressure is that it isn't all bad. In fact, in many cases it is good for you. Without it you couldn't sustain life. Take your blood pressure as an example. If it is too high, it can kill you. But if it is too low the same thing can happen. Life without pressure would be empty and brief. You need pressure to provide not only life itself but motivation, variety, and activity.

In 1982-83 I went through the greatest pressure period of my life. After successfully pastoring churches for thirty years, I felt led of God to resign and launch a national television ministry. Instantly I was in pressure unlike anything I have ever known. I was unfamiliar with the field, had no base from which to operate, and found that television gobbles money faster than the federal government. God marvelously met my needs in those days of incredible pressure and inspired me to write *How to Manage Pressure Before Pressure Manages You*. In the process I discovered that all temperaments do not face pressure the same way. So I thought it wise in this book on temperament to include the different responses of the temperaments to this universal problem of mankind.

SPARKY SANGUINE   Sanguines rarely get ulcers; we have already
FACING PRESSURE   seen that they usually give them to everyone
else. Since people are a major cause of
pressure and sanguines love to be around people, they are never far
from pressure, which usually they helped to create.

These light-hearted people are often very disorganized, generally
arrive late for meetings, and are rarely prepared for whatever they are
supposed to do. I have watched sanguine songleaders select the songs
for an evening service while walking down the aisle of the church.
Despite their lack of preparation, they usually do a creditable job
because they exude so much charisma. Sanguines are such good actors
and people-responders that they often do a better job on the platform
than other temperaments who prepare carefully. One can't help but
wonder how effective sanguines could be if they would only learn to plan
for whatever lies ahead. Unfortunately, each time they get by with
improvising under pressure, they learn that advance planning is not
really crucial for success.

This could be the reason why sanguines are often "short-termers."
That is, they run out of material after a time and must move on to their
next job. Sanguine preachers, for example, usually stay in a church for
only two or three years. Pressure tends to drive them to the golf course
rather than to the study.

Because they are prone to be late, undependable, undisciplined, and
unprepared, sanguines are never far from pressure. Can you visualize
the personable, people-oriented homemaker who welcomes the neighbor
in for a "fifteen-minute coffee klatsch," only to talk too long and discover
that the party has ended only minutes before her husband is due home?
She furiously whips through the house, trying frantically to set things in
order for his arrival. Dinner is late, the house is a mess, and she is not
prepared for his sarcastic insults; she lashes out in self-defense about her
"overworked schedule" or "the pressures of three small children." Such
reactions do little for a loving relationship.

Sanguines are quick of speech and often use their vocal chords to
defend themselves when pressed. More aggressive types learn that in
verbally attacking other people they can often intimidate them into
submission, so they cover their mistakes by pressuring others. I know
one sanguine who reminds me of the Saint Bernard dog we once had
who after knocking me down at the front gate and breaking my glasses,
put both paws on my shoulders and licked my face. Even though you
are right in a disagreement with a sanguine, he will attack you and

bluster; and when you leave, you have failed to confront him with the problem. In fact, he has made you feel that it was all your fault for bringing up the matter in the first place.

Women sanguines are often screamers. That is, their frustration is never far from the surface, so they scream at their children, husband, neighbor, or whoever is near. Male sanguines tend to talk too loudly, making demands or speaking more dogmatically than their grasp of the facts would allow. If one gives a sanguine enough rope, he will usually hang himself verbally.

One of the most uncomplimentary tendencies of a sanguine under pressure is his difficulty in honestly taking the blame for his mistakes. Because he commands a giant ego, needs the love and admiration of others, and lacks discipline, it is easy for him to pass the buck, blame others for his mistakes, and in some cases lie to get out of a trap. This is why parents of sanguine children need to concentrate on teaching them self-discipline and truth-telling. Otherwise they will develop a flexible conscience.

Some sanguines resort to weepy repentance when confronted with the pressure caused by their unkempt ways. Such repentance is usually short-lived; the sanguine has learned little or nothing from the experience.

Sanguines are easily intimidated by more forceful, cruel personalities. I have seen many highly emotional wives, with tremendous capacities to love and be loved, become distraught because their husband cold-bloodedly used their quest for self-acceptance to browbeat them into taking the blame for anything that goes wrong. It always pains me to hear a woman cry, "I know it is all my fault," when that is rarely the case. One woman was intimidated into accepting her husband's infidelity because he convinced her she was inadequate in bed; actually he acted immoral because he was sinful.

Lying never solves anything. The Bible enjoins us, "Speak every man truth with his neighbor" (Eph. 4:25). It takes sanguines a long time to learn that it is much easier to face those unpleasant pressures of life squarely, take full responsibility for mistakes, and then do two things: (1) solve the present difficulty; and (2) learn from the experience.

Most sanguines cannot endure emotional pressure very long. They will start talking, tell an unrelated joke, or run away from the problem. An example of this occurred in the rental car of a nationally famous minister in January 1980. Twelve of us had breakfast with former President Carter and asked several questions: Why did he not oppose abortion?

Why had he endorsed the Equal Rights Amendment in view of the harm it would do to the family? Why did he refuse to support a voluntary school prayer amendment for our public schools? Five of us drove out of the White House grounds in deep silence. I was very depressed by what I had heard, and so were the others. Suddenly the most sanguine of the group split the silence with an unrelated and rather bizarre joke. He was reacting naturally to the emotional pressures that he felt at the moment.

As we have noted, sanguines often give ulcers to others because they will not face their problems and do something constructive about them. A sanguine manager, administrator, or minister, for instance, has an interesting way of trying to solve personnel problems. If he senses another's displeasure, he will tactfully take him out for coffee, lunch, or an evening of entertainment. He will rarely discuss the problem, preferring to use his charismatic charm to disarm his friend's hostility or displeasure. He leaves that encounter feeling that he has solved his problem, whereas in reality he has only delayed judgment-day for a while. As a husband he will bring home a "peace offering" or "take the family out to dinner" to solve a problem. But as you know, that only relieves the immediate pressure; it does not really change anything. If only he would face issues realistically and do something about them, he would reduce most of his life pressures.

Because sanguines cannot tolerate the discomfort of pressure, they always react in some way—an explosive outburst, tears, jokes, lies, change of subject, or "fellowship." They cannot suffer pressure in silence. Fortunately their happy disposition easily forgets unpleasant circumstances; the first moving object or person that catches their eye gains their attention, and they mentally or physically separate themselves from the cause of their pressure temporarily. If sanguines could learn to use pressure as motivation toward problem-solving, their lives would be greatly enriched, and I believe they would be 25 to 50 percent more successful in their chosen fields.

CHOLERICS   No one can create more pressure than a
UNDER PRESSURE   choleric. He thrives on it—until his body
                   breaks down with ulcers, high blood pressure,
heart attack, or other physical adversities.

Some of the choleric's high pressure quotient is occasioned by his "god complex." Perhaps it would be better to label it an "omnipotence complex." Cholerics are always overinvolved. They are willing to tackle anything that needs to be done. They never ask, "Why doesn't someone else do something about this?" To almost any need they respond, "Let's get organized and put the troops to work!" Then they start barking orders to others.

Cholerics rarely get depressed when a project fails, because they have thirty other irons in the fire to keep their overly active minds occupied. Instead of wallowing in self-pity over an insult, failure, or rejection, they busy themselves with their next project.

However, this penchant for taking on more than anyone could possibly accomplish often proves to be the cause of greatest pressures. Cholerics are extremely goal-oriented, but unless their secondary temperament is melancholy, they will not be adept at planning, analyzing, and detailing. In fact, they usually don't like it. Cholerics are doers. Consequently they may rush into battle before establishing a plan of attack, thus creating a great deal of pressure.

Many of the frenetic activities of the choleric should be put on a back burner. He is successful in the business world, not because his ideas are so well designed, but because he launches them while others are still determining theirs. Some of his better notions die on the drawing board, for a choleric has usually implemented his ideas and projects before he realizes that a better way exists. However, dogged determination stands him in good stead, for he usually finishes what he starts.

The choleric typically responds to pressure by refusing to give up. When he encounters an impossible situation, he glibly retorts, "Nothing is impossible." A choleric I know contends, "I never take no for an answer unless I hear it eight or ten times." Even then he is apt to press doggedly onward. Pressure discourages some people, but not the choleric; it simply serves as grist for his mill. Thriving on opposition, in some cases he will clench his teeth and press on regardless. At other times his creative mind will envision a crafty device to achieve his ends. It may not be legal, honest, or fair, but that doesn't always deter him.

Because of their penchant for adopting excessive loads and their natural inability to delegate responsibility, cholerics tend to take their extra time away from the family. Their ten-hour days soon increase to twelve and fifteen hours, the day off becomes another working day, and vacation time never seems to arrive. Consequently the family suffers.

Interpersonal relationships are not a choleric's strength, and work pressures compound this. He tends to be impatient with those less motivated than himself, critical and demanding of others, even unappreciative of people when they do well. If he is an employer, he usually experiences a high turnover at his place of business. His family members tend to give him a wide berth. Cruel and unkind by nature, he can be very cutting and sarcastic under pressure. Unless he seeks the help of God and walks in the Spirit, he will be prone to leave many damaged psyches and wounded egos in his wake. One choleric supervisor was reported to be "very productive, but leaves a trail of weepy subordinates." Gentle spirits should think twice before getting involved with cholerics.

The choleric's principal weapon is his tongue. No one can use it with greater dexterity and brutality. Because he enjoys pressure, he delights in heaping it upon others. His motto: "We do better under pressure."

Cholerics need to understand that there is more to life than money, success, or even accomplishment. Jesus said, "Man's life consists not in the things which he possesses" and "What shall it profit a man if he gain the whole world and lose his own soul?" (see Luke 12:15; Matt. 16:26). Mr. and Mrs. Pressure-building Choleric may successfully launch projects, develop businesses, and construct churches—all to the benefit of others—but if such endeavors succeed at the expense of their relationship with spouse, children, parents, and others, "What shall it profit?"

In short, a choleric must establish the best priorities for his life and concentrate on them. A man without priorities may become engrossed in activities that may better have been left alone. The choleric needs to set his priorities in this order:

1. God
2. Wife
3. Family
4. Vocation

Then he needs to establish clearly defined goals, rejecting creative ideas that do not contribute to the realization of these goals. He also must develop a love for people, learning to encourage others and become interested in them. His time spent on people will be returned to him multiplied, because others will extend themselves in appreciation, thus relieving him of many of his pressures.

MARTIN MELANCHOLY UNDER PRESSURE

Like everyone else, melancholies face pressure in life. But because of their sensitive, creative, and perfectionistic ways, everything in life is intensified, especially pressure. Probably no temperament bears more pressure in his heart and mind than does the melancholy. This may be why his mortality rate is approximately seven years lower than that of other types.

We have already seen that one's mental attitude can increase or decrease realistic pressure. That is bad news for a melancholy. One of his biggest problems in life relates to his mental attitude. A perfectionist by nature, he is extremely negative, critical, and suspicious—as critical of himself as he is of others.

One of a melancholy's consistent pressures is his desire to do everything perfectly. While commendable to a point, this trait can become maddening to others, for he often spends an inordinate amount of time on trivia or nonessentials at the neglect of more important matters. Sometimes he will neglect one assignment altogether until finishing a lesser project at 110 percent perfection level. Some melancholies cause pressure in their employer because they are perfection-oriented rather than production-oriented; consequently they don't produce enough to pay for their perfectionist productivity level.

Melancholy housewives and mothers are easily the best housekeepers and cooks. Dinner is always on time. But they may lack gracious flexibility. Woe to the child who tracks mud all over the freshly scrubbed kitchen floor! Or woe to the salesman husband who gets home late for dinner because he had to finalize that "big sale" at quitting time!

The melancholy's penchant for advance planning can drive the rest of the family off a cliff. Everything should be faithfully worried about! He often creates so much pressure contemplating and designing a vacation that all spontaneity and fun is eliminated.

Melancholies can worry themselves into pressure even when none exists. Most of the things they fear never materialize, but the pressure they build through worry is real. Such unnecessary fears often keep them from venturing out into something new, and as a result they build pressure through boredom, performing the same tasks repeatedly.

Since a melancholy person is predominantly an introvert, he will rarely externalize his pressures by angrily kicking things, swearing, or screaming—at first. His style is to internalize his pressure, comply with what is immediately expected of him, and mull it over until he gets himself so worked up that he lashes out in a manner totally out of character for him—anything from tears to murder. Some of the most vicious crimes committed by people with no criminal records have been accomplished by melancholies under intense pressure. Fortunately, few melancholies react in violence. Most say things of a cutting, hurtful

nature for which they are later very repentant. Others ponder the
problem and lapse into sulking silence.

Melancholy/cholerics—people who are predominantly melancholy
with a secondary temperament of choleric—are the epitome of
workaholics. They react to pressure with intensified work. Their choleric
suggests new projects, and their melancholy tries to do everything
perfectly. Such individuals are often frustrated by "the pressure of not
getting anything done." Others can frustrate them, because they never
quite measure up to melancholy perfectionism.

Everyone needs to deal with people by showing concern for them.
Melancholies are usually so interested in themselves and their persistent
brand of perfectionism that they have little sympathy for and acceptance
of other fallible human beings. They would certainly attract more friends
if they had more sensitivity. People interested in others never lack for
friends.

Everyone needs a diversion—"All work and no play makes Jack a
dull boy!"—but melancholies can become so work-oriented that they
eat, sleep, and think work. Vacations make them feel guilty. The
pressure of unfinished work makes it impossible for them to enjoy a
simple game of golf. They can turn a relaxing walk through the park
into a pressure-filled afternoon.

This inability to relax and learn to cope with the everyday pressures
of life will ultimately lead to a breakdown emotionally, mentally, or
physically. The melancholy's natural inability to cope with these problems
by himself may account for the number of melancholies I have seen
come to Christ, dedicate their lives to him, and learn to walk in the
Spirit. When they are truly filled with the Spirit, they experience
incredible changes that are immediately apparent to all. However, when
they regress spiritually, their friends quickly sense the change. I have
great respect for the potential of the person with a predominantly
melancholy temperament, but only when he avails himself of the power
of God. When he doesn't, his powerlessness is all too evident.

EVEN PHLEGMATICS   Phlegmatics detest pressure. In fact, they will
FACE PRESSURE   do almost anything to avoid it. As we have
                            seen, they do not thrive on controversy, but are
peacemakers by nature. Consequently they will always steer around a
problem if possible. Unfortunately, ignoring a real problem doesn't make
it disappear.

It is easy to diagnose a sanguine's reaction to pressure, for he

explodes loudly enough for everyone to see. Phlegmatics are different;
as very internal people, they do nothing to excess. For this reason you
must observe their responses carefully.

Their compulsion to avoid pressure causes many phlegmatics to
become gifted procrastinators. This eventually increases their pressures,
because tasks must be completed sooner or later and final decisions
have to be made. Some phlegmatics use the old dodge, "we need more
information" as an excuse for delaying an unpleasant deed. "Remove the
pressure, not the problem" often becomes the phlegmatic way of life.

How well I remember three phlegmatics on a deacon board who
appealed for "more time to study the matter" before deciding to expel a
leader in the church who had divorced his wife of many years and
married another woman. Actually he had made the mistake of marrying
the second wife before his divorce was final, and the chapel
inadvertently sent his new wedding certificate—signatures, dates, and
all—to his home, where Wife #1 opened it. The man was a bigamist!
Yet the phlegmatics wanted to delay one more month. Why? They
rotated off the board before the next meeting.

Problems seldom vanish with time. Rather, they tend to return more
robust and intimidating than before. I have found that it is usually best to
solve them when they are still small enough to handle.

The phlegamatic under pressure frequently exhibits one exasperating
trait: he flees from the pressured situation. Fathers of rebellious
teenagers are likely to sneak out to the garage and putter in their
workshop rather than take on their hostile youth. This does nothing for
the wife, who laments, "He always leaves the discipline of the children
up to me." Phlegmatic wives and mothers often are weak disciplinarians,
not because they fail to recognize their children's need for discipline, but
because they personally dislike the friction generated by confrontation.
Many a phlegmatic employee puts up with years of second-rate
treatment at work because he does not relish a confrontation with his
boss. But "peace at any price" is not really a solution to anything.

Those who have lived with phlegmatics will acknowledge that they
are stubborn. This stubbornness invariably surfaces when someone tries
to pressure them into doing something they are unwilling to do. Like a
burro, they will dig their feet in, arch their back, and stall. If they fill a
place of authority, they can be maddening. Experts on trivia themselves,
they can think of more reasons why a building permit or license should
not be granted than ever occurred to those who made the laws. Have
you ever tried to get something approved by the security-conscious

inspectors at city hall? It is nothing short of amazing that the free enterprise system has succeeded in the face of phlegmatic foot-dragging.

Married phlegmatics are quite interesting sexually. A sexuality survey of 3,404 people included a question about temperament. I found that male phlegmatics were less promiscuous before marriage, registered less frequency of sex after marriage, and experienced less satisfaction than their female counterparts. Reflecting on this finding for several years while counseling hundreds of couples, I have come to the following conclusions. Phlegmatics are perfectly normal regarding the place of sexual activity in marriage, and they can be as sexually expressive and loving as anyone else. They enjoy tenderness, love, and affection, as long as it is not displayed publicly. However, they do not like pressure, conflict, or rejection; consequently they tend to let their partners lead.

I was surprised to discover from my sex survey that a rather high percentage of phlegmatic wives had indicated promiscuity before marriage. Because by nature they like to please others, they would often succumb to the pressure of an aggressive lover's advances. Since opposites usually attract, we should note, phlegmatics often find themselves in the company of more aggressive temperaments. Many of these women indicated that their premarital activity had burdened them with years of guilt. (More will be said about temperament and its effect on sexual expression in a later chapter.)

Phlegmatics are apt to blame other people for their mistakes. Adam must have been phlegmatic, for he started it all by complaining to God, "The woman whom Thou gavest to be with me, she gave me from the tree, and I ate" (Gen. 3:12, NASB). This still seems to be the phlegmatic pattern. When phlegmatics are confronted with a mistake, a sin, or an error, they will try to cast the blame onto someone else. It's not that they want to be deceitful; they just don't like the pressure of taking the full responsibility for their behavior. Others find this maddening: parents whose children point the finger at other siblings in the family, or the boss whose otherwise loyal, dependable, and careful employee blames a coworker under pressure.

The disadvantage of this trait to the phlegmatic himself is that he seldom learns from his behavior. Because blaming others frees him from the immediate pressure, he goes his cheerful way, not admitting that he needs to improve in this regard. As a result, he tends to repeat his mistakes.

Phlegmatic children are great daydreamers. They escape the nasty now by drifting off into a fantasy land. Some have trouble reading, spelling, or learning math because of this. When they grow up, this mental habit will serve as an escape hatch from unpleasant circumstances. No doubt many unhappily married phlegmatics have endured to the end by letting their minds drift to the Land of Oz. But this is not what the Bible means when it says, "Be content with what you have" or "Learn to be content whatever the circumstances" (see Heb. 13:5, NIV; Phil. 4:11, NIV). True contentment comes from God to those who walk with him. Daydreaming can become a form of unproductive phlegmatic escapism.

SUMMARY

Whatever your temperament, you will face pressure in life. You cannot change that, nor are you responsible for it. But you are responsible for the way you respond to pressure regardless of your temperament. For there is one thing more important than your temperament in relation to how you respond to pressure, and that is your mental attitude. With God's help *you* can control your mental attitude.

One of the most important truths I have discovered since becoming a Christian is the need to maintain a thankful attitude—about everything. There are only two kinds of people: gripers and thankers (some identify them as groaners and praisers). Gripers are never happy; thankers always are. You have the capacity to be either, but if you allow the Spirit of God to control your mind, you will be a thanker.

We have referred several times in this book to the biblical command to "be filled with the Spirit" (or controlled by the Spirit) (Eph. 5:18). It should be noted that the second result of his "filling" or "control" will be thanksgiving—"always giving thanks to God the Father for everything, in the name of our Lord Jesus Christ" (Eph. 5:20, NIV).

In Psalm 1:1 God warns us against sitting around with gripers. Throughout the Old Testament God denounces and condemns gripers (Israel in the wilderness, Moses, Elijah, Jeremiah, and others). By contrast, in both the Old and New Testaments we read hundreds of challenges to be thankful. First Thessalonians 5:18 makes it clear that anything less is to be out of the will of God: "Give thanks in all circumstances, for this is God's will for you in Christ Jesus" (NIV).

I am convinced that one cannot be lastingly happy or learn how to control pressure unless he develops the mental habit of thanksgiving. And that is not easy. Personally I have to work on it constantly. After all these years of teaching, writing, and trying to practice a thankful mental attitude, one would think it becomes automatic. Not so! I look on the development of a habitual mental attitude of thanksgiving as if it were a large boulder which I consciously push uphill everyday. If I unconsciously forget thanksgiving, the stone rolls back down the hill a few yards, and I must start pushing again. It gets easier only as I walk in the Spirit and try to be grateful by thanking God for his goodness in the things I understand, and by thanking him by faith for what he is going to do in the things I do not understand. Thanksgiving is an imperative in God's Word. Most Christians consider it an option. Without it you will drift into griping, which will destroy your positive mental attitude and increase your pressures.

Thankful living is a matter of daily developing a mental attitude of thanksgiving. It is not only "the will of God" for your life, but the secret to developing a positive mental attitude, which in turn is the key to controlling pressure. Admittedly, thanksgiving is not an easy habit or way of life to develop, but it is absolutely essential.

Some temperaments find thanksgiving to be easier than others, but I do not read in Scripture that God commands only sanguines and phlegmatics, "In everything give thanks." This is a universal command to us all, and it must be obeyed. Otherwise our life's pressures will control us instead of our controlling them.

Anyone who desires to work seriously on developing such a mental attitude should do the following:

> Do a daily Bible study on all the verses related to thanksgiving. Write down your findings.
>
> Memorize one thanksgiving verse per week, starting with 1 Thessalonians 5:18 and Philippians 4:6, 7.
>
> Read Philippians through daily for thirty days.
>
> Make a list of ten characteristics about your spouse (if married) or closest relative or friend (if single), giving thanks for each one daily for three months.
>
> Make a list of ten other items for which you are grateful, thanking God for them daily.

Do not permit your mind to think negatively, critically, or ungratefully—and never repeat such thoughts verbally. If you do, repent as soon as you realize what you have done, confess it as sin, and replace the thought with something for which you are truly grateful. Then quote one of the thanksgiving verses you have been memorizing.

Without consciously practicing thanksgiving, you will never develop a lasting positive mental attitude.

**LEARN
CONTENTMENT**

"But godliness with contentment is great gain" (1 Tim. 6:6, NIV).

"Keep your lives free from the love of money and be content with what you have, because God has said, 'Never will I leave you; never will I forsake you' " (Heb. 13:5, NIV).

"I am not saying this because I am in need, for I have learned to be content whatever the circumstances. I know what it is to be in need, and I know what it is to have plenty. I have learned the secret of being content in any and every situation, whether well fed or hungry, whether living in plenty or in want. I can do everything through him who gives me strength" (Phil. 4:11-13, NIV).

The man who popularized contentment "whatever the circumstances" and "in every situation" was the church's most celebrated jailbird. Paul had been imprisoned many times for faithfully preaching the gospel. Instead of griping and groaning, he had "learned to be content." How? By practicing the art of praise in a situation that would naturally breed complaints. Our modern jails are luxurious palaces by comparison with the Mamertine prison in Rome where Paul was incarcerated. I have seen it—or one like it—and it was dreadful. Lacking doors, lights, or creature comforts, it was a cold, damp cave with one opening at the top through which the prisoner was lowered. After he was placed inside, only his sparse food supply passed through that opening. Yet Paul had *learned* to be content.

Your prison may be an overcrowded apartment with more children than bedrooms, an office without windows, a car that barely runs, or a job well beneath your ability and income needs. It may be an unhappy marriage or overly possessive parents. Whatever the privation or predicament, have you learned to be content? If not, you can never gain contentment by moving to a bigger apartment, getting a new job, or leaving your partner. Most people want to change their circumstances as a means to achieving peace. To the contrary, satisfaction is learned by developing a thankful attitude where you are. Your present circumstances may not be Shangri-la, but they are your training ground. Since God wants to teach you contentment, learn your lesson as quickly as possible so he can speed you on to where he wants you to be. I am inclined to believe that many Christians spend their lives in the prison of discontent because they refuse to learn the lesson of satisfaction where they are.

Remaining cheerfully serene in the face of unpleasant circumstances is possible only through developing the art of "thanksgiving living." Thanking God for your present address in life is the first giant step toward learning contentment.

Learning to be content where you are *and* learning to develop a godly mental attitude of thanksgiving will reduce life's pressure down to an enjoyable level—regardless what temperament you are. Work on it— you'll be glad you did.

CHAPTER
ELEVEN

Temperament and Depression

When I wrote my book *How to Win Over Depression* ten years ago, it was because depression had reached "near epidemic proportions," according to *Newsweek* magazine, "and suicide was its all too often result." During that time my travels took me through the Dallas Airport where I picked up a newspaper and read, "Depression—The Leading Cause of College Suicide." I remember thinking, what would cause a young person in the prime of life (18-23 years) to take his life? The article made it clear—depression.

During this past decade the problem has gotten worse, not better. Today the leading cause of death in junior high school is suicide, and depression is usually the cause. The self-preservation instinct is powerful in human beings, and a person has to be so depressed that he overpowers that instinct before he can take his own life.

You may well ask, "What would cause a fifteen-year-old at the prime of life to deliberately end his life?" The emotional aftermath of a broken home through divorce is one factor, and certainly easy access to harmful drugs is another. It has been my observation, however, that some temperaments have a greater problem with depression than others.

THE SANGUINE AND DEPRESSION

A sanguine is rarely depressed when in the company of others. He is such a response-oriented person that the sight of another individual usually lifts his spirits and brings a smile to his face. Whatever periods of depression he does experience almost invariably commence when he is alone.

The most pleasant characteristic of a sanguine is his ability to enjoy the present. He does not look back on unhappy experiences in his past, and he never worries about the unknown future. A delightful sanguine friend of mine affords a classic example. While traveling across the country he commented on the many people who approached me for counseling due to depression. Spontaneously he exclaimed, "You know, I've never had much trouble with depression; I guess it's because God has been so good to me. Actually, I can't remember ever having any real problems or difficulties in life." His statement really astonished me, for I knew the man well. I was forced to recall that he failed to finish high school until he was almost forty years of age because he ran away from home and joined the Merchant Marines. While in the service he married, and after two children were born, one of them died of a rather strange and rare disease. This caused some bitterness on the part of his wife, who after several unhappy years divorced him and remarried. At the time my friend made his statement, he had been single for six years. Only a sanguine could recollect that type of life and say, "I've never really had any problems in life." But there would be much less depression if all temperaments could think that way.

Many undisciplined sanguines experience depression during the fourth or fifth decade of life. Their lack of discipline and weakness of will has usually made them rather unproductive, much to their own chagrin and self-disappointment. They are also prone to obesity by this time because of their inability to refuse fattening desserts and other delicacies. This lowers their self-esteem and heightens their tendency toward depression. Although they usually go through the motions of responding happily to other people, their tendency toward mild depression will increase. One writer likened them to Peter Pan—they wish never to grow up. Although they are well-liked and attractive, they are often undependable and without real substance.

As these charming sanguines, who usually act like overgrown children, become aware of their own shallowness, their insecurities are heightened. They become defensive, sensitive to slights or criticism, almost obsessed with others' opinions of them. It is not uncommon for them to become depressed at this point by engaging in self-pity. They may even blame their parents for indulging them so much in childhood that they never developed self-discipline; but it is very difficult for them to blame themselves, confess their sin, and seek the filling of the Holy Spirit for the strength of character they so desperately need.

If they do not face their problem realistically and learn to walk in the Spirit, they will fluctuate up and down between depression and happiness for a time until, in some childlike way, they settle for the life of mediocrity which they have brought on themselves, and then go through life fixed in a playful position far beneath their level of potential.

The Spirit-filled sanguine is different! The Holy Spirit not only convicts him of his self-pitying thought-patterns as sin, but guides him to those areas of productivity that make it easier for him to accept and appreciate himself. When a sanguine is filled with the Spirit, like the Apostle Peter in the Book of Acts, he becomes a productive and effective person, untroubled by lasting depression.

THE CHOLERIC AND DEPRESSION

The hard-driving, steel-willed choleric rarely gets depressed. His active, goal-conscious mind keeps him so motivated that he projects fourteen different programs simultaneously. If one of them proves baffling or frustrating, his disappointment is short-lived and he quickly pursues a fresh challenge. Cholerics are happy when busy, and thus they have little time to be depressed. Their frustration in life is that there are not enough hours in the day to engage in their endless supply of goals and objectives.

The rejection or insults that often set other temperaments off into periods of depression never faze a choleric. He is so thick-skinned, self-sufficient, and independent by nature that he rarely feels the need for other people. Instead of feeling sorry for himself when alone, he spends the time originating new plans.

Emotionally he is the most underdeveloped of all the temperaments. For that reason he usually experiences very slight mood changes. Although he quickly becomes angry, he rarely indulges in self-pity. Instead, he explodes all over everyone else. Because he is so insensitive to others' opinions of him, he is not vulnerable to depression occasioned by people. If a choleric ever battles depression, it will come as a result of frustration, retreat, or what he considers the incompetence of other people.

By the time a choleric has reached the fourth or fifth decade of life, his activity-prone brain can often create a mental activity syndrome that makes his thoughts cancel or short-circuit each other, much like an overloaded switchboard. As a Christian, the choleric must learn to rest in the Lord and commit his way to him. An indomitable will and a spirit of self-sufficiency often causes him to be a useless, unproductive Christian because he insists on doing everything in the flesh instead of the Spirit. If he does successfully promote Christian activities, his pride makes him spiritually myopic and he fails to discern his carnal motivation.

The peace of the Holy Spirit that passes all understanding will modulate his thinking pattern, causing him to concentrate on the Lord first and then on the task. He must learn that God's program does not depend on him; rather, he needs to depend on God. He must further recognize that fulfilling the work of God is not enough; he must do it in the power of the Spirit. As the Bible says, "Not by might, nor by power, but by my spirit, saith the Lord of hosts" (Zech. 4:6). The Apostle Paul, possibly the best illustration of a Spirit-filled choleric used of God, had learned this well, for he said, ". . . when I am weak, then am I strong" (2 Cor. 12:10).

The flesh-filled choleric Christian can become depressed until he realizes this principle, because he gets frustrated by the lack of spiritual results from his hard-driving, fleshly efforts. Instead of blaming himself for his carnal, self-willed spirit, he may swell up in self-pity and withdraw from his church activities. His carnal spirit is often easily discerned by others in the congregation, and thus he may be bypassed when officers are elected. "I don't understand," he complains. "Isn't my hard work sufficient proof of my devotion to Christ?" Happy is the choleric who learns with James to say, ". . . If the Lord will, we shall live, and do this, or that" (James 4:15). If he seeks the priorities of the will of God through the leading of the Holy Spirit in his life, he will not only be more productive but also more composed. When once he comprehends that walking in the Spirit is the secret to spiritual productivity, he will gain consistency in his Christian life.

Another period of life during which a choleric is vulnerable to depression is retirement. Though he usually does not retire until age seventy or later, he must program into his thinking some added form of productivity or give way to depression.

A former business executive was forced to retire at sixty-five. Within six months he went in to see his pastor in a state of depression. It did not take the minister long to perceive that the unproductive inactivity of retirement was the culprit. In addition, of course, the executive was indulging in the sin of self-pity that laments, "My life is over, the period of my productivity is past, I am no longer good for anything." The pastor was leading a very dynamic church much in need of a businessman to coordinate and direct the business affairs. He challenged this man to be a $1.00 a year Christian worker. Today that church rates among the most efficient in the nation, and the energetic choleric business manager is thoroughly enjoying his retirement.

The ability of the Holy Spirit to literally transform a choleric tendency toward depression is illustrated superbly in the life of the Apostle Paul. If ever a man was an illustration of choleric temperament, it was Saul of Tarsus before he became a Christian. After his conversion, his indomitable choleric will, now directed by the Holy Spirit, surged forward throughout the Book of Acts. His response to confinement offers a classic illustration of depressing circumstances overcome through the invasion of man's spiritual nature by the Holy Spirit. Confined to the cold, clammy Mamertine Prison in Rome for preaching the gospel, he manifested not one sign of self-pity. Instead, this dynamic Christian took advantage of the opportunity to share his faith personally with every new Roman soldier assigned to him as a guard. Many of these men were converted—"All the saints salute you, chiefly they that are of Caesar's household" (Phil. 4:22). In addition, from this prison he penned the prison epistles, including his epistle of joy, the letter to the Philippians, in which he stated, "I have learned, in whatsoever state I am, therewith to be content" (Phil. 4:11). Spirit-filled cholerics will never become depressed.

Contentment is not natural, particularly when you are confined to a prison. Contentment is a learned mental attitude that requires the supernatural power of the Holy Spirit, particularly difficult for a choleric; but it can be learned.

Your prison is doubtless not a cold clammy prison in Rome. It may be a job you detest. It may be an unhappy marriage or a host of other circumstances. But whether it becomes a cause for depression or contentment is up to you. The Bible commands, "Gird up the loins of your mind" (1 Pet. 1:13). In other words, don't let your mind float along thinking of those things it wants to think about. If you do, it will take your emotions downhill—by thinking of self-pity, or selfish or self-centered thought-patterns.

What causes depression? Many things really. If you have a problem in this area you should examine my book *How to Win Over Depression,* where I give eleven of the most frequent causes. The most common, however, is the self-pity we indulge in after rejection by someone we love or admire, an insult, or an injury. The real culprit is self-pity. The greater your self-pity, the greater your depression. That's why Paul challenges all of us to *learn* contentment—even in the face of rejection, insult, or injury.

Everyone knows what contentment is, or at least they think they do. But few people realize that it is the emotional result of mental thanksgiving—regardless of the prison they're in. Cholerics are rarely content. But they can "learn," by learning to be a thanker and a praiser.

THE MELANCHOLY AND DEPRESSION

Melancholies often are easily depressed because they are perfectionists. Most people could profit by having more perfectionist tendencies, but the true perfectionist is made miserable by them. In the first place, he measures himself by his own arbitrary standard of perfection and gets discouraged with himself when he falls short of that standard. The fact that his standard is usually so high that neither he nor anyone else could live by it rarely occurs to him. Instead, he insists that his criterion for perfection is "realistic."

In addition to perfectionism, he also is very conscientious and prides himself on being dependable and accurate. Naturally, all of his friends fall short of this standard, so it is not uncommon for him to become depressed about himself and his associates. Very rigid and inflexible, he finds it difficult to tolerate the slightest deviation from what he considers to be the measure of excellence.

Such perfectionist-prone melancholies can love their children dearly while at the same time becoming depressed by them. Children are notoriously disorganized and unpredictable; they follow their own schedules and insist on acting like children. A rigid melancholy parent finds it difficult to cope with such unpredictability, and consequently may experience depression. Sometimes a melancholy mother may become ambivalent toward her own children, loving them intensely while at the same time being filled with anger and bitterness at them. The carefree, happy-go-lucky little tyke who insists on trekking across the clean kitchen floor with his wet rubbers can be a source of irritation to any mother, particularly to a melancholy. Before she was married, she probably could not retire for the night until her shoes were lined up properly and the bathroom was in perfect order. Children automatically change that, but perfectionists find it difficult to cope with such change; consequently, depression is their outlet. They become angered at the lack of perfection in others and indulge in self-pity because they are the only ones striving for lofty goals. Such thought patterns invariably produce depression.

In fairness to melancholy people, they are as critical of themselves as they are of others. As a result, they tend to develop an inadequate view of themselves. From early childhood they construct a disparaging self-image on the screen of their imagination. As they get older, unlike some of the other temperaments who learn to accept themselves, they tend to reject themselves even more. Consequently their periods of depression increase. If they were permitted to verbalize their criticisms in childhood, they are apt to be verbally critical in adulthood. Each time they indulge in oral criticism, they only embed the spirit of criticism more deeply in their mind; and critics are never happy people!

One day I had an opportunity to see this principle in action. As I submitted to an airport examination before boarding a plane, the security officer began to criticize the individuals who flew on that airline as "slovenly, inconsiderate, disorganized, and ungrateful people." I took it just about as long as I could, but finally, looking at him with a big smile (I find one can say almost anything if he smiles) I observed, "You must be an unhappy man!" He looked at me rather startled and replied, "Why do you say that?" "Because you're so critical. I've never met a happy person who is a critical person." After inspecting my baggage, he said, "Thank you, sir, I needed that." To my amazement he turned to the next customer and said, "Hello, how are you? So glad to have you on our airline." I don't know how long he will profit by that experience, but I am certain that he has the capability of making himself happy or miserable in direct proportion to the way in which he thinks and talks to people.

Not only are melancholy people rigid perfectionists and conscientious individuals, but they possess a low threshold of anxiety and tension. The American way of life is not conducive to happiness for such people. We live in a hyperactivity-prone, choleric society, as Dr. Paul Tournier verifies in a chapter on temperament in his book entitled *The Healing of Persons*. It seems that Western civilization, where the gospel of Christ has had its most profound influence, reflects a highly choleric population.

This would be characteristic of the Teutonic or Nordic race, whose people tend to represent a high percentage of choleric temperament. Such individuals settled in Scandinavia, Germany, parts of France, Ireland and England, the very countries producing most of the American settlers. Although it would be difficult to prove, it would seem that the most courageous, hearty, and choleric members of Europe came over to settle this country. Consequently, their progeny would include a high level of choleric, activity-prone citizens, which may account for our industrialized, fast-moving, high-pressure environment. Such an atmosphere is not the best for a melancholy, for he is not interested in achieving massive production, but perfection and quality. It is not uncommon to hear a melancholy professional man complain, "We just don't have time to be accurate anymore."

This may explain why so many of the hippy or "freak" people drop out of the mainstream of society today. Rejecting its mad pace and witnessing its lack of perfection through the eyes of idealism, they seek a more passive culture. This may be one reason some of them will speak favorably about a governmental system that has totally enslaved people into passivity in contrast to the free enterprise system, which they think has enslaved people to activity.

I have repeatedly observed that many of the young people who have "copped out" of our society are very sensitive, gifted, idealistic young people indulging in escape rather than making an honest attempt to alter society. Dr. Tournier notes that some of the Indian or Oriental cultures place a higher priority on the mystic or passive individual. Thus Mahatma Gandhi, whose fastings were symbolic of passive resistance, became a national hero. By contrast, in the Western world the dynamic, productive choleric is the hero. Whatever its cause, the frantic pace we live in today contributes heavily to the melancholy's tendency toward depression.

Two characteristics of the melancholy which mutually short-circuit each other are his natural desire to be *self-sacrificing* and his *self-persecution* tendency. Unless he is careful, this conflict will likely make a martyr out of him. Ordinarily he chooses the most difficult and trying location to ply his vocation. When others seem to be more successful or gain more renown, instead of facing realistically the fact that he has chosen the path of self-sacrifice, he indulges in self-pity because his journey winds uphill and leads through arduous straits.

The determination of a melancholy to gripe and criticize merely compounds his negative thinking and ultimately brings him to despair.

For that reason 1 Thessalonians 5:18 can come to his rescue! If he painstakingly and consistently follows its formula, he will never become depressed. "In every thing give thanks: for this is the will of God in Christ Jesus concerning you."

Although everyone is vulnerable to his own mental thinking pattern, none is more responsive than the melancholy. Among his other creative gifts, he harbors the great ability to suggest images to the screen of his imagination—probably in living color with stereophonic sound. Because melancholies are moody by nature, they may regard their moods as spontaneous, but it has been learned that moods result directly from thinking patterns. If a melancholy guards his thought processes and refuses to indulge in the mental sins of anger, resentment, self-persecution, and self-pity, he will not yield to his predisposition toward depression.

The powerful influence of the mind on our moods can easily be illustrated by an experience I had with my sons when they were growing up. One Sunday night as they were going to bed we reminded them, as millions of children are faithfully reminded by loving parents, "Don't forget—tomorrow you have to get up early and go to school." In unison they sang, "Do we have to go to school tomorrow?" Assuring them that this was a necessary part of their lives and accepting their grumbling with customary parental long-suffering, I sent them off to bed. Needless to say, Monday morning they woke up in a sour mood. I sincerely hated to foist them off on their schoolteacher that day.

The next week the same boys were lying in the same bed at night. As I tucked them in I admonished, "Don't forget—you've got to get up early tomorrow because we're heading for Disneyland!" You can imagine the happy chorus that greeted my announcement. The next morning both boys bolted out of bed excited and expectant, as they anticipated the thrilling trip ahead. As I sat at the breakfast table that morning, I contemplated the difference in moods within just one week. Their metabolism seemed to function better, their eyes were clearer, their faces shinier; the whole world looked better because they reflected an improved mental attitude. The melancholy who recognizes the power of the subconscious mind to influence his moods will seek the power of the Holy Spirit to orient his thinking patterns positively.

It is hard to select one period in life that a melancholy finds more depressing than another. Usually his depressions become apparent in early childhood; unless he is spiritually motivated by the power of God, they tend to follow him all his life. Because he is supersensitive and self-centered, he reads things into every activity, at times becoming almost obsessed with the idea that people don't like him or that they are laughing at him.

One day the business manager of Christian Heritage College, my wife (who was the registrar), and I were having lunch together in a restaurant. Suddenly a melancholy college-age man with a gaunt look on his face appeared at the edge of our table and asked, "Pardon me, but may I ask you folks if you were laughing at me?" Naturally we were shocked into silence. Finally I explained, "Young man, I don't think we've ever seen you before in our lives." With that he excused himself and walked away. Reflecting on the incident, we concluded that during our laughter and conversation we must have looked in his direction, which gave that troubled young man the impression that we were laughing at his expense. Equally as substantial are many of the depression-causing events in the life of the average melancholy.

Fortunately for the melancholy, he possesses an unusual *creative ability* to project all kinds of images on the screen of his imagination. Once he fully realizes that his feelings are the direct result of constructing wholesome mental images of himself and his circumstances, he is well on the road to recovery and prevention of future bouts of depression. Melancholy people risk depression primarily because of the continual misuse of their creative imagination. That is, on the imagination screen of their mind they project negativism, self-pity, helplessness, and despair. Once they realize that their creative suggestions can either work for or against them, they can carefully project only those images that are pleasing to God. Such thoughts will lift their spirits, stabilize their moods, and help them to avoid depression.

Through the years, more melancholy temperaments found their way into my counseling room than any other type. At first I thought it was because I have a magnetic attraction for depression-prone individuals. Later I realized that the creative melancholy has a greater difficulty getting his act together. His creative thought process can find just too many problems and imperfections or conjure up too many imagined rejections, insults, or injuries.

Even more than the choleric, he needs to concentrate on thanksgiving as a way of life. Griping, criticizing, and complaining always have a depressing effect on a person's mood. If you are going to "learn" contentment and inner peace, it will be through thanksgiving. And interestingly enough, that is the will of God for your life anyway (1 Thess. 5:18)!

THE PHLEGMATIC AND DEPRESSION

As a general rule, a phlegmatic person is not easily depressed. His unique sense of humor signals a happy outlook on life, and rarely does he reflect much mood fluctuation. It is possible to know a phlegmatic all his life and never see him truly angry, for no matter what the occasion, he tends to mentally excuse the person who has offended, injured, or rejected him. His ability to adjust to unpleasant circumstances is unbelievable to the other three temperaments, which find it easy to gripe or criticize mentally and verbally.

If a phlegmatic ever does experience depression, it is usually aimed at his own lack of aggressiveness. Many times his practical, capable mind devises a suitable plan of action for a given set of circumstances, but because of his passive inclination or his fear of being criticized by others, he keeps it to himself. Consequently, driven by family or other group pressure, he may find himself pursuing a plan inferior to his own. This can produce irritation which, when followed by self-pity, will make him depressed. Fortunately, his depression is short-lived most of the time, for in a brief time one of those amazingly interesting characters called a human being comes along to amuse and entertain him.

At one critical period in life the phlegmatic is most vulnerable to depression. During the fifth or sixth decade he often becomes aware that the other temperaments have passed him by vocationally, spiritually, and in every other way. While he was passively watching the game of life as a spectator, his more aggressive friends were stepping through the doors of opportunity. His security-mindedness has checked him from attending upon daring adventures in life, and thus his existence may seem rather stale to him during this period. If he indulges in self-pity, he will definitely become depressed.

Instead of blaming his fear or indolence, he finds it much easier to reproach "society" or "the breaks" or "my luck." Such a person should learn from the Lord Jesus early in life to attempt great things for God, for Christ said, "According to your faith be it unto you" (Matt. 9:29).

No one is in greater need of external motivation than a phlegmatic. But he often spends his life resisting pressure. Rarely does he take on more than he can do or become overinvolved. The only thing I have ever seen a phlegmatic become overinvolved in was keeping from getting overinvolved.

Frankly, he needs to get overinvolved. He is the *only temperament* I say that about. Sanguines take on everything and finish nothing. Cholerics take on everything and wear themselves out doing it. Melancholies take on the most difficult things that others won't do and ruin their health. Not phlegmatics. They live to a ripe old age protecting themselves. Someone has said, "A phlegmatic is the only type of person who can jam fifty years of living in a 100-year lifetime." And most of those years will be basically depression-free.

SUMMARY

You can't help being the temperament you are. And there is no one temperament that is better than another. Each is unique with its own set of strengths and weaknesses, including the tendency to easy depression or a carefree way of life. But you can control your mental attitude or thinking process. If you inherited a choleric or melancholy temperament, it is wise to face it honestly and realize you will have to fight all your life against indulging in self-pity and criticism. If you are a combination of the ChlorMel or MelChlor temperaments, you will have to fight off those thought-patterns particularly hard. But it can be done! With God's help you can learn to be a thankful, content person, but you will have to work on it all your life.

Every time you find yourself griping in the spirit of your mind, confess it as sin and begin praying to God for who and what he is in the midst of your circumstances. Don't indulge your natural inclination to self-pity. You will be both out of the will of God and miserable. Make thanksgiving a way of life, and depression will lose its deadly influence on you. "Give thanks in all circumstances, for this is God's will for you in Christ Jesus" (1 Thess. 5:18, NIV).

CHAPTER
TWELVE

How to Cope with Anger and Hostility

Fear may be the first emotional problem ever to face the family and it may even afflict more people than the second; but it is not the family's Number One enemy. That dishonor is reserved for anger, which sometimes takes the form of hostility and wrath.

More wives have been battered, children abused and psychologically destroyed by the violent outbursts of anger than anyone knows. It is impossible to overexaggerate the damage this emotion does to the family, marriage, and all other interpersonal relationships.

A pastor friend in Northern California called to ask if I would meet with a dedicated couple from his congregation who happened to be in San Diego, trying to work out their marriage problems. This ChlorSan husband and MelPhleg wife had been married seventeen years and acknowledged two problems. First, both admitted, "We cannot communicate." Second, the wife added, "He turns me off sexually. I am absolutely dead toward him." Sue's story was pathetic. Raised in a German immigrant family with five children, her father "ruled the roost with an iron hand." She lamented, "Mealtimes were always a terror for me, because if Father got upset, he would pound his fist so hard that the dishes and silverware would leap off the table. I always promised myself that I would never marry a man like my father." When Bill came along, he seemed so sweet and kind that she fell in love with him and they soon married. "Three weeks after our wedding, it happened," she continued. "Something set him off, and he pounded his fist on the table so hard that the dishes and silverware leaped into the air. As they clattered down onto the table, I thought, I've married a man just like my father!"

ANGER AND FEAR   Sweethearts rarely have trouble
STIFLE   communicating before marriage. In fact, they
COMMUNICATION   can talk on the phone by the hour. But to
                        destroy that relationship it only takes the angry
action of one to set up a fear reaction in the other. Oh, they usually
make up and renew their tenderness and communication, but the
damage is done. Each has seen the other in his true light. Consequently,
the spirit of free communication will be inhibited. The anger of one
builds a formidable block in the wall that obstructs communication. The
self-protective reaction of fear keeps the other from expressing himself
freely, and thus another block is added to the wall. Gradually such
outbursts and reactions build an impenetrable wall until the former
lovebirds are not really communicating at all, apprehensive that the
anger of one will be ignited or the fear of the other will cause added
pain. Tears, silence, and pent-up feelings all play their part, and before
long they need counseling because "we can't communicate anymore."
Lack of communication is not the problem. Anger and fear are the
culprits! In this chapter we will examine its results and its remedy.

PRESSURE DOESN'T   Bill defended his actions by saying, "She has
MAKE YOUR SPIRIT   no idea of the pressures I'm under, and she
                       takes my outbursts too seriously because of
her background. What she doesn't realize is that all men have to let off
steam. I don't really mean the things I say, but she won't forgive me
when I apologize." In other words, Bill doesn't want to change. He
expects Sue to live with an angry man just as her mother did.
    What Bill didn't recognize is that pressure does not make your
spirit—it merely reveals it. What a man is under pressure is what he is!
If you explode under pressure, you are admitting that underneath a
carefully constructed facade you are an angry person. Some people have
more tolerance and can take more pressure than others, of course, but if
you are an angry individual, your weakness will show up sooner or later
by the way you act, react, or think. And we all know that the home is
potentially the world's greatest pressure cooker. That is why anger and
its various forms of hostility are the family's Number One problem.
    One hostile husband told me, "Well, I have to find someplace where I
can be myself." Yes, he did, and that was his problem—himself. A
person at home always reveals his true nature. We can put up a front
outside the home, but under the pressures of family living the real
individual manifests himself. I have found only one remedy. Let God

change the real you so that your hours at home can be pleasant and those who love you most will not be threatened.

ANGER AND MASCULINITY

Many men seem to have the strange idea that anger is a justifiable masculine trait. "Every man gets angry," they exclaim. Some would insist that a man who doesn't have an anger problem isn't a real man. Nothing could be further from the truth! Man's natural tendency toward anger has probably started more wars, created more conflict, and ruined more homes than any other universal trait.

Anger seems to be a man's way of expressing his frustrations, but it is a mistake to deem it a beneficial emotion. In fact, it inhibits sound judgment and thinking. A nineteen-year-old lad who had a fight with his girl friend backed out of her driveway and "laid a hundred and five feet of scratch" in front of her house. In seven minutes he was dead. His anger robbed him of good judgment as he floorboarded the gas pedal at ninety-five miles an hour, failed to navigate a freeway curve, and sped straight into eternity. Anger struck again.

Newspapers have been carrying reports lately from hospital emergency wards and welfare agencies that child abuse is alarmingly on the increase. Over 10,000 children died last year due to such mistreatment. What could cause any adult to so abuse a helpless child? Frustration due to anger! Broken-hearted parents have wept as they related stories of their "abnormal behavior," registering amazement that they were capable of such action. They aren't basically "abnormal"; they just never learned to control their anger, and when a sufficient level of frustration was reached, they committed an act which they regretted for life. Such anger-laden behavior is not limited to the lower socioeconomic members of society, although their living conditions may accelerate frustrations. I have seen otherwise respectable people destroy their children through anger.

A minister asked me to counsel his wife for an unrepentant "affair" she was having. Expecting to see a siren walk into my office, I was surprised to find a gracious, soft-spoken woman of forty-five who told her story through her tears. Her husband was a dynamic minister, very successful in his church and admired by everyone. But he had one sin she could not excuse. He was an angry, hostile man whom she considered "overstrict and physically abusive of our three children. He cannot control his anger and has on one occasion beaten our oldest son unconscious." When the boy reached nineteen, he ran away and joined a hippie group. Broken-heartedly she said, "From that day on I lost all feeling for my husband."

An extreme situation like that never occurs suddenly. It had been building up for years, primarily related to major disagreements over disciplining the children. She had learned to live with his other angry explosions but could not endure his manhandling of the children. Too fearful to voice her real feelings, she witnessed her husband's angry frustrations worked out on the heads, faces, and backsides of their children. Although she only interrupted on extreme occasions, she acknowledged "dying a little" each time he abused them. As it turned out, her "affair" was simply retaliation to spite her husband.

When the minister came in, he was obviously desperate. I was never sure if he sought help because he really loved his wife or if he was just trying to save his ministry. When confronted with his hostilities, he retorted, "If a man can't let down and be himself at home, where can he?" I was silent for a long time. As he sat there thinking he finally admitted, "That sounds pretty carnal, doesn't it?" Before leaving, he realized that his anger was as bad or worse than her adultery. Although this man was able to salvage his marriage, as far as I know he has never regained his son. In all probability, more sons have been alienated from their fathers because of Dad's anger than anything else. And the tragic part of it is that the son will probably treat his son the same way. Angry fathers produce angry children.

THE DEVASTATING CONSEQUENCES OF ANGER

Anger, hostility, or wrath—or, as the Bible calls it, "enmity of heart" or "malice"—is as old as man. Doubtless you recall the first family squabble in recorded history. "Cain was very wroth (angry) and . . . rose up against Abel his brother, and slew him" (see Gen. 4:5-8). Ever since that tragic day, millions have died prematurely, and countless marriages have broken up because of anger. The number of children subjected to emotional tension in the home due to the anger of adults staggers the mind. Any counselor will acknowledge that most of his emotionally scarred clients are the victims of someone's anger. It is a nearly universal emotional problem with devastating consequences, particularly in the home. Even as I write this chapter, our local newspaper carries the story of a pro-football player whose wife killed him in his sleep with an eight-inch kitchen knife. Only protracted anger which turned into the white heat of rage would make a person take another's life.

**TEMPERAMENT
AND ANGER**

The only temperament that will not have an
inherent problem with anger is the phlegmatic.
But since no one is 100 percent a phlegmatic,
even he will encounter the difficulty to one degree or another, depending
on his secondary temperament. As we have seen, a PhlegMel will
experience the least problem with it, depending of course on the
percentages of his two temperaments. The two temperaments that have
the greatest problem with it are the two extremes, as shown on the next
chart. Sanguines, you will recall, are instantly eruptive and forgiving,
cholerics eruptive and grudging. Melancholies take longer to explode,
preferring to mull over self-persecuting thoughts and to harbor
revengeful plans until they, too, are capable of unreasonable expressions
of wrath.

The gravity of this problem cannot be overestimated! Of the 949
couples I have joyfully united as husband and wife during my years in
the ministry, I am happy to say that only two dozen, to my knowledge,
have divorced. Perhaps this is because I have asked each couple to
make a sacred promise that "before you ever spend a single night
separated by duress, you will come to see me." Except for a few
couples whose problem in the early days pertained to sexual difficulties
which were resolved in a short period of time, every other couple's
problem was anger!

Anger not only destroys home life but ruins health. A book we
mentioned previously, *None of These Diseases*, lists fifty-one illnesses
that can be caused by tension produced by anger or fear—including
high blood pressure, heart attack, colitis, arthritis, kidney stones, gallbladder troubles, and many others. For years I have quoted Dr. Henry
Brandt, who says, "Approximately 97 percent of the cases of bleeding
ulcers without organic origin I have dealt with are caused by anger." At
a seminar in Columbus, Ohio, a medical doctor identified himself as an
"ulcer specialist" and reported, "I would take issue with Dr. Brandt—it's
more like a hundred percent!" At the same seminar a young doctor who
identified himself as an internist informed me, "Yesterday afternoon I
treated five patients with serious internal complications. As you were
talking, I made a mental note that all five were angry people."

Doctors have warned us for years that emotionally induced illness
accounts for 60-85 percent of all sicknesses today. What they mean is
that tension causes illness. Anger, fear, and guilt are the primary causes
of tension, and are clearly the major culprits of poor health.

Suppressed anger and bitterness can make a person emotionally upset until he is "not himself." In this state he often makes decisions that are harmful, wasteful, or embarrassing. We are intensely emotional creatures, designed so by God; but if we permit anger to dominate us, it will squelch the richer emotion of love. Many a man takes his office grudges and irritations home and unconsciously lets this anger curtail what could be a free-flowing expression of love for his wife and children. Instead of enjoying his family and being enjoyed by them, he allows his mind and emotions to mull over the vexations of the day. Life is too short and our moments at home too brief to pay such a price for anger.

Dr. S. I. McMillen makes these interesting statements:

"The moment I start hating a man, I become his slave. I can't enjoy my work any more because he even controls my thoughts. My resentments produce too many stress hormones in my body and I become fatigued after only a few hours' work. The work I formerly enjoyed is now drudgery. Even vacations cease to give me pleasure . . . the man I hate hounds me wherever I go. I can't escape his tyrannical grasp on my mind. When the waiter serves me porterhouse steak with french fries, asparagus, crisp salad, and strawberry shortcake smothered with ice cream, it might as well be stale bread and water. My teeth chew the food and swallow it, but the man I hate will not permit me to enjoy it . . . the man I hate may be many miles from my bedroom, but more cruel than any slavedriver, he whips my thoughts into such a frenzy that my innerspring mattress becomes a rack of torture."

So many real-life situations come to mind as I write about the appalling effects of anger that I scarcely know where to begin. I have seen it produce impotence in a twenty-seven-year-old athlete, make normal women frigid, render a twenty-four-year-old physical education teacher incapable of expressing love to her husband, and, in short, annihilate normal love responses. I have visited hundreds of people in hospitals who could have avoided the entire problem had they been relaxed in the spirit instead of being angry. I have even buried many before their time because, like Moses before them, they indulged the secret sin of anger.

In my opinion, the physical damage caused by anger is only exceeded by the spiritual harm it fosters. Anger shortchanges more Christians and makes more spiritual pygmies than any other sin. It has caused more church strife and "turned off" more young converts than anything else. It grieves the Holy Spirit in the life of the believer (see Eph. 4:30-32) and almost destroyed my own health, family, and ministry.

**ANGER IS
SIN, SIN, SIN**
In two of my previous books (one written ten years ago) I deliberately identified anger as a sin and offered a scriptural remedy that not only changed my own life but has been used by thousands of others to resolve the problem. Since then several writers have taken issue with my premise and tried to justify anger, insisting: "It is natural," "Anger is universal," "All anger is not sin," or, as one indicated, "The person who never consciously feels any anger is emotionally ill." Some counselors get so agitated that they write lengthy epistles to correct my "misunderstanding of the universal problem of anger." One man was so irritated that he ended his letter by saying, "You're wrong! Wrong! Wrong!"

I agree that there is a place for short-term unselfish anger that is not injurious to others and does not involve sin. But such anger is objective, on behalf of others. I am convinced there are two reasons that self-induced anger is sin. (1) The Bible, my base of reference, is extremely clear in condemning anger—over fourteen times; (2) It is essential to accept the sinfulness of anger in order to effect a cure.

Consider these Bible verses carefully.

> Cease from anger, and forsake wrath. (Ps. 37:8)

> Be not hasty in thy spirit to be angry: for anger resteth in the bosom of fools. (Eccles. 7:9)

> Better is a dinner of herbs where love is, than a stalled ox and hatred therewith. (Prov. 15:17)

> Better is a dry morsel, and quietness therewith, than an house full of sacrifices with strife. (Prov. 17:1)

> It is better to dwell in the wilderness, than with a contentious and an angry woman. (Prov. 21:19)

> A wrathful man stirreth up strife: but he that is slow to anger appeaseth strife. (Prov. 15:18)

> He that hath no rule over his own spirit is like a city that is broken down, and without walls. (Prov. 25:28)

> Make no friendship with an angry man; and with a furious man thou shalt not let go: Lest thou learn his ways, and get a snare to thy soul. (Prov. 22:24, 25)

> He that is slow to anger is better than the mighty; and
> he that ruleth his spirit than he that taketh a city.
> (Prov. 16:32)
>
> Hatred stirreth up strifes: but love covereth all sins.
> (Prov. 10:12)
>
> But now ye also put off all these; anger, wrath, malice,
> blasphemy, filthy communication out of your mouth.
> (Col. 3:8)
>
> Wherefore, my beloved brethren, let every man be
> swift to hear, slow to speak, slow to wrath: for the wrath
> of man worketh not the righteousness of God. (James
> 1:19, 20)

Many other verses could further illustrate that God condemns anger in the human heart. In fact, the meaning is so clear and easily understood that I shall resist the temptation to comment on them and simply let the Word of God speak for itself.

The best verses to use if you wish to justify anger are Ephesians 4:26, 27—

> "In your anger do not sin": Do not let the sun go down
> while you are still angry, and do not give the devil a
> foothold. (NIV)

Since this is the only biblical text that seems to condone anger, we ought to examine it carefully. It carries two serious qualifications: to be angry (1) without sinning, and (2) without carrying it into the next day.

Qualification 1 forbids any sinful thought or sinful expression of anger. Frankly, people never visit my counseling room with emotional distress from that kind of anger, because "righteous indignation" (which is my label for anger without sin) does not create hang-ups. And qualifier 2 obviously demands that this innocent anger not linger past sundown. Those who terminate their anger at sundown will not cultivate emotional problems either. Incidentally, verse 27 suggests that if innocent anger is permitted to burn past sundown, it "gives the devil a foothold."

The solution to the apparent conflict between the fourteen verses that condemn anger and Ephesians 4:26, 27, which seem to condone it, is really quite simple. The Bible permits righteous indignation and condemns all selfishly induced anger. You experience righteous indignation when you see an injustice perpetrated on another. For example, when a bully picks on a child, you feel a surge of emotion (righteous indignation) and go to the aid of the child. You do not sin in this, nor is it difficult to forget such externally induced anger after dark. But when someone rejects, insults, or injures you, that is a different matter. Is your emotion without sin? And do you forget it after dark?

The Lord Jesus' earthly expressions of anger provide another example. When he drove the moneychangers from the temple, his action was impersonal—"You have made my Father's house a den of thieves" (see Matt. 21:13). His anger at the Pharisees later was kindled because they were spiritual wolves leading the sheep astray, not because they were hurting him. In fact, when his beard was plucked out, or when he was spat upon and nailed to a cross, he showed absolutely no anger. Instead we hear those familiar words, "Father, forgive them, for they know not what they do." Our Lord never showed selfishly induced anger! Why? Because as a human emotion it is always a sin.

Those who use Ephesians 4:26 to justify the human frailty of anger tend to overlook a very important fact. Just five verses further on in that same context we read:

> Let all bitterness, and wrath, and anger, and clamour, and
> evil speaking, be put away from you, with all malice:
> And be ye kind one to another, tenderhearted, forgiving
> one another, even as God for Christ's sake hath forgiven
> you. (Eph. 4:31, 32)

It is quite clear from all of this that righteous indignation is acceptable, but personally induced sin is wrong. What is the difference? Selfishness! Selfishly induced anger, which is the kind most of us experience and that which causes so much personal and family havoc, is a terrible sin. That is why Scripture says, "Let all bitterness, and (all) wrath, and (all) anger be put away from you." As we shall see, it is curable, but only after you face it as a sin.

THE SUBTLE
PROBLEMS OF
BITTERNESS AND
RESENTMENT

A woman once commented, "I never get angry; I just become bitter." Many others would admit the same about resentment. Let's understand something very clearly—the Bible condemns all human bitterness, resentment, and indignation. They are just subtle forms of anger.

At a seminar many years ago, Bill Gothard made a statement to the effect that every couple he counseled for marital disharmony had either

married without the approval of their parents or had developed a
conflict with one or both parents that eventually created conflicts
within the couple's relationship. When a person who had attended the
conference shared that thought, I remember considering it a bit extreme.
Since then, however, the Christian counselor on our church staff, Pastor
Gene Huntsman, and I make this question concerning the couple's
relationship to their parents a standard inquiry, and without exception we
have found Mr. Gothard's formula to be correct. People who harbor
bitterness and resentment toward a parent, brother, sister, or boss are
bound to let it spill over and injure their relationship with others.
Resentment and bitterness preserved in the recesses of the mind are like
cancer; they grow until they consume the whole person. That is why
people who cannot forget an unfortunate childhood, rejection, or injury
are invariably miserable people.

One of my favorite secular writers, a plastic surgeon, counselor, and
lecturer, has authored three self-help books that have benefited millions.
In one of his best-selling books he tells about two counselees with
"choking sensations." One, a middle-aged salesman who suffered from
an inferiority complex, occasionally woke up dreaming of being choked
to death by his mother. The other was a young father who loved his
wife but on two occasions awakened from a dream with his hands
clutching her throat with such a resolute grip that he was terrified. The
good doctor accurately diagnosed both problems. The salesman hated
his mother, and even though he had not seen her in years, she filled his
thoughts. The young husband hated his father and subconsciously
transferred it to his wife. These cases may seem extreme to you, but
they are not really unusual, for they demonstrate the natural result of
harboring bitterness, resentment, and anger in your heart and mind.
Remember this: bitterness and love cannot burn simultaneously in the
same heart. Bitterness indulged for those you hate will destroy your love
for those most precious to you.

One of my most pathetic cases concerned a young mother of two
who tearfully confessed to feelings of such anger at her infant when he
screamed that she sometimes entertained "thoughts of choking him."
She then added, "I'm afraid I will do something harmful to my baby."
Upon questioning, we discovered that she had been rejected by her
father and clung to bitter thoughts about that rejection. Her rancorous
attitude was eating her up, in spite of the fact that her father had been
dead for five years.

SEVEN STEPS FOR
CURING ANGER,
BITTERNESS, OR
RESENTMENT

Many years ago, after over thirty years of being an angry, hostile ChlorSan, I had a life-changing experience with God. Gradually my anger responses lessened from "most of the time" to "only occasionally." Today they are so infrequent that I enjoy an inner peace I wouldn't trade for that old hostile way of life, even for the youth it possessed. Since than I have shared the following remedy with thousands of people, many of whom will testify that it has changed their lives. It may not seem "scientific" to some, but I like it for two reasons: it is biblical, and it works.

1. *Face your anger as sin!* The giant step in overcoming anger is to face it squarely as sin. The minute you try to justify it, explain it, or blame someone else, you are incurable. I have never known anyone to have victory over a problem unless he was convinced it was wrong! That is particularly true of anger. If you have any question at this point, then just reread the Scriptures on pages 199-201 and consider the commands you find there.

2. *Confess every angry thought or deed as soon as it occurs.* This is a giant step too. First John 1:9 says, "If we confess our sins, he is faithful and just to forgive us our sins, and to cleanse us from all unrighteousness." Inwardly I groaned as I read the advice which the plastic surgeon prescribed for the two men who came to him with anger-induced emotional problems. Essentially, he urged them to replace their hateful thoughts by concentrating on some successful or happy experience in life. I remember asking, "But what does that do for guilt?" Absolutely nothing! The blood of Jesus Christ alone, which is adequate to cleanse us from all sin, is available to all who call upon him in faith.

3. *Ask God to take away this angry thought-pattern.* First John 5:14, 15 assures us that if we ask anything according to the will of God, he not only hears us but also answers our requests. Since we know it is not God's will that we be angry, we can be assured of victory if we ask him to take away the habit. Although secular man may remain a slave to habit, the Christian need not. We are admittedly victims of habit, but we need not become addicted to patterns of conformity when we have at our disposal the power of the Spirit of God.

4. *Forgive the person who has caused your anger.* Ephesians 4:32 instructs us to forgive "one another, even as God for Christ's sake hath forgiven you." If a parent, person, or "thing" in your life occupies much of your thinking, make a special point of formally uttering a prayer of

forgiveness aloud to God. Each time the hostile thoughts return, follow the same procedure. Gradually your forgiveness will become a fact, and you will turn your thoughts to positive things.

A charming illustration of this came to me after a seminar for missionaires in South America. A lovely missionary had been plagued with anger problems that almost kept her from being accepted by her board. A Christian psychologist challenged her that she must forgive her father, but she replied, "I can't." He said, "You mean you won't! If you don't forgive him, your hatred will destroy you." So in his office she prayed, "Dear Heavenly Father, I do want to forgive my father. Please help me." She acknowledged having to pray that prayer several times, but finally victory came and with it the peace of God. She is a well-balanced and productive woman today because she forgave. You cannot carry a grudge toward anyone you forgive!

5. *Formally give thanks for anything that "bothers" you.* The will of God for all Christians is that "in every thing give thanks . . ." (1 Thess. 5:18). Thanksgiving is therapeutic and helpful, particularly in anger reduction. You will not be angry or depressed if in every insult, rejection, or injury you give thanks. Admittedly that may be difficult at times, but it is possible. God has promised never to burden you with anything you cannot bear (1 Cor. 10:13). Naturally, at times such thanksgiving will have to be done by faith, but God will even provide that necessary faith. Learn the art of praying with thanksgiving.

6. *Concentrate on thinking positive thoughts that include love for others—including the former object of your wrath.* The human mind cannot tolerate a vacuum; it always has to dwell on something. Make sure you concentrate on what the Scripture approves, such as things that are ". . . true, honest, just, pure, lovely, of good report . . . virtue [and] praise (Phil. 4:8). People with such positive thoughts are not plagued by anger, hostility, or wrath. It is essentially a matter of subjecting every thought to the obedience of Christ. Anger is a habit—a temperament-induced, sinful habit—ignited through the years by unpleasant distresses and circumstances that can control a person every bit as tenaciously as heroin or cocaine, making him react inwardly or outwardly in a selfish, sinful manner. Unless you let the power of God within you change your thinking patterns, your condition will gradually ruin your health, mind, business, family, or spiritual maturity. In addition, it grieves the Holy Spirit (Eph. 4:30), robbing you of the abundant life which Jesus Christ wants to give you.

7. *Repeat the above formula each time you are angry.* Of the

hundreds who claim that this simple formula has helped them, none has indicated that it happened overnight. In my case, I had over thirty years of practice at being angry. Fortunately, it didn't take that long to gain victory.

IT REALLY WORKS   One reason God has given me the opportunity to minister to so many angry people is because I know where they are coming from. First Corinthians 1:3, 4 tells us we can comfort others with the same comfort God has used in comforting us. Basically what that means is that we can minister to others in the same areas we have been ministered to. That doesn't mean we can't minister in areas we have never experienced, because when you help people with the Word of God you are using truth, and truth works no matter who uses it. But it seems God often uses us in a special way with those who have similar troubles as those in which he ministered to us.

Although I am not proud of it, I must confess that in the early years of my ministry, I was a dedicated, hard-driving choleric minister with an anger problem. God met me in a very personal way at a conference where my dear friend, Dr. Henry Brandt, was speaking on anger. That experience changed my life. The Holy Spirit brought in a new peace and joy that transformed my habit of anger, bitterness, and wrath. It didn't happen overnight. It started that day by facing anger as a sin and was followed by many applications of the formula. I have found that anger destroys peace; confessing the sin restores it. The first day I must have used the formula fifty times. The next day it was only forty-nine times. But gradually the habit pattern of anger began to diminish and I became a new man. Today some of the things that used to enrage me only serve to make me laugh. I can't say I never get angry; after all, I still have the same predisposition to anger I've always had. But the expressions are so less frequent I wouldn't go back to that old way of life for anything in this world. And very honestly, my wife agrees. We both know that the most enriching thing to happen to our marriage in over thirty years was when God's Spirit began a special new work on my natural anger. I would never trade love, joy, and peace for anger, bitterness, and wrath. Anger never did anything positive to a marriage, but the Holy Spirit's love, joy, and peace really do.

IT WORKS   A seventy-year-old man came to me after a
FOR ALL AGES   seminar in his church and said, "Dr. LaHaye, I
                  should have heard your message on anger over

forty years ago. I have been an angry man all my life. Do you think a man seventy years old is too far gone or would your formula work for me?" As I looked into his eyes—I'll be honest—I really didn't know. I had only been teaching the formula about two years at that point and my church, counseling, and seminar ministry was mainly with under-fifty types. As I looked at him, I prayed silently, "Lord, what should I tell this man?" I have learned that when you pray that prayer he usually calls Scripture to mind, so I blurted out, "With man this is impossible, but with God nothing is impossible to you!" Then I heard myself say, "My God is able to supply all your needs." These verses encouraged him, and he walked away to try the formula for himself.

Two years later I was holding meetings in Phoenix, and he and his wife attended. Afterward he came up to give me a "progress report." He said, "I am a changed man. If you don't believe it—here, ask my wife." That is the acid test! For what we are at home is what we are. The smile on her face and the nod of her head made it clear—God the Holy Spirit had given her a new husband. You're never too old or too far gone to change. God is for you and will give you all the help you need. It's up to you.

PART Five

TEMPERAMENT IN LOVE AND MARRIAGE

CHAPTER
THIRTEEN

Do Opposites Really Attract?

Self-understanding is only one benefit gained from knowing the theory of the four basic temperaments. In addition, it helps you understand other people, particularly those closest to you. Many a matrimonial battleground is transformed into a neutrality zone when two individuals learn to appreciate their partner's temperament. When you realize that a person's actions result from temperament, rather than being a tactic designed to anger or offend you, this conduct is no longer a threat or an affront.

"We are so hopelessly mismatched that we have to get a divorce," lamented a couple one Tuesday evening in my office. To my question, "Where did you get that idea?" they replied, "We have been to a Christian counseling center which gave us a battery of psychological tests, and that's the conclusion our counselor came to." I spontaneously responded, "That is the worst advice I have ever heard given by a Christian. It is unbiblical in your situation and will only compound your problems." The husband groaned, "Do you mean God wants us to be this miserable the rest of our lives?"

"No," I replied, "there is a much better way! God is able to give you the grace to adjust to and accept each other's temperament." Since they knew nothing about temperament, I proceeded to show them my chart, and before long they could determine the true nature of their completely opposite temperaments. Upon my promise to counsel them, they agreed to cancel their scheduled appointment with an attorney the following Thursday and delay further talk of divorce.

This chapter contains the principles I shared with them. I am

convinced that any couple—with God's help—can understand and
accept each other's temperament, ultimately reaching a perfect
adjustment, if they want to.

I proceeded to teach them the four-temperament theory which you
have already studied in this book. It was obvious he was a strong
choleric with sanguine traits, and she was about equally balanced
between phlegmatic and melancholy. That is about as opposite as you
can get.

They were quite amazed to find that they were not so different from
other married couples and that most people marry opposites. Fascinated
by the theory and concerned about their three teen-age children, they
agreed to come in for counseling once a week. During that time they
began to grow spiritually and rededicated their lives to Christ and today,
seventeen years later, are happily married. So happily that when I was in
their home socially a few months ago I was impressed that people
meeting them today would not believe they had ever had marital
problems.

Interestingly enough, they are still opposites, and they will be as long
as they live; but they have learned, with God's help, how to accept and
get along with their opposite partner. It hasn't always been easy, but
neither is divorce! I've had to go through divorce with many couples,
and without exception it has always been worse than they had expected.
Even the most friendly divorce I know has produced emotional
disturbances in the two children that neither couple anticipated. And in
addition to the guilt they bear for the weight they have heaped upon
their children, they have to live with the knowledge they disobeyed
God's standard. Now that they are both remarried, they discover they
have a new opposite partner with whom they must learn to adjust.

No matter who the couple is and no matter how much they love each
other, every couple goes through an "adjustment stage" that experts say
lasts about three years. Divorce is three times lower among those
married longer than three years. Those first three years are crucial.
They often make or break a marriage. And the reason? It is during that
period we all discover two things about our partner, (1) they are not
perfect, and (2) in the areas where we are opposites, we clash.

The notion that opposites attract each other did not originate with
me; it has been around for a long time. World-famous psychologist Dr.
Carl Jung believed that opposites not only attract each other, they hold
a particular fascination for each other. An article published in USA Today
(September 15, 1983) reported on a new theory that showed that

"thinkers tend to attract feelers," and that both types need to understand that tendency in their mate. I find that very interesting because sanguines make judgments on feelings (intuitively) while mels and phlegs have to analyze everything before reaching a decision. And these are the groupings that usually attract each other.

WHY OPPOSITES ATTRACT EACH OTHER   What could be more opposite than male and female? Yet they still attract each other after thousands of years. In fact, the future of the race is dependent on such attraction.

Unfortunately, they fail to realize that their physical differences are only symbolical of the many other differences in their natures, the most significant of which are their temperaments.

A negative is never attracted to another negative, and positives repel each other in any field—electricity, chemistry, and particularly temperament. Instead, negatives are attracted to positives and vice versa. I have found that almost universally true of temperaments.

Have you ever wondered what attracts you to other people? Usually it is the subconscious recognition of and appreciation for their strengths—strengths that complement your own weaknesses. Consciously or otherwise, we all wish we could eradicate our particular set of weaknesses, and we blissfully admire the strengths of others. If given enough association with the person who sparks our attraction, we experience one of two things. Either we discover weaknesses in them similar to our own and are understandably turned off by them, or we discover other strengths we are lacking, which translates admiration into love. If other factors are favorable, it is not uncommon for such couples to marry.

Like temperaments rarely cohere. For instance, a sanguine would seldom marry another sanguine, for both are such natural extroverts that they would be competing for the same stage in life, and no one would be sitting in the audience. Sanguines, you see, need an audience to turn them on. Cholerics, on the other hand, make such severe demands on other people that they not only wouldn't marry each other, they probably would never date—at least not more than once. They would spend all their time arguing about everything and vying for control or authority in their relationship. Two melancholies might marry, but it is very unlikely. Their analytical traits find negative qualities in others, and thus neither would pursue the other. Two phlegmatics would rarely marry, for they would both die of old age before one got up enough

steam to propose. Besides, they are so protective of their feelings that
they could "go steady" with a person for thirty years before saying or
otherwise communicating, "I love you." One phlegmatic man had
courted an exceedingly patient Christian lady for four years. Finally her
patience snapped and she asked, "Have you ever thought about our
getting married?" He replied, "A time or two." She countered, "Would
you like to?" He then answered, "I think so." "When?" He responded,
"Whenever you would like." Years later he acknowledged that he had
wanted to marry her for two years but was afraid to ask. Can you
imagine how long they would have waited if she, too, had been a
phlegmatic?

In the Western world, where couples choose their own partners, you
will find that generally opposite temperaments attract each other. For a
previous book, I surveyed several hundred couples who understood the
temperaments and fed their responses into a computer. Less than .4
percent indicated that they matched the temperament of their spouses.
Ordinarily I found that sanguines were attracted to melancholies and
cholerics to phlegmatics, although that is by no means universal.

Sanguines, who tend to be disorganized and undisciplined themselves,
are apt to admire careful, consistent, and detail-conscious melancholies.
The latter, in turn, favor outgoing, uninhibited individuals who
compensate for the introvert's rigidity and aloofness. The hard-driving
choleric is often attracted to the peaceful, unexcited phlegmatic, who in
turn admires Rocky's dynamic drive.

After the honeymoon, the problems from this kind of selection begin
to surface. Sparky Sanguine is not just warm, friendly, and uninhibited,
but forgetful, disorganized, and very undependable. Besides, he gets
quite irate if his lady love, a melancholy, asks him to pick up his clothes,
put away his tools, or come home on time. Somehow Rocky Choleric's
before-marriage "dynamic personality" turns into anger, cruelty, sarcasm,
and bullheadedness after marriage. Martin Melancholy's gentleness and
well-structured life-style become nitpicky and impossible to please after
marriage. Philip Phlegmatic's cool, calm, and peaceful ways often seem
lazy, unmotivated, and stubborn afterwards.

Learning to adapt to your partner's weaknesses while strengthening
your own is known as "adjustment in marriage." Hopefully, it will
comfort you to know that no matter who you marry or what
temperament you select, you will have to endure this adjustment
process to some degree. Additional encouragement will be found in the
fact that God, by his Holy Spirit, has given you ample resources to
make a salutary adjustment.

I am not suggesting that single people look for a person that is opposite for a mate. What's wrong with marrying for love, in the will of God, of course? Actually, I know several happily married couples that are very similar in their temperament. For example, one couple we know well are both introverts. She is a PhlegChlor and he is a MelPhleg. Because of his walk with God, he is a happy, well-adjusted person. And most of their friends think they are alike, but they aren't. I also know a pair of extroverts who married. She is a ChlorMel, and he is a SanMel. Theirs was a stormy household for a time, because both were volatile and clashed a great deal until they learned about temperament.

One of the reasons I favor long courtships is because they usually give a couple time to expose the weaknesses of their temperament to their proposed partner. Another reason is that it allows for explosions like those they will encounter in marriage to reveal themselves. However, the couples that come to me "hopelessly mismatched" are already married to a person who thinks differently, feels differently, and responds differently than their partner. Some of these differences are just the natural difference of the sexes. In spite of what the feminists say, men and women are different.

Personally, I don't believe there are any "hopeless" cases with God. You show me two people who are willing to trust God and obey his rules for interpersonal behavior, and I will show you a couple that has learned to be happy in marriage. It isn't easy, but it certainly is an improvement over the disharmony experienced in many families today.

Through the years I have developed a series of steps these couples need to take to rekindle their love. If these steps are followed, any couple can have happiness.

God is the author of marriage. He intended that it be the happiest, most fulfilling experience in a person's life. And millions have found it so long before anyone had discovered temperament. Now that we have this theory to assist us, the adjustment to a happy marriage should be every couple's goal. And these steps to temperament adjustment will help.

1. *Slam the divorce door.* Easy divorce has done nothing to help the longevity of marriage. In the state of California I warned our leaders that if they reduced the waiting period for a divorce decree from one year to six months it would double the divorce rate in ten years. I was wrong; we doubled it in seven years.

I have found that as long as the divorce door remains open, it retards the adjustment to a happy marriage. And if you are a Christian, it is not a legitimate option for you. God has made it clear in his Word that you are wed for life. So acknowledge that and close that door. Never use it as a threat to your spouse, or even entertain it as an option in your mind, for if you do Satan will entice you with the idea every time you experience pressure and unhappiness. By slamming that door in your mind, you open yourself fully to the resources of God to bring the sparkle of love back into your relationship.

2. *Admit to yourself that you are not perfect.* Humility is the best possible base for establishing any relationship between two people. That is true particularly of marriage, because the couple spends so much time together. True love for another person is built on humility.

A healthy look at your own temperament will enable you to recognize that you have not brought only strengths into your marriage and that God is not finished with you yet. He is strengthening your weaknesses and improving you all the time. In fact, you probably have a long way to go. Realistically facing the fact will help you accept step three.

3. *Accept the fact that your partner has weaknesses.* Repeatedly we have discerned through the study of temperament and temperament blends that all human beings reflect both strengths and weaknesses. It cannot be otherwise until the resurrection, when we will be made perfect in Christ. The sooner you face the fact that anyone you marry will have weaknesses to which you must adjust, the sooner you can get to the business of adjusting to your partner. Resist all mental fantasies of "If only I had married _____!" or "If only I had married another temperament." That is not a live option, so why not accept your partner's weaknesses?

4. *Pray for the strengthening of your partner's weaknesses.* God is in the temperament-modification business. By his Holy Spirit and through his Word, he is able to provide the strengths your partner needs for the improvement of his or her temperament weaknesses. But it will never happen if you are on his or her back all the time. If a temperament weakness produces a consistent pattern of behavior such as tardiness, messiness, legalism, negativism, and so on, it may be advisable to talk lovingly to your partner about it once; but after that, just commit the matter to God. If you take the place of the Holy Spirit in your partner's conscience, he will never change; but if you remain silent on the issue and love your partner as he is, then the Holy Spirit can get through to him.

The Bible says, "The effectual fervent prayer of a righteous man availeth much" (James 5:16). As you pray, God will work on your partner.

5. *Apologize when you are wrong.* Everyone makes mistakes!

Fortunately, you don't have to be perfect to be a good person or partner. A mature person is one who knows both his strengths and weaknesses and develops a planned program for overcoming his weaknesses. That presumes you will make mistakes. We must ask, then, Are you mature enough to take full responsibility for what you have done? If in anger you have offended your partner in word or in deed, you need to apologize. God in his grace has given us the example and the means for repairing mistakes and offenses. An apology reaches into another's heart and mind to remove the root of bitterness that otherwise would fester and grow until it choked your relationship. That is why the Bible exhorts, "Confess your faults one to another . . ." (James 5:16).

6. *Verbalize your love.* Everyone needs love and will profit from hearing it verbalized frequently. This is particularly true of women, whatever their temperament. I once counseled a brilliant engineer, a father of five, whose wife left him for another man whose salary was one-third her husband's. After a bit of probing, I learned that he had not expressed his love for ten years. Why? He didn't think it was necessary. Verbalizing love is not only a necessity for holding a couple together, but an enrichment of their relationship.

After five or ten years of marriage the man is responsible for 80 percent or more of his wife's self-acceptance. That is more important than most people realize, for if a person doesn't love and accept himself he will have a very difficult time loving and accepting others. And the best way for a man to help his wife gain self-acceptance is by verbally reassuring her of his acceptance and love. Instead of harping on her weaknesses and beating her down continually, he should comment positively on her strengths. It enriches her self-esteem and motivates her to try harder. Some ill-advised men are afraid of the procedure, thinking it will make her complacent. Just the opposite is true. Women thrive on approval, compliments, and love. Disapproval and humiliation destroys; approval enriches. The man who wants a wife who thinks well of herself can help her become that way.

This is not just psychologically sound advice. More importantly, it is a command. "Husbands, love your wives" occurs four times in Scripture. Once (Eph. 5:26-30) we are commanded to love her as Christ does the church. Such love illustrates the way our Lord reassures the church of his love—through his Word. You know yourself that occasionally you entertain doubts about God, his love, and perhaps his forgiveness. What reassures you? His Word. That is one reason I advise that we all read it daily. But that is the same way you can reassure your wife of your love—by verbalizing it. Giving her jewelry and gifts and providing other thoughtful and tangible expressions of your love is important. But she will never cross beyond the need to hear your "Honey, I love you!" or "Honey, I admire your ability to _____." (And wife, neither will he.)

SUMMARY   We are not today what we once were, nor are we what we will be, particularly if we let God work in our lives. And that person you are married to is not in their final form. Trust God to gradually conform him or her to the image of his Son.

In the meantime learn to be friends, partners, and lovers. That is rarely easy, and for most of us it takes a long time, but with God's help it can be done. As God and time wear off some of the rough edges of your and your partner's natures, you will find more pleasure in your relationship than irritations—provided you are not selfish. Nothing destroys like selfishness.

Adjusting to another person, particularly one with a temperament opposite your own, is not easy and it is not done quickly. But like anything of real value, it is worth the investment. And someday you will realize you are married to your best friend. That is the ideal marriage.

CHAPTER
FOURTEEN

Temperament and Sexuality

We are all sexual creatures. That is nothing to be ashamed of—we were made so by a holy and loving God. The idea that sex and sexual feelings are evil is a distortion of the devil. History reveals countless individuals who were shipwrecked by refusing to come to grips with their sex drive. Some try to pretend it isn't there, others abuse it to their own destruction. Like everything else in life, sex has its place and proper function.

The Bible makes it clear that the only place for sexual expression is marriage. History shows the untold human suffering that is caused when that standard is violated. Everything said about our sexuality in this chapter is said in the biblical context of one man and one woman as long as they both live. That is still God's plan, and it is still the best way for anyone to express his sex drive.

When my wife and I wrote *The Act of Marriage,* it was not popular for ministers to write explicit manuals on sex. But I had been a pastor and family counselor for so many years I knew that sexual inadequacy was one of the basic causes for adultery and divorce among Christians. I had counseled many Christians who had been married from one month to forty-one years who found sex "unpleasant, distasteful" or "the worst part of marriage." God never intended it to be so.

Think about it a moment. Would a loving God design two human beings to have an experience an average of one hundred twenty-five times a year for fifty years that was "unpleasant" or "ugly"? Hardly! And the Bible is not silent on the subject. Sex in marriage is not just for the propagation of the race; it is for love, communication, oneness, and just plain pleasure. If you do not find lovemaking pleasurable, you need to read *The Act of Marriage*. God has used it in the lives of many people to open up to them a lifetime of enjoyment.

We had two major purposes in mind in writing that book. One was to prepare innocent Christian young people who had kept themselves sexually pure to read one manual that would open the door to a lifetime of meaningful sexual enjoyment when they married. Today, with a million and a half copies in print, it is the one book most often recommended by pastors for the couples they marry to read before and during their honeymoon.

The second reason was to help Christians already married who were not getting all the benefit from this God-designed experience to read one book that could change their attitude, inform them on this delicate subject, and answer the many questions they might have on the subject from a Christian perspective.

I saw the "sexual revolution" coming. I knew that although it would never be approved by the Bible-believing church, it would have a great influence on many of the people in our churches. That has happened in our generation. The permissivism, the overemphasis and near-obsession with sex in our society has destroyed far too many homes even in our churches. I believe the two best safeguards to help a couple keep their sacred wedding vows and maintain sexual purity all through their marriage are: (1) a strong spiritual life, and (2) a healthy, expressive sexual relationship.

Sexual dysfunction or disharmony was said by one researcher to be 90 percent of the cause of the breakdown between divorced couples. That seems high to me, but even if it is only 60 percent we can see how powerful an influence sex is to a marriage. And since we have already established the fact that temperament is the most powerful single factor in influencing all of human behavior, it follows that a person's temperament will have an extremely powerful influence on a man or woman's sexual behavior.

Everyone knows that men and woman are different sexually—not only from a physical equipment standpoint, but mentally and emotionally. Their appetites are different, and so are their inhibitions. But their different temperaments also have a bearing on their different attitudes, appetites, and requirements. Many writers and sex researchers fail to take into account the influence on a couple's sexual functions or the drives of their different temperaments. That failure has led to a lot of inaccurate conclusions.

It is wrong to say that "women are sexually less aggressive than men." For example, sanguine women can be more aggressive than some phlegmatic men. However, much more research is necessary in this area to be definitive. For this chapter, I have made some observations about the differences in the sexual attitudes, appetites, and pleasures of each of the temperaments, both male and female, based on my counseling experiences. These observations will have to suffice until more complete research is done. But all married people will benefit if they understand the sexual needs and likely responses of their mate. I try to cover them in this chapter. If you are not married, it would probably be best that you skip reading the following.

SPECIAL   Sexual expression is not just a physical
CONSIDERATIONS   experience. It involves emotions, mind, body,
                       mental attitude, temperament, physical fitness,
sex education, and other factors. Two identical people of the same sex and temperament can have entirely different sexual capabilities and demands. For example, a melancholy wife, raised by a loving, thoughtful father who welcomed her into his heart anytime she wanted to sit on his lap, is likely to be a warm, affectionate wife who thoroughly enjoys lovemaking. (Incidentally, the best preparation for sex in marriage for a young woman is to have enjoyed a healthy relationship with her father all through life.) If, however, that same young woman has been rejected by her father as a child, she is likely to be frigid. After the wave of libido that encouraged her to marry has subsided and after the novelty of marriage is over (three to nine months for a melancholy), her *amour* may decline and her frigidity take over. Her response may have nothing to do with her husband's behavior or personality, and it may have nothing to do with her true love for him. Such women need counseling, patient husbands, and the power of God to overcome such difficulties.

Traumatic experiences can also make a vast difference in the sexual expression of both men and women. Even sanguine men can be warped in their mind and feel insecure if they were molested by a homosexual as a child. Melancholies can be almost rendered impotent by the guilt, shame, and insecurity of such an experience. And we hear all too frequently today of the tragic psychological blocks to sex in women caused by child molesters. One choleric woman confessed that she was "totally dead sexually. When my husband makes love to me, I cannot feel a thing; it is as if I am sexually insensitive." At my probing it was revealed that she had been molested by a stepfather regularly from six

years old until she was seventeen years of age and could not gain the
maturity to put a stop to it. What caused her insensitivity? Blind rage!
She hated that man so much, it killed her capacity to love anyone else. I
am happy to say she is perfectly normal today, but it took time and
much forgiveness.

Now you see why I say that sex is complex. Like a 125-piece
orchestra, it works best when all the instruments are in tune and
functioning in unison. If one instrument is out of tune, it won't have too
much ill affect; but if a dozen instrumentalists don't play on cue, it may
be terrible. Fortunately, there aren't that many components to good
sexual harmony, but it still is best when all the factors contribute toward
the same goal—mutually satisfying expressions of love. Like a great
orchestra, great sex takes training and practice. The difference is that in
God's plan sexual training in marriage must be conducted with another
person who knows as little about it as you do. That is why the more
you know about your partner's needs in advance, the easier it is to
relate to them. It is also essential to maintain open lines of
communication between each other; this hastens the training process.

Married couples will find the analysis of the sexual responses of the
four temperaments as presented in this chapter very helpful. After you
have read them all for both the male and female, you should go back
and study the temperament presentation of your partner and your own.

SPARKY SANGUINE'S Sparky Sanguine is so responsive that it
SEXUAL RESPONSES   doesn't take much to "turn him on," and since
                       he is so obvious about everything he does, his
wife is instantly aware of his mood. A natural charmer, he thinks he
can turn the head of a female marble statue with his flattery. And he
can—unless he is married to her. He usually has a great appetite for
everything, including lovemaking.

Most sanguines have very few hang-ups about sex and usually make
it clear they enjoy it. If it isn't the most important thing in life for them,
it's a close second. The sanguine husband is usually reluctant to take
no for an answer; in fact, he can easily be hurt or deflated if his
partner does not respond to his gestures of love. He may outwardly
project the idea that he is God's gift to women, but underneath he has a
great need for affection. If he is not satisfied at home, Sparky, more than
any other temperament, may seek affection elsewhere, for two reasons:
(1) the conquest of another woman is necessary to satisfy his powerful

ego, and he finds lonely, unfulfilled women easy prey to his charm;
(2) he is weak-willed and emotionally excitable; consequently, he is
vulnerable to the unscrupulous woman.

The supersex emphasis of our day is very hard on Sparky, for he is
easily stimulated. He has four basic needs in this area:

(1) Moral principles deeply ingrained in his heart and mind from
childhood that show God's plan of one man for one woman "so long as
they both shall live."

(2) The concept of "walking in the Spirit," particularly in his thought-
life. Romans 13:14 says, "Make not provision (forethought) for the flesh,
to fulfil the lusts thereof." If a sanguine indulges in immoral "fantasies,"
he will soon fan his passions out of control and will commit the sin of
adultery to the heartache of his wife and himself. Once the moral barrier
is broken, it is easy for him to repeat his sin. Sparky particularly needs
to avoid all use of pornographic material whether magazine, movie, or
television. He is visually stimulated, and such material is like pouring
gasoline on his fire. It artificially stimulates his sex drive.

(3) A loving, responsive, affectionate wife who freely lets her husband
know how much she enjoys his love and who rarely refuses his desires
for sex. Husbands treated like that rarely stray, regardless of their
temperament.

(4) Sparky Sanguine needs to learn to control his sex drive. He is an
instant gratifier in everything, including sex. Many a wife who dearly
loves her sanguine husband complains, "He is too quick" or "He doesn't
wait for me" or "He takes too many shortcuts." Sparky needs to
understand women and make a study of lovemaking. Most sanguines
assume they know all about it. Nothing could be further from the truth.
Good lovemaking is an art that must be learned. And sanguines need to
learn to control their sex drive and hold off its expression until the wife is
properly prepared.

Sanguines can be romantic, and most women like to be romanced.
Sparky needs to control himself to adapt his satisfaction to his wife's
need. The sexually satisfied wife will naturally enjoy sex more and want
to engage in it more frequently. All husbands should make a quest of
learning the art of bringing their wife to orgasm. This is a safeguard to a
long and happy marriage. Sanguines can learn to be good lovers in
marriage, but it takes learning, practice, and self-control.

One thing Sparky can do that will enrich his bedroom life is stop his
lifetime habit of flirting with other women. He doesn't mean anything by

it (usually), but his melancholy wife is sure to see him; and although it may turn other women on, be sure of this—it is a giant turnoff to his wife. Be friendly, but not flirtatious.

THE SEXUAL RESPONSE OF MRS. SARAH SANGUINE

Very few differences in sexual response distinguish a sanguine man from a sanguine woman. Sarah Sanguine is a cheerful, happy, affectionate cheerleader-type who has the gift of making men feel "comfortable" in her presence. Her charming personality makes her a "hit" with all types of men, and in her naivete she can turn them on without realizing it. She usually thinks she is "just being friendly."

As a wife, Sarah has a tremendous amount of love to impart to her husband and family. Lovemaking is very important to her, and it doesn't usually take too much coaxing to get her into the mood. Even if hurt or angry, she rather easily can moderate her attitude. Sanguines rarely carry a grudge, a trait essential for any marriage. She is the most likely type to greet her husband at the door with a "kiss with a future." Of all the temperaments, she is the one most likely to jolt her husband, after reading *The Total Woman*, by meeting him at the door dressed in boots and an apron.

Sarah rarely has hang-ups about anything, so she usually maintains a good attitude toward sex, often in spite of disastrously distorted misconceptions handed down from her mother. Her natural ability to express herself overcomes her inhibitions, and she quickly finds that she heightens her lovemaking enjoyment by being aggressive. Unless unwisely stifled by her husband, she usually learns early that passivity in lovemaking is not for her. Her sanguine moodswings vary, bringing great delight to her partner. These wives have a tremendous desire to please their partners. With a reasonable amount of encouragement and cooperation, they usually succeed in this area of marriage, provided their shortcomings in other areas do not become their partner's obsessions.

Fun-loving Sarah Sanguines start out in marriage expecting to enjoy sex. The following suggestions will help them to realize that potential:

(1) Cultivate a strong spiritual life by walking in the Spirit, regularly studying the Word of God, and obeying his standards of moral behavior.

(2) Recognize your ability to excite men other than your husband and avoid flirtations that would provoke his jealousy or confront you with unnecessary temptations.

(3) Soften your extroversion so you will not embarrass your husband. A loud, overbubbly wife may gain the attention of other men, but she is certain to earn the disapproval of her husband.

(4) Sarah needs to concentrate on tenderly loving her mate, who will assure her of his approval and acceptance and dispense tender words of encouragement, attention, and affection. If she receives these, she will give attention to proper grooming, fashion, manners, good housekeeping, and whatever else will make her pleasing to her husband.

Sexually satisfying lovemaking is important to Sarah. She can happily endure almost anything in life if she is not starved for love. And let's face it—sex is an expression of love. It is a wise husband who does *not* pander it out for good behavior, but adapts himself to his wife's needs.

ROCKY CHOLERIC AS A HUSBAND

On the surface a choleric suitor appears to be a great lover. Candy and flowers in abundance, politeness, kindness, and dynamic leadership make him appear to be the embodiment of manliness. Somehow that tends to change shortly after marriage as he takes the romance out of their marriage. Cholerics are such goal-conscious creatures that they are willing to do almost anything to attain their desires. Since the "sweet young thing" is subconsciously a goal before marriage, the choleric is willing to pay any price to win her hand. Once married, however, the goal is changed; now he wants to support her properly. Consequently, he may work from twelve to twenty hours a day. The hardest thing for a choleric male to understand is that his partner did not marry him for what he could give her, but for himself. When confronted with his wife's complaint that he doesn't love her anymore, he responds, "Of course I love you; I work like a slave to give you what you want." The truth of the matter is, he enjoys work.

Emotionally, a choleric is an extremist; he is either hot or cold. He can get furiously angry and explode over trifles, and his bride becomes terrified when she first sees these outbursts. His impatience and inability to lavish affection on her may produce a difficult adjustment for her. Showing affection is just "not his thing." One woman married to a choleric said, "Kissing my husband is like kissing a marble statue in the cemetery on a winter day."

The choleric's impetuous traits likewise hinder his proper adjustment to marriage. Just as he is apt to set out on a trip before consulting a road map, he is prone to take his wife to the bedroom without the slightest sex education. Somehow he thinks it will all work out!

Fortunately, a choleric possesses one important trait that helps his love life—he is always practical. Once he realizes that lovemaking involves more than preparing for a 100-yard dash—that he must be tender, gentle, affectionate, thoughtful, and sensitive to his wife's needs—he learns quickly. In the learning process he finds that affection is exciting and that watching the woman he loves respond to his touch is extremely fulfilling.

The most underdeveloped part of a choleric is his emotional life. And since lovemaking at its best is motivated by emotion, he has many needs:

(1) To show love and compassion for others. Nothing short of the personal experience of receiving Christ as Lord and Savior and learning to "walk in the Spirit" will provide the choleric with this ability. Even after his conversion, it often takes some time before the "love of God" characterizes his life.

(2) To understand that many people are not as self-sufficient as he. Even though they may be as capable, they will not be as confident that they can perform well. Rocky must realize that other people may tend to harbor doubts much more easily than he. If he will patiently show kindness and encourage his partner, she will be a better performer.

(3) To develop tenderness and affection for his wife and children and to voice his approval and commendation of them. He must learn to say "I love you" quite frequently to his wife and act proud of her. Because the choleric is a natural leader, others tend to look to him for approval, love, and acceptance. He can wither them with a disapproving look and condemning word, or he can lift their spirits by going out of his way to approve and commend them. Those who have been rejected by him may tend to build a shell around their egos in order to protect themselves and to ward off future injuries. When the choleric father and husband becomes sensitive to the emotional needs of his family, he can even spark emotions within himself that would otherwise remain dormant. To say, "I love you" is not easy for him; but when he forgets himself, recognizing the importance of these words to his loved one, and concentrates on her emotional well-being, Rocky will learn quickly—and will thoroughly enjoy the response it brings.

(4) Rocky also needs to eliminate sarcasm and disrespectful speech from his vocabulary. Unkind and resentful words never turn a wife on.

(5) To learn to overcome his inner hostilities and anger for two reasons: first, "grieving the Spirit" through anger (Eph. 4:30-32) will keep him a spiritual pygmy all of his Christian life; second, the threat of

instant choleric explosion inhibits the emotional expressions of his wife. It is difficult for a choleric Christian to realize that his spiritual life will affect his bedroom life, but it does—one way or the other.

THE CHOLERIC WIFE'S SEXUAL RESPONSES

Clara Choleric is usually an exciting creature, particularly if one does not have to live with her. She is extremely active in every area of life—a dynamic, forceful individual with multiple goals in mind. At the same time, she may feature a spitfire personality and a razor-blade tongue, dominating and controlling every activity in which she is involved.

In my late teens there was such a girl in our youth group. Many guys dated her because she was fun to be with, but they kiddingly remarked behind her back, "Don't marry Evelyn unless you want to be President of the United States."

The necessity of having a positive mental attitude toward lovemaking in marriage comes into focus when dealing with the choleric wife. If she observed a warm love relationship between her parents while she was growing up, she will probably enter marriage expecting to enjoy lovemaking. Cholerics usually achieve what they set out to do, and she will probably not be disappointed—nor will her husband.

On the other hand, if she has been raised by unhappy, bickering parents, if she has been molested or has endured other traumatic experiences in childhood, or if she has been taught that "sex is dirty" for either religious or other ill-conceived reasons, she may encounter serious difficulty in relating properly to her husband. Cholerics are so opinionated that once obsessed with the idea that "sex is not for nice girls," they might reject the angel Gabriel carrying a message on a stone tablet saying "marriage is honorable in all." But once convinced that God wants her to enjoy sex, she can usually make a quick transition to a happy love life.

Choleric wives often acquire several potential hang-ups in this department. They are not usually given to open affection, and thus they often stifle their husbands' advances before their own motor rolls into action. In addition, if not Spirit-filled they tend to demasculinize a man by dominating and leading him in everything—including sex. It takes a Spirit-led, thoughtful choleric woman to recognize that she ignores her husband's ego at her own peril.

We have observed that opposites attract each other in marriage; consequently, a choleric woman will usually select a passive partner. If she isn't especially fond of lovemaking, they may go for long periods without it because he may be too passive to say or do anything about it. Whether or not he raises the issue, you can be sure he doesn't enjoy the abstinence! Ultimately an explosion occurs and almost always with serious consequences.

It is to the choleric wife's credit, however, that she will usually adjust and become a very enjoyable partner once she learns how important a good bedroom life is to her husband. She must realize that the success of her marriage may well depend upon her performance and willingness to let her husband maintain leadership in this intimate area of their life.

Like her male counterpart, Clara Choleric has many needs. These are some of the most important for her to consider:

(1) To "walk in the Spirit" in order to provide victory over her hot temper and sarcastic tongue, and to develop her emotional capability in showing love and affection. Being loving and affectionate is certainly easier for some temperaments than others, but God would never have commanded that we love one another if he had not known it was possible for all. Cholerics may need to work at it a little harder than some, but the more they express it, the easier it comes.

(2) To learn forgiveness—especially for her father, if necessary. No woman can fully enjoy her husband if she hates her father. This is especially true of strong-minded, opinionated, willful cholerics. They will vent their frustrated wrath on their husbands, stifling their expressions of love. One reason a choleric woman may have this problem is that as a little girl she may have resisted her father's affections; and because he did not understand, he closed her out of his heart and had little to do with her—he simply did not know how to reach her. Not realizing why she was rejected by her daddy, she increasingly withdrew from showing any normal expressions of emotion toward him and fostered a growing resentment toward men.

(3) To avoid heaping sarcasm, criticism, and ridicule on her husband, particularly in the lovemaking area. Cholerics exude so much self-confidence that, even without saying anything, they cause others to feel inadequate. The choleric woman needs to let her husband know how much she values him as a man and a lover. No compliment is sweeter and cherished longer than one which appreciates the masculinity or femininity of one's partner.

(4) To take time to express love to her husband. Cholerics are often night people. Early-bird husbands may crawl into bed at ten or eleven o'clock, hoping for a little tenderness and love. But they fall asleep while

their choleric wives finish a book, clean the house, or pursue countless other activities which their active minds suggest. Many choleric wives could improve their love lives just by going to bed earlier.

(5) To learn submission by biblical standards. A choleric likes to lead and usually makes a good leader, but by the grace of God and in obedience to his Word, such a wife needs to bring herself into submission to her husband. If she attempts to assume the husband's role and responsibilities in the home, she is courting disaster. A passive husband will give his wife more love, respect, and flexibility if she encourages him to take the responsibility and leadership of their home.

THE MELANCHOLY HUSBAND'S SEXUAL RESPONSES

Marvin Melancholy is a supreme idealist. He usually goes into marriage without any sex education because he idealistically believes that "everything will work out." If he is blessed with an amorous and exciting wife who has no hang-ups, everything usually does work out; but if he marries someone as naive as he, they may come home from their honeymoon in a depressed state. When the love life of a couple is deficient, it can create a shaky experience for a melancholic husband. His wife will especially be turned off by his depression, further complicating matters. It is usually quite difficult for him to seek counseling until his marriage enters a precarious phase.

The melancholy, more than any other temperament, has the capacity to express true love. He is a loyal and faithful partner unless he overindulges in impure thoughts and becomes involved in pornography. When Marvin Melancholy enjoys a good sex life with his wife, he will almost overextend himself in every other area of their marriage in thoughtfulness, kindness, and emotion.

Among the melancholy's greatest assets is his romanticism. He does the work of preparation beautifully: soft music, dim lights, perfume— those things that delight the romantic heart of a woman.

Because he is extremely analytical, Martin quickly learns what his wife finds pleasurable and enjoys bringing her fulfillment. If everything goes well for them, this couple can become great lovers.

Melancholies are such perfectionists that they almost refuse to accept anything less than perfection. Many a melancholy man can come home all "revved up" for his wife only to have his ardor cooled by dirty dishes in the sink or kids' toys in the middle of the floor. In fact, I know one melancholy husband who could be turned on by watching his wife get undressed for bed and turned off because she didn't hang up her clothes.

At a time like that, a sanguine or choleric wouldn't even notice the clothes!

The sensitive traits of the melancholy that on most occasions make him aware of his wife's needs for tenderness and love may also work against him at times. He is prone to interpret his wife's lack of immediate response when he first initiates lovemaking as rejection. If his wife is in a coy mood, as women frequently are, and wants mild pursuit, he is apt to think she doesn't desire him and gives up before she can reveal her true feelings.

The melancholy individual has a tremendous amount of love to give to others if granted the slightest encouragement. These are some of his most obvious needs:

(1) Maintaining a vital, personal relationship with God, and a daily Spirit-filled experience that keeps him "others-oriented" instead of obsessed with himself. No selfish or self-centered person will be a good lover, no matter what his temperament. A real test of whether or not a melancholy is walking in the Spirit appears when he breaks that self-centered syndrome.

(2) Learning to give unconditional love, not rewarded love. A wife once told me that her husband was a natural-born nitpicker. "He has a long checklist for housekeeping, and if I don't rate an 'A' before we go to bed, he will not make love to me," she complained.

(3) Avoiding a critical and pessimistic attitude, the two biggest problems of a melancholy. Because of his perfectionism, he often has unrealistic standards of achievement for himself and others. This in turn causes him to become frequently disillusioned when things and people don't measure up.

(4) Maintaining a positive and wholesome thought life (Phil. 4:8). He should never indulge in revengeful thought patterns of self-pity, but always "in every thing give thanks" (1 Thess. 5:18).

(5) Being married to a woman who is not easily offended and can cheerfully encourage him when he is down, reassure him of his manhood when he is insecure, and take his criticism lightly. As long as she knows he is moody, she can patiently wait a little while for his mood to change.

(6) Concentrating on God and thanking him for his partner's strengths. He must regularly encourage her with verbal assurances of love and approval. I have seen many a sanguine wife go through a personality change under the constant criticism of a melancholic husband. Unfortunately, when he is finished even Martin Melancholy doesn't like his creation.

THE MELANCHOLY
WIFE'S SEXUAL
RESPONSES

Martha Melancholy is an unpredictable love partner, for she has the greatest of all mood swings. On some occasions she can be as exciting and stimulating as any sanguine. On others she has absolutely no interest in anything—including love. She may meet her husband at the door and sweep him off his feet right into the bedroom, or she may ignore his arrival completely.

Martha Melancholy is the supreme romantic, and her moods are as apparent as the noonday sun. When in the mood for love, she resorts to dinner by candlelight, soft music, and heavy perfume. (If she's married to a sanguine, that works quite well; but if her husband is a choleric, she may be in trouble, because he often detests perfume.)

Although she has the capability of enjoying ecstatic love at heights that would asphyxiate other temperaments, she rarely is interested in setting world records for frequency. To her, quality is always preferable to quantity. Of all the temperament types, she is the most apt to engage in bedroom roulette—that is, she dispenses love as a reward for good behavior. However, no man worthy of the title will put up with that!

A melancholy is often plagued with unreal prudishness, especially if her mother had a problem in this area. She may use trumped-up religious arguments to excuse her sexual abstinence; her real problem, however, probably stems from her premarital resolution that sex is undesirable, and she has never given herself the opportunity to learn otherwise. She is the type that saves lovemaking only for propagation— rarely for pleasure. A study of the Scriptures can teach her differently.

Little things can quickly be turned into mountainous problems for Martha Melancholy. Her husband's inability to balance the checkbook, his forgetting to run an errand, or his forgetting to bathe may thoroughly upset her and send her into frigid revenge. She feels he didn't keep his part of a bargain, so she need not keep hers—and thus she refrains from lovemaking. What she doesn't realize is that she is cheating herself out of both the enjoyment of lovemaking and the loving approval of her husband.

I counseled a melancholic wife who had not made love with her partner for several weeks. She was only interested at night, but by the time she was ready for bed, he had collapsed. She complained, "He goes to bed tired, and he never even takes time to bathe or brush his teeth. In the morning I am a zombie and he is charged up. But I can't stand his body smells and bad breath then!" I suggested that she learn to accept her husband and not try to change him. This was hard medicine for a wife to take, but before long she discovered that by cooperating with him, he was quite willing to modify his habits for her.

Another hang-up common to Martha Melancholy is jealousy. Not given to "insincere flirtation," she often marries a man who is outgoing and friendly to all. It is not uncommon for her to ride home in icy silence after a party because her husband "flirted with every woman there." Since her husband's male ego gets so little food at home, he unwisely seeks it at social gatherings. And he may often think, "Nothing I do ever satisfies that woman!"

Seated across from the beautiful wife of a wealthy and dynamic Christian businessman, I was startled to hear his melancholy wife ask me, "Would you explain why I am so jealous of my husband even when I know I have no reason for it?" It seems that he had dismissed three successive secretaries and finally hired the homeliest gal he could find just because of his wife's jealousy, but it still didn't solve her problem. I responded, "The problem is not with your husband; you just don't like yourself." Tears ran down her cheeks as she admitted to strong feelings of self-rejection. Later her husband commented concerning their love life, "When her groundless suspicions make her jealous, I can't touch her. But when she is sorry for her accusations, she can't get enough of me. I never know whether to expect feast or famine!"

Martha's biggest problem in life will be the tendency toward self-pity. A melancholy can follow the slightest insult or rejection with self-pitying thoughts that plunge her into a state of depression until she is not interested in love or anything else.

The emotional capability of a melancholy is so extensive that she has the potential of being an exciting and fulfilling love partner if her weaknesses don't overpower her strengths. Here are some of her specific needs:

(1) A vital and effective relationship with Jesus Christ, walking in his Spirit, so that she may enjoy the love, peace, and joy he gives to make her an effective person.

(2) A thankful attitude for all the blessings God has given her, never thinking or verbalizing criticism for the things that don't please her. She will discover that a positive mental attitude combined with thanksgiving can give her a happier outlook on life and make her a more pleasant person for others to enjoy. This attitude will also help her to accept herself as she is; self-condemnation will destroy her. It is very difficult for others to like her if she does not like herself.

(3) Acceptance of her husband as he is, permitting God to make any changes that are needed. Her submission to him should not be

dependent on his behavior, but on her obedience to God.

(4) Encouragement and reassurances of love from her husband. A thoughtful and verbally expressive husband who proves his love in many other areas of their marriage will be rewarded in this one.

(5) The request that God give her an unconditional love for her husband and the ability to love him to the point that she forgets about herself. She needs to realize that married love is beautiful because it is God's plan for married partners. Our Lord promises that a woman who gives herself without reservations to her husband will be loved. He said, "Give and it shall be given unto you," and "Whatsoever a man soweth, that shall he also reap." If a woman sows love, she will surely reap it in abundance.

(6) The lesson of forgiveness. Almost every durable marriage requires forgiveness along the way. Because an unforgiving attitude will always destroy a relationship, the partners must realize that their harmony requires it and God commands it (Matt. 18:35; Mark 11:25).

THE PHLEGMATIC HUSBAND'S SEXUAL RESPONSES

Not much is known about the bedroom life of Phil Phlegmatic. He is without doubt the world's most closed-mouth individual, particularly concerning his personal life. What is known about this intimate area usually comes from an irate partner; consequently, the information could well be biased. In fairness to the phlegmatic male, therefore, any suggestions we make concerning his lovemaking responses have to be evaluated on the basis of deductive analysis and hearsay reporting. His secondary temperament will also have a powerful influence on his expression, as will his background and mental attitude.

Some assume that because a phlegmatic is easygoing and prone to be unmotivated, he may not be a very spirited lover; but that may not always be true. If a study of the habits of phlegmatics is indicative, we find that they usually accomplish more than they are given credit for. They just don't make noise and attract much attention to their achievements like other temperaments. Rather, they make good use of the effort expended. When they want to do something, they follow through effectively and promptly in their own quiet way. We suspect that is the way they make love.

One characteristic of phlegmatics should help their love life: their abundant kindness. Rarely, if ever, would Phil Phlegmatic embarrass or insult his wife; sarcasm is just not his way. Women usually respond to a man who is kind to them. On that basis he should have little trouble gaining love from his wife, if he desires it.

Another trait that is surely a great advantage is that a phlegmatic rarely gets angry and seldom creates irritation in others. If his fiery partner screams at him for some reason, his response usually extinguishes the fire because he is a master of the "soft answer." Consequently, the storm has usually passed by bedtime, and he can conveniently act as if it never happened.

Phlegmatic men often have a way of getting things to go their way by waiting for them. They are patience personified, apparently able to outwait others into action. Their love life is probably like that. As the intensity of their youthful sex drive cools down somewhat, they patiently teach their partner to originate lovemaking. And it may be that phlegmatics may get used to a less frequent than average lovemaking schedule as their drive cools. This could be habit. Sexual frequency in marriage is often related to habit. Those who perform three times a week develop a habit for that frequency level. The same person's life-style could change and sex could develop into a once-a-week habit. Phlegmatics are great for developing habits for everything.

One observation I have made about phlegmatic husbands is that their wives sometimes complain about lack of frequency. The only wives I have had decry this lack of loving have been married to phlegmatic husbands. Whether this lack of sex drive is induced physically, temporarily, or is the result of quiet resentment is difficult to determine. However, most of these men are not aware of how important it is to their wives' self-image and self-acceptance for them to make love to her frequently—particularly as she gets older.

Three areas may cause the phlegmatic man serious trouble. First, he tends to be reluctant to assert himself and take leadership unless it is thrust upon him. When he does lead, he performs his tasks admirably. However, when he fails to take the leadership in the home, his wife can become very disillusioned. The wife who expects such a husband to assume the initiative in the bedroom may soon feel unloved. Sometimes she loses respect for her phlegmatic husband because he doesn't seem to assert his manhood.

A second danger spot is phlegmatic selfishness, making him stingy, stubborn (in a polite way), and self-indulgent. Yielding to these weaknesses can produce resentment in a wife who complains, "He doesn't give me enough grocery money, and he never takes me out. All we ever do is what he wants to do." As we have already seen, resentment stifles love.

The third potential danger area to a phlegmatic is that he tends to crawl into a shell of silence when things fail to work out. Since he usually finds it difficult to talk about anything, he probably finds it hard to teach his partner what he finds exciting in lovemaking. Consequently, he may silently endure subpar relations for years and cheat both himself and his partner out of countless ecstatic experiences which God meant them to enjoy.

The kindhearted, soft-spoken, gentle phlegmatic may appear to outsiders as a man who has conquered his weaknesses, but those who live with him recognize his quiet needs. These are some of the most pertinent in the area of his love life:

(1) A dynamic relationship to Jesus Christ that motivates him to think of the needs of his wife and family rather than indulge in his own feelings and solitude.

(2) A more aggressive attitude in everything, especially in consideration of his wife's needs in lovemaking.

(3) Greater expression of his love and approval for his wife. He must learn to talk more freely about his own desires and needs, especially if the couple is confronting problems. This need to communicate requires his continual efforts.

(4) A wife who will understand and accept his seeming lack of motivation without resentment, one who will tactfully use her feminine wiles in arousing him at the appropriate time.

(5) A wife who will try to adapt her metabolic timetable to her partner's to maximize what vitality he has, one who appreciates his strong, silent tendencies and recognizes the depth of his nature, giving thanks for it rather than chafing at his inclination toward passivity. If she starts nagging, he will crawl into his shell and shut her out.

THE PHLEGMATIC
WIFE'S SEXUAL
RESPONSES

As a general rule, the easiest person in the world to get along with is a phlegmatic, especially a woman. She loves to please people and usually gives in to her more forceful mate rather than create turmoil. She is easily satisfied and often turns her affection and attention on her children if trouble arises between her and her husband.

Her passive personality will usually characterize her bedroom life; she rarely initiates lovemaking, but because she wants to please her partner she almost never turns him down.

One of the most powerful influences in a phlegmatic's life, an influence which will strongly affect her lovemaking, may be fear and the anxiety which it causes. Such a woman may fear pregnancy (although she doesn't have a corner on that problem), disclosure, embarrassment, and a host of other real and imagined dilemmas. One of her fears is that her husband may lose respect for her if she appears eager or forward in lovemaking, though quite the opposite is the usual reaction.

In spite of her gracious, kind, and pleasant spirit, Polly Phlegmatic has several needs to become a better wife and love partner:

(1) To accept Jesus Christ as her Lord and Savior. Many phlegmatics have a hard time acknowledging that they are sinners (and they act so nice that others will likely agree, but self-righteousness has kept many out of the Kingdom of God). As she learns to "walk in the Spirit" each day, the phlegmatic woman will gain motivation to overcome her passivity, love to overcome her selfishness, and faith to overcome her fears. When armed with such attributes from God, she can become an exciting partner.

(2) To create and maintain an interest in her appearance. Phlegmatic mothers often get so tired after their babies arrive that they become careless about their personal appearance—their hair, their attire, and often their weight. When a wife ceases to care how she looks to her man, she has clearly lost her self-esteem. Her husband's love and respect will also fade. A wife need not be a raving beauty to maintain the high regard of her husband, but her appearance night after night will indicate what she thinks of herself and of her husband. Any man should appreciate the fact that his wife is tired once in a while, but five nights a week is a cop-out.

Some Christian women have used 1 Peter 3:3 as an excuse to let their "outward appearance" run down—at the expense of their marriage. That passage says that a godly wife will spend more time cultivating her spiritual life than her physical, but by no means does it teach that she is to neglect either one. Remember, a woman is the most beautiful flower in a man's garden, and even roses need to be cultivated, pruned, and cared for.

(3) Polly needs to organize her daily life and sustain a regular schedule. A phlegmatic wife finds it easier to neglect her housekeeping chores than anyone else except a sanguine. She enjoys "coffee klatches," and before she realizes it hubby is due home. Since opposites attract each other, it is not uncommon for a phlegmatic wife to create such resentment in her more fastidious partner that it spills over into their bedroom life. His uncharitable outburst may cause a stubborn phlegmatic to "refuse to clean up," producing further disharmony.

Consequently, she needs to take pride in homemaking; her husband will respect and treat her better, and even more importantly, she will respect herself more.

(4) She needs to appreciate a thoughtful lover and strong, gentle husband. She requires a lover who learns how a woman functions best and takes time to arouse her to orgasm. Once she has learned that art, her desire for the experience will overpower her tendency to passivity, and she can learn to be an exciting partner. He needs to be a strong, gentle husband from whom she can draw courage to overcome her fears, one who will encourage and not browbeat her. A wise husband will verbally assure his wife of her worth and his love.

(5) She needs to learn to overcome her inability to speak the words she feels and communicate with her husband and family. Words do not come easily for her, especially about the intimacies of her love life. Phlegmatics need to push themselves in every area of life, and lovemaking is no exception. Polly Phlegmatic needs to remember the needs of her partner and forget her own; they will both be happier for it.

OTHER   There are a number of other things that
CONSIDERATIONS   influence harmonious sexual relations during
                 the length of a fifty-year marriage. I have
noticed that young mothers with two or more children at home are not as interested in lovemaking as they were at twenty or as they will be at thirty-five and forty. Partly due to physical exhaustion and partly due to fear of pregnancy, their interest can wane. Men, on the other hand, react to pressure. Loss of employment can stifle even the most powerful male sex drive, as can financial pressures. Job advancement in his thirties can become a god to a man, making his sexual activity perfunctory or deficient. And sometimes nothing his wife does is able to change him.

One of my observations, shared by other counselors with whom I have discussed the matter, is that wives tend to get more interested in lovemaking as they get older while men tend to require it less frequently. That is particularly true after her children leave the nest and she feels unneeded by anyone but her husband. He then becomes the special object of her love in every way, including sex. Lovemaking at that point in time becomes a psychological need. And why shouldn't it? Everyone needs to be needed, and everyone needs love. In addition, the children are out of the home and the fears of discovery or interruption that bothered her in her twenties and thirties are now gone.

During her menopause a good wife may become sexually erratic.

Hormonal changes going on in her body over which she has little or no control can cause her to be amorous one day and cold the next. Her usual supply of vaginal fluid may dry up or run out right in the middle of lovemaking. All women at this stage of life need much love and understanding. They also need to see their doctor. He can not only help shorten this period of her life, but he can recommend medication that will help control her emotions and body functions. Many women testify that heavy doses of Vitamin E during that period are also helpful.

Men, too, need patience as they mature. For some men, it is the retirement stage that turns them off. It is still true that a person's most important sex organ is his brain. Once he begins to realize his life is not over at sixty-five, he can be sexually active on into his nineties if his health permits.

Every couple goes through stages, changes, and adjustments in their sex life, just like everything else in their relationship. And although their temperament is not the only influence on their sexual responses, as we have seen, it is certainly one of the most powerful.

All four temperaments possess the capacity to become loving, satisfying marriage partners. As we have seen, each has its area of strength and weakness. Consequently, each is capable of over-compensating in an area of strength or developing a hangup in an area of weakness. For that reason, it is helpful for every partner to know their mate's temperament so that they can approach each other in the most suitable fashion. Remember—love gives! When a partner administers love, he will in return receive all the love he needs.

One of the advantages of knowing the four temperaments is that it becomes easier to appreciate why your partner acts or reacts the way he does. That in turn helps you to accept his individual foibles and work with them, not against them.

We have a lovely sanguine friend named Molly who told me how God used the temperaments to resolve a pet peeve that was hindering her love life. Her husband, Pete, a melancholy/phlegmatic, regularly checked up on her. When he put his arm around her in bed as she snuggled close to him and warmed up to his mood, he would ask, "Molly, did you lock the back door and turn the heat down?" Though she answered, "Yes, Pete," he would jump out of bed, run through the dining room and kitchen, and check the back door and the thermostat. By the time he returned, her mood had turned to ice and she gave him the cold shoulder. This went on night after night—except when he became amorous enough to forget to ask the aggravating question.

One night Pete, an accountant by profession, brought home several income tax reports, spread them out on the dining room table, and began to work. Molly stood in the doorway, watching a strange charade: four times he added up a column of figures, put the answer on a slip of paper, and turned it over. When he finished the fourth one, he turned them all right side up and smiled to himself. They all agreed, so he wrote the answer on the tax form. Suddenly Molly realized that Pete didn't just check up on her; he even double-checked himself! She was proud of his reputation as an accurate accountant, and now she realized that the striving for perfection which made him successful in business was the same trait that caused him to check up on her.

That night she was ready for him! He put his arm around her, and she snuggled up close as usual. But when he asked, "Molly did you lock the back door, and what about the heat?" she sweetly replied, "I sure did, honey, but if you want to check, it's okay by me." He got up and trotted through the dining room and kitchen; as usual, the door was locked and the thermostat turned down. But that night when he crawled back into bed, he didn't encounter a frosty iceberg!

Once you have diagnosed your partner's temperament you can lovingly cooperate with it instead of clash with it and will enjoy a long and enjoyable love relationship.

PART Six

TEMPERAMENT AND YOUR SPIRITUAL LIFE

CHAPTER
FIFTEEN

Temperament and Spiritual Gifts

During the past few years we have heard a
great deal in the church about spiritual gifts. Much of it has been healthy
in that it pointed out that God wants to use all of his children in some
positive way in his kingdom. It also makes everyone realize he has real
worth. Without God in their lives many people never feel they make any
significant contribution to life. A Spirit-controlled Christian should not
have that feeling.

Bible teachers are not in complete agreement on what spiritual gifts
are and where they come from. I have been silent on the subject up until
now, even though I have written several times on the Spirit-filled life.
Basically the reason was because when I finally did put something in
print I wanted to have my thoughts well in mind so that my ideas would
be a positive help to people. The differences among Bible teachers on
this subject indicate that no one has the last word on spiritual gifts. And
after you have read this chapter you still will not have the final teaching.
But it will be related to you and your temperament and hopefully will
make you think and be helpful to you.

First of all, I don't think spiritual gifts are things you do not have any
aptitude for before you become a Christian. I believe they are God's
control of our naturally inherited temperament, directing its use in a
manner that will glorify his Son Jesus Christ.

Most Bible teachers treat spiritual gifts as if they are additives, things
we did not have before receiving Christ and had access to the power of
the Holy Spirit to overcome our weaknesses. I do not agree. My father
had a beautiful Irish tenor singing voice and an ear for music (neither of

which I inherited). He could play a piano by ear and accompany himself. So when he accepted Christ, he kept right on singing—only different songs in different places and for a much different purpose. Gaining the power of God allowed him to use the talent he already had to communicate the gospel of Christ and glorify him. I believe that is the way spiritual gifts always work, except sometimes he uses gifts or talents we had before salvation that were unused and may have been unknown. For example, a person may have had the gift to teach before his salvation and never knew it. His vocation may not have provided an opportunity to express that gift, and he didn't even know he had it. But after salvation, the pastor or Sunday-school superintendent, under inspiration of the Holy Spirit, may have asked him to take a class, and before long he has a spiritual gift used to the glory of God. He didn't get a new gift; he was inspired by the Spirit of God to use his natural talents.

The same thing has happened to people who had never felt they were public speakers, or because of traumatic experiences when children were too afraid to speak. After their conversion God puts a burden in their heart to preach the gospel and they do a beautiful job. New gift? No; God unlocks the restrictions of fear that kept the natural talent silent prior to salvation.

There is a close kinship between talent and human temperament. We have seen in our study of the four temperaments that each of us has at least ten strengths which we inherited at birth. (Personally, I have found at least five more plus the secondary temperament's contribution, making a total of more than twenty-five talents or temperament strengths available to every person.) When a person is touched by the Spirit of God and has a corresponding strength through the Spirit available to him, he is now able to be used of God in the area of his naturally inherited temperament.

God is abundantly able to perform miracles and do with any of us as he sees fit. After all, he is the Sovereign God. If he chooses to give some an added talent they did not have before salvation, that is his divine right. Usually, however, he uses our existing talents—whether they were known previously to us or not. The following, however, is my definition of a spiritual gift.

A spiritual gift is the use God makes of an individual's natural talents when touched by his Holy Spirit. Such use will always glorify him. Rulers, for example, were rulers before salvation. They could have been rulers if they had never become Christians. Now, however, that they are

born-again children of God, they no longer run roughshod over other
people; they rule honestly, and their basic motive is no longer selfishness,
greed or pride. It is now one of love, gentleness, and longsuffering. The
same is true of the car salesman whose natural spirit of charisma makes
it possible for him to sell a car even with a bad paint job. Such a person,
when filled with the Holy Spirit, may have the gift of evangelism and
will, as he walks in the Spirit, lead many to the Savior. However, some
who receive the gift of evangelism were so psychologically straitjacketed
before salvation they did not realize they had that potential until filled
with the Spirit.

In addition, the gift of evangelism is one gift every Christian has to
one degree or another. I have seen the most introverted individuals lead
many people to Christ. It is a matter of obedience, availability,
persistence in sharing the Word of God through the power of the Holy
Spirit. Anyone who has heard the gospel can receive Christ, if he so
chooses. Faith comes by hearing "the word of Christ" (Rom. 10:17,
NIV). That doesn't mean faith comes by hearing the Word from a person
with the gift of evangelism, nor does it mean faith comes by hearing the
Word from a sanguine. Faith can come by reading the Word of God
without the presence of any human instrument—except to put that
Bible in the motel room or print that gospel tract. In that sense, all
Christians have the potential of the gift of evangelism either directly or
indirectly. And I believe that is our primary purpose for being on this
earth—to be used of God to evangelize. When Christians give their
tithes and offerings to God through their church and other ministries,
they are being used of God to evangelize. When they open their home
for Bible studies, they are exercising the gift of evangelism. The reason I
harp on this gift is two-fold—first, to point out that we all have the
potential to use this spiritual gift. Paul told timid Timothy, "Do the work
of an evangelist," and he says it to each of us.

ALL CHRISTIANS   The other reason I used the gift of evangelism
HAVE ALL OF THE   as an illustration was to point out that we all
GIFTS   have all of the gifts to one degree or another,
                            depending on our temperament. Cholerics
have the gift of ruling much more than they have the gift of serving or
giving, but they can serve. Those who have the gift of mercy are not
usually endowed with a strong dose of the gift of ruling. But they can
rule, and they can always rule better when controlled by the Holy Spirit.

I do not agree with the theory advanced by some Bible teachers that we all receive one spiritual gift and ought to find out what it is and exercise it. That is a nice theory, but there is no scriptural support for such an idea and it doesn't fit my observations of people in the real world. It is more accurate to recognize that we all have all of the gifts, but depending on our individual temperament combination they will be in differing priorities. To some, ruling will be first. To others, serving will be first. Knowing your temperament will help you determine your spiritual gifts. But before we get to pointing out the various priorities of gifts according to temperament, we should examine the definition of the gifts.

SPIRITUAL GIFTS   There are thirteen different spiritual gifts that
DEFINED   are operative today that are referred to in
                         three passages of Scripture. These gifts should
not be confused with the nine fruits of the Spirit (Gal. 5:22, 23). The fruits of the Spirit are external gifts given to us by the Spirit of God when he comes into our lives to strengthen, lead, and empower us. Our spiritual gifts are the natural traits or talents we received at birth which now the Holy Spirit will use to some degree in our lives if we make ourselves available to him.

The three basic passages that contain these thirteen spiritual gifts are Romans 12:3-9; 1 Corinthians 12:7-31; and Ephesians 4:11-13. Some are repeated in each section. Some, like apostles, were for first-century use only. The following thirteen are the spiritual gifts I believe are operative today, along with their definitions applied to you. Those with asterisks require a special calling from God to enable us to use them in the offices given in the church today. However, they may be used in some parallel manner. For example, you may not be called of God to be a "pastor" to shepherd a flock of Christians. Yet, you may be serving as a Sunday-school teacher, department superintendent, or youth leader and doing the work of pastor-shepherding a group. You may not be called as a missionary-evangelist, yet you may be evangelizing regularly. Look on these as ministry gifts, and don't limit them in your mind to an office of the church. Look on them as potential areas in which you may serve your Lord.

1. Mercy: The ability to cheerfully suffer the hurts of
                         others, enabling you to minister to them in
                         their time of need.

*2. Pastor
shepherding:

Guiding, feeding, and protecting the flock of God.

*3. Teaching:

Communication of biblical truth; your greatest joy is in helping others to understand the truths of God.

4. Helps:

The ability to thoughtfully anticipate the needs of others and joyfully assist them in fulfilling their calling and duty.

5. Wisdom:

The ability to apply the principles of God's Word to the practical, everyday problems and choices of life in order to determine the will of God both for oneself and others.

*6. Evangelism:

The ability to proclaim the gospel to individuals or groups for the purpose of winning them to Christ. In a sense, all Christians have this gift for direct or indirect use. The Christian that never uses this gift to some degree has an unfulfilled feeling.

*7. Prophesying:

Spirit-empowered preaching that clearly sets forth the Word of God primarily to Christians, calling them to righteous living.

8. Exhorting:

The capacity to encourage, motivate, and strengthen others in the faith, to confront them with their behavior, and to challenge or advise them in conforming to the will of God as it is revealed in his Word.

9. Knowledge:

The ability to learn the facts of God's creative universe and relate them to his revealed Word.

10. Government:

The ability to lead others in administering the work of God. Such a person is capable of enlisting others in serving the Lord.

11. Discernment: The capacity to distinguish between truth and
                        error and the ability to make good decisions.

12. Giving: The ability to make money and joyfully give it
                        to the work of the Lord.

13. Faith: An unusual trust in God, enabling you to
                        launch divinely ordained projects that turn
                        vision into fact.

As a person matures in his Christian life, he will naturally increase in his effectiveness in expressing these gifts. The two areas over which you have control of the expansion of these gifts are the Word of God and faith. The more you know the Word of God, the better each of these gifts will function in your life. It's as though God gave them to you in infancy and you are to develop them. You are to exercise these gifts by faith. If you don't use a gift, it tends to atrophy, like the muscles of your body. If you step out by faith and use it, it becomes stronger. God leads us from "faith unto faith," from little steps of faith to larger. Teach a small group and God will give you an opportunity to teach a larger group. So it is with all our gifts; they need to be used or exercised regularly.

TEMPERAMENT AND THE PRIORITY OF SPIRITUAL GIFTS

Temperament is one of the factors that makes us unique from other human beings. Not only are there four basic temperaments and twelve blends of temperament, but there are differing degrees of these temperaments (a 70 percent sanguine, 30 percent phlegmatic might well be somewhat different than a 55 percent sanguine and a 45 percent phlegmatic). In addition, you must consider the differences of the sexes, I.Q., education, and background.

As you can see, many things go together to make up the total you. For that reason, it is impossible to predict exactly what priority scale every temperament combination will have. However, for vocational purposes and to help Christians find the place in their local church for which they are best equipped to serve their Lord, I have in "The LaHaye Temperament Test" prioritized the spiritual gifts according to the blends of at least two temperaments—one primary, the other secondary. I arbitrarily established a 60 percent to 40 percent split. That seems to be a common balance. The following are the priorities I have worked out.

SanChlor
MERCY
EVANGELISM
PASTORING
TEACHING
EXHORTING
PROPHESYING
GIVING
HELPS
FAITH
KNOWLEDGE
DISCERNMENT
WISDOM
GOVERNMENT

SanMel
MERCY
EVANGELISM
PROPHESYING
TEACHING
EXHORTING
PASTORING
GIVING
WISDOM
KNOWLEDGE
DISCERNMENT
HELPS
GOVERNMENT
FAITH

SanPhleg
MERCY
EVANGELISM
PASTORING
TEACHING
PROPHESYING
EXHORTING
WISDOM
GIVING
KNOWLEDGE
HELPS
DISCERNMENT
GOVERNMENT
FAITH

ChlorSan
TEACHING
EXHORTING
GOVERNMENT
PROPHESYING
KNOWLEDGE
DISCERNMENT
EVANGELISM
FAITH
GIVING
PASTORING
WISDOM
HELPS
MERCY

ChlorMel
TEACHING
EXHORTING
PROPHESYING
GOVERNMENT
KNOWLEDGE
WISDOM
DISCERNMENT
EVANGELISM
GIVING
PASTORING
FAITH
MERCY
HELPS

ChlorPhleg
TEACHING
EXHORTING
GOVERNMENT
PROPHESYING
KNOWLEDGE
WISDOM
DISCERNMENT
GIVING
PASTORING
EVANGELISM
FAITH
HELPS
MERCY

MelSan
PROPHESYING
EXHORTING
WISDOM
EVANGELISM
PASTORING
MERCY
TEACHING
KNOWLEDGE
GOVERNMENT
GIVING
HELPS
DISCERNMENT
FAITH

MelChlor
PROPHESYING
EXHORTING
TEACHING
WISDOM
GOVERNMENT
PASTORING
MERCY
KNOWLEDGE
DISCERNMENT
EVANGELISM
GIVING
FAITH
HELPS

MelPhleg
WISDOM
PROPHESYING
TEACHING
EXHORTING
MERCY
PASTORING
KNOWLEDGE
GOVERNMENT
HELPS
EVANGELISM
GIVING
DISCERNMENT
FAITH

PhlegSan
MERCY
PASTORING
TEACHING
HELPS
WISDOM
EVANGELISM
PROPHESYING
EXHORTING
KNOWLEDGE
GOVERNMENTS
DISCERNMENT
GIVING
FAITH

PhlegChlor
PASTORING
MERCY
GOVERNMENT
WISDOM
HELPS
TEACHING
EXHORTING
EVANGELISM
PROPHESYING
DISCERNMENT
KNOWLEDGE
FAITH
GIVING

PhlegMel
PASTORING
MERCY
WISDOM
HELPS
PROPHESYING
EXHORTING
TEACHING
GOVERNMENT
EVANGELISM
KNOWLEDGE
DISCERNMENT
GIVING
FAITH

These lists are not as complicated as they may seem, in that you only need to study one of the twelve—yours. Once you have diagnosed your temperament combination, you will just need to study that list that pertains to you to discover the priority list of your spiritual gifts. One indication would be to refer to the results of Chapter 5, "Give Yourself a Temperament Test." However, if you wish a more thorough analysis of your primary and secondary temperament and the appropriate list of twenty-four or more places you can serve your Lord in your own church and the fifty secondary vocations for which you are the most suited, you will want to order, "The LaHaye Temperament Analysis" available at special discount because you are a reader of this book. See page 351.

USING YOUR SPIRITUAL GIFTS

The above priority list indicates intensity of gifts in your life, the first gift being your most intense or the one that is your priority gift. Keep in mind, you have all of the thirteen gifts, but not in the same intensity. You will probably find that you feel more comfortable doing the first four gifts, reasonably comfortable doing the next five, but the last three or four may be difficult for you. Don't give up on these as the Lord directs your life. But I have found that we get our greatest satisfaction out of life in serving our Lord in the top three to five priority gifts. This accords with the popular teaching today that the thing you do that gives you greatest pleasure in life is probably the exercise of your most significant spiritual gift.

It is my prayer that this chapter has helped you locate your primary spiritual gifts. Now dedicate them to God (Rom. 12:1, 2; 6:11-13; 1 Cor. 6:19, 20). By faith anticipate that he will use your life to glorify him. You may wonder why I repeatedly have said in this chapter to glorify the Lord Jesus Christ. It is because that is the test of the work of the Holy Spirit. Our Lord said of the Holy Spirit, "He will bring glory to me" (John 16:14, NIV). If you and I fulfill the will of God for our lives, it will be to glorify Jesus. And that is why he gave us his Holy Spirit, who will make your gifts holy and use them to glorify the Son of God.

CHAPTER
SIXTEEN

Temperament and Your Relationship with God

Any Christian, regardless of his temperament, can become a spiritual person. However, his temperament will influence both his spirituality and its expression. One thing we have learned so far in our study of human temperament is that we are not all cut out of the same mold. We are unique individuals. I have been studying temperament and people for eighteen years and so far have never met two people with the same combination of temperaments. When people come to Christ, he meets them where they are and has the same plan for all to be conformed to his image (Rom. 8:29). That is true spirituality.

What is Spirituality?

Before we can examine the influence of temperament on a Christian's spiritual life, we must first determine what spirituality is. It certainly is not an emotional feeling that transports us into a mystical relationship with God. It is a state of being that takes time for the Holy Spirit to develop in any temperament. You can be saved in an instant and raptured in a "twinkling of an eye," but it takes a long time to become a spiritual person.

I combine maturity and spirituality. A baby Christian may be spiritual momentarily, but only a mature Christian will be spiritual in the sense of true spirituality. Paul must have had that in mind when he told the Corinthians, "And I, brethren, could not speak to you as to spiritual people but as to carnal, as to babes in Christ" (1 Cor. 3:1, NKJV). These Corinthian Christians were babies because they were still carnal.

They had not matured or grown up spiritually. They were saved, but they were factious, critical, contentious, and had other problems not associated with a truly spiritual person. Paul had spent a great deal of time in Corinth with these people, but they had not abandoned the influence of the Greek world around them. Consequently they were baby Christians—even long after they should have been mature.

We should be careful not to confuse true spirituality and seniority. As a pastor for over thirty years, I know all too well the problem the local church gets itself into when it elects people to its boards and committees on the basis of seniority rather than spiritual maturity. Just because a person is an active tithing man of a congregation does not make him qualified for service on the deacon board—or to be the pastor of the church. Seniority may qualify you for retirement, but it does not make you a spiritually mature person.

By contrast, you don't have to wait a decade to be a spiritually mature person. Most of the early Christian leaders were active leaders before they had been saved more than five to ten years. We see the same thing today. We have four- or five-year Christians who are far more spiritually mature than some who have spent fifty years as active church members.

A spiritually mature Christian is one who is controlled by the Holy Spirit (Eph. 5:18) and manifests the nine fruits of the Spirit (Gal. 5:22, 23), who walks in holiness, who knows the Word of God and diligently seeks to do his will because he loves him (John 14:21). While that does take time, it does not take a lifetime. The Apostle Paul spent three years in Arabia after his conversion before Barnabas brought him up to Antioch to begin serving as an elder. By this time he was spiritually mature enough to take a position as a teacher of the Word. Several years later he became a leader in his own right. But this was a gradual process.

Although it is impossible to say when a person becomes spiritually

CHILDREN	YOUNG MEN	FATHERS
Sins forgiven	Overcomers	Know God

mature, I think we can gain insight from 1 John 2:12-14 where we find three stages of growth compared to the spiritual life: "little children," "young men," and "fathers."

A spiritual child is one who is newly born again. While salvation is a free gift, spiritual growth is the result of growing in grace and the knowledge of our Lord through study of his Word and faith. A newborn "babe," as Peter calls him, or a "little child" as John labels him, is not going to be a victorious Christian most of the time. He may experience an up-and-down life spiritually for a time until his commitment to the Word makes him an overcomer. At that point, he is a "young man" in Christ; that is, he overcomes the "wicked one" by "the word of God [which] abideth in you" more often than he is overcome. Note the gradual growth process. Finally, as this person continues studying the Word, walking in the Spirit and in obedience to the Word, he believes such a faith is based on knowing God and becomes a father of the faith. One thing about fathers—they spiritually reproduce themselves in other people. That will be the result of being conformed to our Lord's image. As he served the Father by seeking that which was lost, so will we, both directly and indirectly.

In this day of instant everything, we need to understand that there are no shortcuts to maturity—physical or spiritual. There is, however, one major difference between physical maturity and spiritual maturity—you. In the physical it is almost automatic. If you eat three meals a day and get a reasonable amount of exercise and rest, you will gradually mature into adulthood. Spiritually, it depends on you. God is for you, the Holy Spirit is available to you, and you have the Word to study (probably in five different translations). How fast you grow depends on how long it takes you to learn the principles, wisdom, and knowledge of God found in his Word and to incorporate this into your daily life.

Of one thing I am certain—there is no such thing as spiritual maturity without Bible study. It may come through hearing in church, TV, cassettes, Bible school, or through reading and studying the Word for yourself. But just as you can't grow physically without food, you can't grow spiritually without the spiritual food of the Word of God. That may be why the Bible refers to itself as milk, bread, and meat.

PERSONAL BIBLE STUDY AND YOUR TEMPERAMENT

The success of your spiritual life is dependent on the effectiveness of your personal Bible study, not your temperament. However, your temperament will influence your Bible study habits just as surely as it influences your physical eating habits.

Sanguines are spontaneous, undisciplined people who really have to work at being consistent about anything. That certainly includes their personal study of the Word. They are as quick to see its importance as any temperament, but their problem is doing on a regular basis what they know to be valuable. They are so susceptible to external stimulation and so interested in everything that it is easy for them to get chased off in other pursuits. And of all people, television can be the slavemaster of the sanguine to the expense of his spiritual life. Mr. and Mrs. Sanguine of all the temperaments need to make the rule that can transform their spiritual life—"no Bible, no breakfast." That is, they should say, If I don't have time to read the Word on a given day, I won't take time to eat breakfast. If he keeps that commitment, he will soon develop a consistent devotional life.

Cholerics are self-disciplined people as a rule, but their problem is that they seldom see the need for personal Bible study. Their attitude usually is, "I go to church to hear the Word, but the Bible is an old book and I have so many important things to think about that it isn't that vital for me." This may be why so many cholerics are shallow spiritually and why they do not experience spiritual growth. They can see how important it is to others, but think it's not necessary for them. And even when they do see the need to be consistent daily in the Word, they may find truths that apply to others and not to themselves. However, once convinced that without God their life is rather futile, they can learn to develop effective spiritual habits.

Of all the temperaments, the melancholy is most apt to be consistent in his daily Bible study, reading, and memorization. He is usually interested in anything that is good for him and once convinced, he will work tirelessly. However, he may get so technically involved, he does little to apply the Word to his own life. Or he may castigate himself for falling so far beneath what the Bible holds out as the word of encouragement and blessing. One thing I suggest to all temperaments is that they keep a spiritual diary of what God says to them on a daily basis. It is really a simple but practical way to be edified by the Word. In fact, I have developed a daily spiritual diary chart that is extremely helpful to keep such a record and help a person get maximum benefit from their study of the Word.

Phlegmatics, the nicest of the temperaments, have a problem with consistency. They procrastinate over everything, including their Bible study. It isn't that they don't believe it's important, but by the time they read the newspaper and talk to their friends on the phone or putter around, it is time to go to work or school or whatever. Naturally, they feel convicted when they go to church and make a vow to be different, but seldom do their Bible study habits change. They would never think of going to church without taking their Bible, but seldom use it between Sundays.

Phlegmatics need to realize that they should get involved with serving God, and that they won't have spiritual depth unless they discipline themselves and develop a regular devotional life. One thing I have noted—regular Bible study never just happens. Those whom I have found who are consistent in having a daily study in the Word set a specific time and usually a specific place and follow a specific formula. This may seem somewhat regimented to a phlegmatic, but he will never be consistent for God or develop a regular devotional life unless he does. And never will any other temperament.

**PRAYER LIFE
AND YOUR
TEMPERAMENT**

Prayer is as essential to a Christian's spiritual life as breathing is to his physical life. All Christians pray. How they pray, however, is almost as varied as people. There are essentially two things that have a pronounced influence on your personal prayer life: 1) your instruction, and 2) your temperament.

The Bible is filled with teachings, commands, and instructions on prayer—from "pray without ceasing" to ". . . let your requests be made known to God." There are hundreds of promises regarding prayer. It seems to be God's means of blessing his children and supplying their needs. If you haven't done a Bible study on prayer you should, and you will find a wealth of material to work with.

But it isn't just formal instruction in the Word that gives you your instructions on prayer. Your pastor-teacher or the individual God sends you to instruct you in his ways will have a profound influence on your prayer life. For instance, prayer patterns will become a model for your own. When you observe the prayer life of a Christian you admire, you are often prone to consider his prayer life to be the secret to his spiritual life. And that is generally speaking not true. His prayer life is the result of his instruction, role model, spiritual life, *and* his temperament.

Remember, temperament influences everything you do. You should have that fact fully implanted in your mind by this point in our study. It isn't the only factor, but it is probably the most important. And certainly you will find that in the case of your prayer life temperament plays an important role.

Sanguines are quick, unpredictable, and spontaneous about everything—why not their prayer life? Sparky is the type who wakes up with the birds in a happy mood, so he probably praises the Lord in the morning. He may even do it during his morning shower. He usually isn't too much on prayer lists or records, but his favorite verse on prayer is, "Pray without ceasing." To him, that means he doesn't have to set aside a specific time for prayer, he just talks to God (and people) whenever he feels like it and about anything he thinks about. One sanguine told me, "I feel guilty when I promise to pray for someone and forget. So now I pray instantly in my heart as soon as they request a place in my prayers, 'Lord, bless this person!' " That's probably better than nothing, but not much. Sanguines, unless they are unusually challenged by God or some friend who has a great deal of influence on them, usually have a rather shallow prayer life. They are not much for solitude and contemplation; consequently, they would rather spend time with people than long periods of time with God.

Cholerics are activists personified. Like Martha, they would rather spend time serving their Lord than talking with him. Their spirit of self-sufficiency has a tendency to limit what they discuss with God. If they can figure out what to do in a given situation, they would rather do it than talk to their Heavenly Father about it. They save "the big ticket" items—that is, the projects or subjects they can't figure out—as the ones to pray over.

Once a Christian learns by the school of hard knocks (and that is usually what it takes) that he must commit "all his ways" to the Lord, he develops the habit of praying while doing something else. Driving, jogging, yard work—anything that does not require concentration becomes an opportunity for him to pray. Paul must have prayed that way; as he walked from city to city en route to serve God he would "pray without ceasing." One of the enemies of a choleric's prayer life is his overactive mind. He no sooner begins his prayer time and he thinks of something that needs to be done. The best way I have found to solve that problem is to keep a note pad by your chair or place of prayer and write down every idea that comes to mind while praying so you can get right back to prayer. It is the best way to maintain your prayer concentration.

Mr. or Mrs. Melancholy, however, usually have the most extensive prayer life. They seem to have a capacity for God and communion with him that is unequalled by any of the other temperaments. I find it instructive that all the prophets were melancholy to one degree or another. They are famous for their ability to commune with God. The melancholy with a high degree of choleric temperament will resort more to a life of prayer than any other. He enjoys solitude and serious contemplation. He is easily regimented to schedule and style. He will often make a prayer list and pray consistently. As a pastor for years, I found the saints with the most effective prayer ministry were usually melancholy. Not always—God can give any of us a burden to be a prayer warrior, but it seems melancholies have more consistent prayer habits.

One area Mr. Melancholy has to work on, however, is to avoid letting his moody disposition or his spirit of criticism lead to griping or complaining to God. This can ruin his prayer life. For him most of all, the advice of Paul is appropriate, "in every thing give thanks, for this is the will of God in Christ Jesus. . . ." Once Mr. Melancholy develops the habit of praying with thanksgiving, which is a lesson we all need to learn, he can develop a very effective prayer life.

The phlegmatic Christian can also become a man or woman of prayer *if* he will guard against drowsiness. He can enjoy worship and does love God, but any time they strike a sedentary position, their enemy is sleep. For that reason I suggest the phlegmatic Christian learn to pray pacing the floor or in a standing position. He does well with a prayer list and is often moved with compassion for the needs of others.

One of the things that helps the phlegmatic Christian is that he likes routine. It is hard for him to work prayer in on a regular basis into his life, but once he does so and develops a routine, it is equally as hard to forget it. Of all the temperaments, he is as likely as any to become effective as a man or woman of prayer.

TEMPERAMENT AND   Many years ago I came to an interesting
LIVING BY FAITH   observation in my Christian life, and today I
                        have seen nothing that would cause me to
change my mind. Very simply, it is this: faith is more important than intelligence or talent.

I came to this conclusion in answering the question, "Why does God seem to use some people more than others?" I think that is a very legitimate question, as is the second that bears on it—"Why does God use some very ordinary people more than some of the more talented and intelligent?" Now that does not mean God does not use gifted people. The Apostle Paul was obviously a brilliant man with the best education available in his day, and God used him mightily. Yet he also

used Peter, James, and John, who were ordinary and "unlearned men."
I have seen the same thing in churches I have served. I have seen God
use brilliant scholars and people with very average talent and low I.Q. I
have seen him seem to bypass some brilliant Christians as well as
ordinary saints.

Then I discovered the common denominator. God is no respector of
persons—he uses anyone, from Balaam's ass to the wisest man who
ever lived or who ever will live. What is that common denomination?
Faith. God himself said, "Without faith it is impossible to please God."
The one thing that raises one Christian above another is not looks,
brains, talent, or even opportunity; it is faith. Second Chronicles 16:9
tells us that "the eyes of the Lord run to and fro throughout the whole
earth, to shew himself strong in the behalf of those whose heart is
perfect toward him." In this context, the "perfect" that God has in mind
is faith. God's eyes are continually running up and down this earth
looking for men and women of faith. The New Testament tells us that
the one thing God requires in stewards is *faithfulness.*

We have already seen that faith comes through the Word of God. It
also comes through the Holy Spirit, for it is one of the nine fruits or
results of the Spirit according to Galatians 5:22. But there is another
way the gift of faith comes into our lives—from one step of faith to
another step of faith (Rom. 1:17). That is, as we take one step of faith, it
stretches our faith for the next step. People who never trust God for the
first step of faith will never become strong in faith and God will not use
them very much—regardless of how much natural ability they might
have. Romans 14:23 says, "Whatsoever is not of faith is sin." Many
Christians limit God's use of their lives by the sin of unbelief. Sometimes
that follows the pattern of their temperament.

Sanguines are the quickest to step out by faith if they are spiritually
motivated. But then they are quicker on the trigger in everything.
Venturesome by nature, it is not hard for them, particularly in their
youth, to launch new ventures or projects impetuously. And surprisingly
enough, God meets their need and somehow blesses what seems to
others a very impetuous move, if their heart is right. Not given to
complex thinking, it is usually easy for them to take God at his Word
and step out by faith.

When it comes to personal soul-winning, the sanguine has the easiest
time. He likes people, is rarely intimidated by them, and if spiritually
motivated will share his faith readily. Success in soul-winning encourages
his faith, and he finds it easier to do it the next time, until someone asks

a theological question he has not thought of. It is perhaps easier for
sanguines to take God at his Word and act upon it than any other, at
least on the short run. Consistency is not one of his gifts, however.

Cholerics can also be men or women of faith. However, they are such
visionary, project-oriented people with a strong sense of self-confidence
that it is sometimes difficult to tell whether their faith is in God or
themselves. If they come to real faith in the living God and that he is
indeed operative in our present day, it is not difficult for him to take God
at his Word and claim the promises of God for himself. He is not usually
troubled by theoretical doubts or self-condemnation. Consequently, he is
willing to venture out on a new project and expect God to supply. Once
he proves God by successfully achieving step one, he is ready for a
second step of faith. And his steps tend to get bigger. There is no
seeming limit to his vision if he continues in the Word and walks with
God. Many of the Christian organizations, mission societies, and
Christian education institutions were founded by cholerics or choleric/
sanguines who, like Paul, "believed God."

Melancholy saints can go either way when it comes to faith. They
either limit God by unbelief and do nothing, or attempt great things for
God and do them. It all depends on their mood at the time, and that is
usually influenced by their spiritual life. Unfortunately for them, they
have a difficult time taking God at his Word, for two reasons. One, they
are naturally endowed with analytical skills and theoretical questions that
if pressed too far always lead to doubt. And two, they often destroy
their potential for faith by self-condemnation. Mr. Melancholy usually
feels unworthy of the blessings of God—even though he may live a
more godly personal life than the sanguine or choleric who ventures out
in faith. The melancholy tends to feel unworthy and asks, "Why me?"
The sanguine and choleric tend to say, "Why not me?"

The melancholy person with his uncanny ability to analyze things can
foresee more negative problems (real or imagined) in any project than
any of the other three temperaments; this does nothing for faith. He
needs to keep his eyes on the Lord's sufficiency, not the anticipated
problems. He is the one kind of builder who will not only plan on the
high side of every anticipated cost, but will program in a 10 to 15
percent contingency factor to cover the unexpected. By that time, the
cost estimate is so high he does not have the resources or faith to
proceed.

One asset a melancholy does have is his vivid imagination. That can
help him in two ways if he concentrates. First, he can visualize the

stories of the men of faith in the Bible, and this can electrify his own faith. And two, if he forces himself to keep his eye on the goal he can see it more vividly than others, and this always results in a forward movement. He also has a good memory, so once he has taken a step of faith he can remember God's faithfulness, which encourages him to take another step of faith.

Living by faith is possible, of course, for the phlegmatic, but it isn't easy. You don't read where Matthew, Bartholomew, Andrew, or James made a mad rush to get out of the boat and walk on water. Who was it? Sanguine Simon Peter, of course. We have seen that fear, worry, and anxiety are a way of life to many phlegmatics. Obviously, these negative emotions do nothing for faith, but rather kill or intimidate it.

One of the things that contributes to the phlegmatic's doubts and unbelief is his passive way in the Word or his procrastination. If he would force himself to study his Bible, the Word would build faith in him; but although he believes in the necessity of a daily quiet time, it is not usually his habit. Consequently, when the door of opportunity opens to him, he lacks the faith to step inside. I have known phlegmatic Christians to attend church faithfully for twenty years and never do anything in the way of church service. It wasn't that they didn't love God or that they did not live a godly life. Their problem was lack of faith. They could always think of enough "respectable" excuses to talk themselves out of the opportunity to walk by faith. Lacking the illustration of God's faithfulness at that first step of faith, it is likely phlegmatics will not take the second. They are capable, intelligent people who limit themselves by unbelief unless they walk in the Spirit and begin trusting God. Once they embark on the life of faith, they experience a whole new dimension to life that becomes contagious. Even for them a step of faith leads to another. Like the melancholy, they must develop the habit of looking at God and his resources, not at circumstance or their anticipation of consequences.

The Apostle Peter is often ridiculed by preachers and Bible teachers for sinking as he walked on the water to Jesus. The truth is, of all the disciples he was the only one with sufficient faith to walk on water. To this day that feat has only been accomplished by our Lord and Peter. What made the difference—bigger feet? More intelligence? Of course not—faith made the difference. At a moment in time Peter had more faith than the other disciples, and he walked on water.

Are there opportunities you have passed up due to lack of faith? Probably! Most of us have. That's why you should develop your faith through regular study of the Word and walk in the control of the Spirit, being obedient to all you know God wants you to do. Take that step of faith.

Be sure of this. No one takes giant steps of faith who has not already taken baby steps. God leads us from faith to faith.

TEMPERAMENT
AND PERSONAL
HOLINESS

This is an unholy age in which to live. And unfortunately we do not hear much about the holiness God requires of Christians. That, in my opinion, is why so much immorality, carnality, and worldliness is creeping into our churches today. Be sure of this—no one will be spiritually mature who does not practice mental holiness, and today you will have to work at it. The best place to start is to examine what the Word says on the subject. Consider the following:

> Be ye holy; for I am holy. (1 Pet. 1:16)

> Pursue peace with all men, and holiness, without which no man will see the Lord. (Heb. 12:14)

> Seeing then that all these things shall be dissolved, what manner of persons ought ye to be in holy conversation and godliness. (2 Pet. 3:11)

> Having therefore these promises, dearly beloved, let us cleanse ourselves from all filthiness of the flesh and spirit, perfecting holiness in the fear of God. (2 Cor. 7:1)

Holiness is not easy, but it is essential. And like faith, little steps lead to bigger steps—in either direction. And your temperament is no help! I have found that all temperaments have a problem with holy thinking, particularly men. Our Lord taught men not to look at women in lust. In so doing, he established the male Christian's principle source of temptation. Godly men, regardless of temperament, have learned to look at women without lusting. Jesus did not say a man could not look at women. It is looking and lusting that is sin. A godly man will learn to look on women admiringly, as he can legitimately look on any beautiful object with approval. But it takes mental discipline and spiritual determination to learn to recognize the line between looking and lusting and to refuse to cross it. And if he fails, he must quickly and silently face his sin, confess it, and look at something else.

Sanguines are so receptive and responsive to sight, they must be particularly careful what they see. It is wrong and dangerous for any

Christian to watch suggestive movies or TV, and pornography should never have a place in any Christian's thought-life. All temperaments are vulnerable to sensual sins; that's why they are usually addressed first in a catalog of sins in Scripture (for example, Gal. 5:19-21), but sanguines particularly so.

Cholerics think they have an advantage in their thought-life. They see beyond the temptation to the consequences, which often has a cooling affect on them—unless, however, they care to justify immorality somehow, and then they are capable of anything. One experienced choleric Christian I know tried to excuse his infidelity by blaming his beautiful but frigid wife with the remark, "Living with her is like having a delicious dish of candy that you can't touch." A cholerically clever retort, but really undisguised unholiness!

Melancholies are less likely to indulge or justify unholy thoughts than all the temperaments. They are usually as critical of themselves as they are of others, so they tend to quickly label unholy thoughts as sin. In addition, once they taste the joy of unbroken fellowship and communion with God, they are unwilling to lose it to unholy thinking. However, their tendency to indulge self-pity can ruin their relationship to God and make them vulnerable to any kind of unholy thinking.

Phlegamtics seem so nice and clean, but they are human too. If they aren't careful, they too can be swept along the tempting road of impure thoughts. They tend to spend more time fantasizing than any other temperament. If unchecked, those fantasies can become impure, ruining their spiritual life.

The best scriptural challenge I know in this regard is 2 Corinthians 10:5; practice it throughout your entire life:

> Casting down imaginations, and every high thing that exalts itself against the knowledge of God, bringing into captivity every thought to the obedience of Christ.

HOW YOU FACE AFFLICTIONS

Everyone has afflictions in life—even Spirit-controlled Christians. Our Lord, who was perfect and sinless and on whom "the Spirit rested without measure," was afflicted, grieved, sorrowed. As you know, he even wept! Job, one of the godliest men who ever lived, suffered the premature death of his children, loss of his cattle and goods, and even of

his health as a testimony to man and Satan that God is able to supply
the needs of the afflicted saint.

You, too, will suffer affliction, if you have not already. Sickness and
death are a part of life. Insult, injury, and rejection are common to all
men, and Christians are not exempt. And your first reaction will often be
the result of your temperament. I say first, because if you are a Bible-
taught Christian, you will follow your natural reaction with the kind the
Bible requires, and that is extremely helpful.

Sanguines explode whenever anything goes wrong, so that is their
first response to affliction. Tears, anger, or laughing are their usual
repertoire of tools, and not always at the most opportune time. In fact,
I'll make a confession. One of the things *some* sanguines do that most
irritates me is laugh at the most inappropriate times and events. It's just
a nervous relief valve that helps them live with the pressures by letting
some steam escape. Then after a short time they rush off to something
else. Have you heard the story of the sanguine golfer on the sixteenth
hole who saw a funeral procession drive slowly by? He put his cap over
his heart and stood momentarily at attention. When his companion
asked, "Was that a friend?" He replied, "Yes. If she had lived five more
days, we would have been married twenty-seven years!"

Escape from reality is a temptation for all temperaments. It can be
overpowering to sanguines—much to the annoyance of friends and
loved ones.

The choleric reaction to affliction can sometimes be as external as the
sanguine, but he will invariably respond with, "What can I do about
this?"—either expressed or implied. He may be aching inside, but hides
his true feelings by activity. He is not too sympathetic, and since most
afflictions are shared by other family members he may be a source of
irritation and grief to them.

Melancholies are predictable in the face of unexpected adversities.
Their response is, "Why me?" or "What have I done to deserve this?"
And it is downhill from there, as they indulge the sinful thinking pattern
of self-pity to the hilt. Finally depression sets in to complicate their life
and get them completely out of fellowship with God. Being creative can
be a disadvantage when you permit it to turn negative.

Phlegmatics seem unflappable, and they are almost. But they still hurt
inside. Just because they don't scream, holler, or laugh hysterically
doesn't mean they aren't concerned or are ignoring the real difficulties
they face. It's just not their style to become external. They are prone to
go off by themselves and grieve quietly. Their chief weapon is silence.

WHAT IS A PERSON   Since all the reactions above are wrong, what is
TO DO?   a person to do? Heed the words of Scripture:
                     "Count it all joy when you fall into grievous
testings (afflictions)" (James 1:2). Instead of reacting in the flesh
(temperament), react in the Spirit by learning to praise the Lord in the
circumstances. Not for them, but in them. There is a difference! There
are some circumstances in life for which we cannot give thanks or
"count it all joy." But there are no circumstances in which we Christians
cannot count it all joy or give thanks for God and what he is able to do
in the midst of our affliction. The key, regardless of temperament, is the
direction of our look. If we look only at the problem, which is normal,
we will respond according to our temperament. If, however, we look to
God, we will respond according to the scriptural power within us.

One thing to keep in mind in evaluating the effects of a person's
temperament on his spiritual life is the fact that all people are a
combination of two or more temperaments. Consequently, there will be a
blending effect on their response to everything. Remember that the
resources of God are more than sufficient for any combination of
temperaments. If a Christian becomes unspiritual, he cannot blame it on
his temperament combination, but on the fact that he refused to avail
himself of God's adequate resources.

Your Achilles Heel

We have already dealt with the weakness of
each temperament and how to apply the Spirit-controlled life to each in
order to avail ourselves of the resources God has made available to us.
However, there is one weakness that seems to follow a sex pattern
rather than temperament, and this is probably the best place to discuss
it.

Men are different, as we have seen, in regard to their temperament.
Consequently, they will have temperament-induced weakness patterns.
The same is true for women. But there is one area that men seem more
vulnerable to than women and vice versa. I refer to finances and
vocation for men, and children and family for women.

FINANCES AND   Nothing seems to test a man's faith more than
VOCATION   financial pressures or economic loss or change.
                 God has not only commanded man to be the
principle breadwinner and protector of his family; he seems to have
wired him psychologically so that anytime he is threatened in those two

areas, it is a threat to his spiritual life. Worry, insecurity, anxiety, and
frustration may grip him, causing his reactions to compound his
problems.

Economical threats can actually strengthen a man if he turns
immediately to God for his power and help. God will not leave or
forsake us in those hours of adversity, and when we are forced to put
him to the test his supply not only solves our problem but strengthens
our faith.

Walt was not only a church member, he was a good friend. I had
discipled him personally for several months, and he was growing very
rapidly when it came time to go on a two-week vacation to Yosemite
with his family. When he picked up his paycheck that Friday night, he
unexpectedly picked up a pink slip saying his services were no longer
required by the company and he was being terminated after twenty-two
years of service.

When his wife said, "What are we going to do?" he said, "Go to
Yosemite as we planned. We have been faithful in our walk with God;
we have double-tithed this year during our Church Building Program. I
am confident our faithful God will provide." So Walt and his family went
on vacation, had a good time, and returned one day early to a ringing
telephone. When he picked it up he heard his supervisor say, "Walt,
where have you been? I've been trying to locate you for a week. We
want you to report for work on Monday to Plant 2." What do you think
that did for Walt's faith? It made a phlegmatic strong in faith, just the
way God intended.

FAMILY   Women, however, are not so troubled by
money problems, and most don't seem to be as
convinced as men about career, etc., depending of course on each
family's circumstances. But children, marriage, and family? That's
another matter! Women never come closer to sheer panic than when
their children are in jeopardy—regardless of their temperament. I talked
to a lovely mother of two teen-age girls who had just gone through a fire
in her home. The second-story bedrooms were completely gutted, and
the blaze almost took the life of one of the girls. The mother was so
terrified that her daughter was still asleep in her bed, she fought through
the smoke and flames to reach her and almost lost her life. Only the call
of a neighbor telling her that the girl had jumped safely out the window
made her turn back from certain death. That mother's life was not
worth living at that moment if her daughter was lost.

Not only will the fear of fire do that, but any threat to her children.

This divorced woman has all kinds of financial pressures, but first on her list is the well-being of her children. That's not unusual; it is part of the maternal instinct and true femininity. Such emergencies, however, are sometimes easier to bear than the long drawn-out threats a woman faces every day. Particularly is this true of single parents. Their understandable response of fear can strip them of their spiritual vitality. Or it can cause them to depend even more on their Heavenly Father.

I am often accused of having a lot of faith. I attribute much of that to my widowed mother who turned her insecurities and problems over to God and developed an abiding faith in her Heavenly Father that we kids found contagious.

Always bear in mind—God's resources are sufficient for any temperament and any sex. Claim them—they are yours for the taking.

THE BOTTOM LINE   Many Christians think they are spiritual but are not. Some don't understand what a spiritual Christian is, and some are just kidding themselves thinking they are spiritual because they go to church regularly, tithe, and are faithful marriage partners. A spiritual person will do all of these things and many more. One thing he will do is walk in the control of the Holy Spirit and thus fulfill the will of God (Eph. 5:17, 18; Gal. 5:16-18). But there is more. In fact, this may be the final test of spirituality.

The *New International Version* of the Scripture gives us new insight on this subject by translating an old familiar verse of Scripture just a bit differently. One of the first verses any Christian memorizes is Romans 12: 1, 2. But the NIV translates the first verse more accurately by changing "your reasonable service" to "spiritual worship." Note the two translations on the next page.

The bottom line to spirituality will be, who uses your body? That's what this life is all about. Who uses your body—God or Satan? A truly spiritual person so dedicates his life to God for whatever use the Heavenly Father wishes to make of it that he will do whatever it takes to be a "living sacrifice" or living vessel of service. He will do all the things mentioned above, including living his life under the control of the Holy Spirit, obedient to whatever God tells him to do. He will not grieve or quench the Spirit (Eph. 4:30-32; 1 Thess. 5:19) by indulging his naturally inherited weaknesses, but will so seek the kingdom of God (Matt. 6:33) that his life will be available to do whatever the Lord commands. His mind will be so renewed by the Holy Spirit through the Word of God that he will not conform to the paths of this world. And be sure of this—he or she, Mr. or Mrs. Sanguine, Choleric, Melancholy, or Phlegmatic, will *be holy. True* spirituality, regardless of the temperament package with which it is housed, will *always* come *clothed* in holiness. And though more difficult for some temperaments, it is possible for all.

King James Version	*New International Version*
I beseech you therefore, brethren, by the mercies of God, that ye present your bodies a living sacrifice, holy, acceptable unto God, which is your reasonable service.	Therefore, I urge you, brothers, in view of God's mercy, to offer your bodies as living sacrifices, holy and pleasing to God— which is your spiritual worship. Do not conform any longer to the pattern of this world, but be transformed by the renewing of your mind. Then you will be able to test and approve what God's will is—his good, pleasing and perfect will.
And be not conformed to this world: but be ye transformed by the renewing of your mind, that ye may prove what is that good, and acceptable, and perfect, will of God.	

PART *Seven*

MINISTERS HAVE TEMPERAMENTS, TOO

CHAPTER
SEVENTEEN

The Influence of Temperament on Preaching

Ministers are as different as people, because they are people. Two ministers can graduate from the same seminary, be the same age, and even look alike; yet they will be very different in their preaching technique and pastoral style. What makes the difference? They have different temperaments. Next to his theological beliefs (liberal or conservative), nothing influences a minister's style more than his temperament. Even his I.Q. does not have all that much to do with his style.

At the outset I would like to make it clear that no temperament is better than another in the Lord's work. However, some temperaments fit into different areas of the ministry better than others. But no temperament has a corner on the work of God. He used all four of the temperaments in the Old and New Testament times.

Peter was a strong sanguine. Yet God used him when he was filled with the Spirit. Saul of Tarsus, that choleric-melancholy persecutor of the church, was ruthless until he was filled with the Spirit of God. Then he became a mighty tool of blessing in the hand of God.

John, the beloved apostle, was a melancholy idealist who served Jesus Christ until he was almost ninety years old, according to tradition. Many of God's faithful servants have been melancholy.

Barnabas, the peacemaker and first missionary with the Apostle Paul, must have been a phlegmatic, and God used him in a mighty way. There is no temperament God cannot or will not use if it is *fully committed* to doing his will.

The reason I stress this in any introduction to this subject is so everyone will understand that his temperament is the right one for him. God makes no mistakes! Our temperament was not the result of the chance fall of the genes, but the creative design of a loving and sovereign God.

Having been a pastor for thirty years and a student of temperaments for twenty years, it is only natural that I would put them together. Actually, I backed into this subject by being invited to speak on the subject at a ministers' conference. When I saw their raucous laughter as I presented the sanguine and choleric temperaments, I knew I was pressing a nerve. When I went to the mission field and spoke to over 8,000 missionaries in 1977, I realized that most of them were melancholy and phlegmatic. Upon my return I began taking notes, making observations, and talking with Christian workers, their mates, and their associates. Now there is no question in my mind that ministers not only come in all sizes, shapes, and descriptions; they also come in a variety of temperaments and temperament combinations.

It is my prayer that this chapter can be the highlight to this book—not just for my preacher friends, but for the many Christians who must hear their sermons, work with them, and go to them for ministry in times of need. I pray that the preachers who read this chapter will come to grips with their God-given temperament and its natural weaknesses and strengths and then go to the Holy Spirit for the strengthening of their weakness so they can make maximum use of their God-given talents. I also pray that church members will accept their pastor in the light of his temperament and work with him accordingly.

So often when I hear ministers criticized, it is a temperament weakness that is the culprit (and often at the expense of his strength). No minister is perfect! At best, they are filled-with-the-Spirit members of a fallen human race. It is a wise congregation that tries to provide their pastor with the staff support that is needed by his temperament, so that he can spend the maximum time doing the things he does best.

Unfortunately, we don't have the space in this book to give all twelve temperament combinations that ministers can inherit. But we can deal with the four basic temperaments in the light of three major areas: (1) his preaching style, (2) his pastoral style, and (3) his major needs or the areas he should concentrate on improving. That third part is primarily designed for ministers; so if you're a layman or woman just skip that.

Meet Pastor Sanguine

You already know that sanguines are superextroverts with charisma to burn who can charm people into almost anything. Many such men answer the call of God for the gospel ministry and usually make good soul winners. If disciplined by the Holy Spirit, they can become great evangelists, pastors, or church builders. No one makes a better first impression than a sanguine, and he often has a powerful influence on thousands of people during his lifetime.

THE SANGUINE MINISTER'S PREACHING STYLE

A pastor's preaching style is usually the most important part of his ministry. Every week he must give a thirty- to fifty-minute sermon Sunday morning and evening, a Bible study on Wednesday, and possibly one or two more Bible studies during the week. Most of his public life is spent in the pulpit, so we shall examine this important part of his ministry in detail. You will find that most sanguine preachers are . . .

1. *Dynamic spellbinders.* Sanguines are articulate. Pastor Sanguine takes that gift with him into the pulpit each Sunday and captivates his congregation with his words. Usually he likes to preach on topics of current interest, depending on his training.

2. *Enthusiastic.* Pastor Sanguine's enthusiasm for the work of God or the subject he is preaching on is presented in a positive manner and his contagious spirit has an infectious effect on his congregation.

3. *Highly emotional.* The sanguine minister is a very emotional person, so don't think it strange that his sermons are full of emotion. People usually cry during his messages, and he is the one temperament most likely to weep during his own stories. He is so compassionate by nature that he is never far from tears. A supersanguine minister friend of mine began wiping away the tears from his eyes while telling me a story and said, "We sanguines are never far from tears. We can cry at laundry lists and telephone numbers." This temperament can be a blessing if it is natural and not overdone. While the sanguine and phlegmatic in the congregation may love that kind of preaching, cholerics and melancholies usually dislike it.

My pastor when I was a boy was a weeper. He could cry at the drop of a hat. I hated it. In fact, I can remember as a teenager saying, "When I preach I'll never do that," and unfortunately I haven't. In moderation, it can be a powerful tool for communicating the message of God's love and mercy.

4. *Fascinating storyteller.* No one can tell a story better than a sanguine; Pastor Sanguine can make a story live. He can make the characters of the Bible come to life and can punctuate any point with an interesting illustration. He does need to be careful not to take too much license with the text or the factual events. He also needs to be careful not to give so many details of a story about people whom his congregation may be familiar with, lest he embarrass someone who expected him to keep his problem confidential.

5. *Dramatic.* Sanguines are naturalborn actors; consequently he has a flair for the dramatic. His sermons will be punctuated by dramatized Bible stories. I shall never forget an evangelist who came to the summer camp where I heard the call of God for the gospel ministry. He dramatized the story of David and Goliath. One minute he was the giant standing fierce and tall challenging the soldiers of Israel. The next minute he was young David twirling his sling and trusting God. The next thing I knew he was the stone hurtling across the stage until it struck Goliath right in the middle of the forehead! Then suddenly he was the giant falling flat on his back, raising a cloud of dust from the old carpet in that tabernacle building. His dramatization really got exciting when he impersonated David taking the giant's sword and cutting off his head. Needless to say, I have never forgotten the story of David and Goliath!

6. *Extemporaneous.* Sanguines have a difficult time following a script. Some can't even stick to an outline. People tend to draw extemporaneous thought out of a sanguine. Unless you are an experienced public speaker you may not realize it, but facing an audience creates a powerful pressure on your mind. I find I do some of my most creative thinking in front of an audience. Some temperaments are so afraid of saying something wrong, they stifle this power until they can think it through carefully. Not the spontaneous sanguine. Whatever comes into his head usually comes out of his mouth. If he overshoots the field and says something in poor taste or inappropriate, his "helpmeet" will hopefully gather enough courage to straighten him out at home.

I have been on the platform with sanguine speakers who whispered, "I sure wish I could think of something to say" or "I haven't the slightest idea of what I'm going to say." But once they get started, you would never guess how ill-prepared they were. People have a way of drawing a message out of Pastor Sanguine.

7. *Charismatic evangelist.* Sanguines, more than any temperament, have the gift of evangelism. Very few evangelists do not have a high degree of sanguine temperament. I don't mean to minimize the work of the Holy Spirit and the necessity of his power in the conversion experience. But as a pastor for many years, I have had many evangelistic meetings in our church. Some call them "revivals," others "crusades," or a dozen other names. The thing that stands out most in my mind is the large number of people who "walked the aisle" when Evangelist Sanguine preached, but how few went on to become faithful servants of Christ.

We had one campaign that resulted in 167 decisions for Christ in eight days. Six months later I could only find twelve of those who came forward. Now don't get me wrong—the spiritual stimulus to the church was a blessing, and anytime you can reap twelve souls (plus whatever else is accomplished for God that we don't know about) it is well worth the investment of time, talent, and money. But I have noticed a lot of sanguine flesh in the so-called "results" that are tabulated. When, however, the Holy Spirit is at work, it doesn't matter what temperament the preacher is; people will find Christ.

POTENTIAL PREACHING WEAKNESSES OF PASTOR SANGUINE

We have already noticed that all temperaments have weaknesses, and so do preachers! Fortunately, no one has to be dominated by their temperament, and that includes ministers. That's what this book is all about. Consider the following weaknesses Preacher Sanguine must work on.

1. *Words! Words! Words!* Sanguines can use more words to describe nothing than anyone I know. Admittedly, they make it interesting—for awhile. Like the couple who left the sanguine pastor's congregation one morning. The wife said, "Oh, Pastor Sanguine, that was a marvelous sermon you preached today." Later on the way home the choleric husband asked, "So you liked the sermon today. What did he say?" The wife thought a moment and replied, "I'm not sure, but he certainly made it interesting!"

Most preachers confuse "preaching" and "teaching." The Old King James translation of the Scriptures usually translated certain passages as "Go into all the world and *preach* the gospel," giving rise to the notion that preaching was energetic, colorful, dramatic, and powerful. The sanguine can do all of that with words, whether or not he is filled with the Spirit, and many times at the expense of teaching the Word of God. Actually, the Greek word "preach" really means to teach or communicate the Word of God. It isn't stories, words, or human reason that lastingly convicts of sin. It is the teaching or communication of the Word of God to another individual or group empowered by the Holy Spirit that God uses to convict sinners and redeem men.

2. *Play on emotions.* It is a temptation to sanguines to use their ability to make people cry, or to play on the emotions of a crowd. As one minister said, "I drilled for water this morning and struck it." Being moved by the Holy Spirit may characterize itself by a convincing show of tears. But a person moved by a sanguine preacher can have the same experience.

In fairness to the sanguine, it must be noted that there is a valid place for emotion, particularly in things involving worship, repentance, and commitment. Oftentimes a sincere sanguine is accused of deliberately playing on people's emotions when in reality he may be extremely sincere and entirely led of the Holy Spirit. Just as sanguines need to be sure they are Spirit-led, some of the rest of us who are not so emotionally responsive need to be understanding with sanguines and recognize that theirs is a gift much needed by the church.

3. *Egotistical and self-exalting.* Sanguines don't have a corner on ego; we all have to fight the flesh or we will be overcome by it in one way or another. But sanguines have to be extremely careful lest they become so self-centered that they become obnoxious bores. The preacher who always tells personal stories that make him the hero or the center of attention wears thin rapidly. There is a fine line between the use of personal or third-person stories, and meaningful illustration. A personal illustration has enormous power, but it can be overdone. The test every sanguine should give his people is, Who gets the glory?

The ministry today is not conducive to humility. There is a lot of pastoral exaltation and adulation going to the pastor that, if taken personally, can turn a man's head. He may humbly mount the pulpit with the prayer that God will use his ministry in a wonderful way. After God sends the blessing, he may be tempted to take credit for what God has done.

Most cult leaders are sanguines who began believing their own press clippings. It is dangerous when a sanguine develops a messiah complex because he can usually get a following. A true man of God will draw people to Jesus, not himself. God will use him as a vessel, but the vessel should be careful never to confuse himself with who is the master and who is the servant. Pastor-Servant Sanguine can be a blessing to any congregation, and sooner or later his real attitude will "out."

3. *Exaggerates.* If he isn't careful, sanguine preachers can so "bend the truth" there is no relation between what really happened and the way he presents it. His treatment of events is never dull, but then his treatment may not be factual either—particularly if he preaches for applause. That is when he gives in to the temptation to embellish the truth. This can be a permanent turnoff to melancholy hearers. Jesus said, let your "yea be yea and your nay be nay," and the Apostle Paul said, "Speak the truth in love." A sanguine should live by the rule: if it isn't true, don't say it.

4. *Doesn't study.* Sanguines are so people-oriented, it is difficult for them to lock themselves up in a room and study. So when they go into the ministry, they have a tendency to let people-pressures that are more pleasurable to deal with take precedence over study habits. Consequently, for most sanguine ministers, Saturday night and Sunday morning are panic palace for them.

I know a minister who outlined his sermons eight years in advance. Obviously, he was not a sanguine. To most sanguines, the biggest problem they have each week is deciding on Tuesday, in time to put their sermon title in the church paper, what they will preach next Sunday. As one sanguine said, "How do I know what I'm preaching next Sunday? It isn't Saturday night!"

This difficulty in studying often makes Preacher Sanguine a short-termer. As an evangelist, he can get by with only ten or twelve sermons, provided he doesn't get invited back to the same church more than twice. But as a pastor, it only takes sixteen to twenty months for him to "run out of gas." That is, it takes him about that long to preach everything he learned in seminary or Bible school. Then it is time to move on to his next church. One denomination that I know that seems to attract a high percentage of sanguines has a pastoral mortality rate of about eighteen months. It is said that the average evangelistic pastor moves about every two and a half years.

One observation I have made is, great church builders are not short-termers. You may be able to build a great church in five to eight years, but if you do you will want to stay and enjoy it. And as we shall see, study is the key to longevity in most churches.

People don't go to church to be entertained. They can stay home and let the humanists who control the idiot-box entertain them. They go to church to learn the Word of God, but the pastor must study the Word to teach them something or they will soon quit coming.

5. *Repetition.* This last weakness of the sanguine which I will mention (and he has others) is based on the previous one. Unless he studies, he will have a tendency to repeat his sermons. Now I realize that repetition is an aid to learning, but there is a point where repetition becomes boring—and church attendance will prove it. Again, study is the key to fresh presentations.

Meet Pastor Choleric

Cholerics as we have seen are *SNLs*—that is, they are strong natural leaders. They seem to have energy to burn, a head full of ideas, goals, projects, and vision. They are drivers, pushers, and field generals. Most people find them to be interesting people, and some go into the ministry. One of the expressions in my lecture to preachers on this subject that gets the biggest laugh is, "You will find that the world's great generals, dictators, kings, leaders, gangsters, and some preachers are cholerics."

THE CHOLERIC MINISTER'S PREACHING STYLE

It rarely takes more than one sermon to betray the choleric temperament in a preacher; he just can't hide it. And as we shall see, this is the day of the choleric-pulpiteer. Here are some of his pulpit traits.

1. *Practical preacher/teacher.* Choleric preachers love to teach the Word of God. They may not be the most emotional people in the world, but once they see the need to teach the Word they have a compulsion to preach to anyone who will listen. The Apostle Paul is a classic example. He taught the Word in synagogues, amphitheaters, and even in jail where only his guard could hear. But wherever he found people, he was bent on teaching the Word.

Cholerics seem to have the hortatory gift. They are rarely guilty of teaching theology for theology's sake. They love to apply it to the lives of their audience. Paul's letters to the churches are much like that; they

start out with instruction in God's revelation of truth and end up teaching
the people how to live or apply God's revelation of truth to their
everyday lives.

2. *Compulsive communicator.* Cholerics are usually not the orators
that melancholies are or spellbinders like the sanguines. Instead, they are
communicators. They're so obsessed with communicating a practical
principle to live by or a life concept or a truth from God for today that
they give very little place to style. It is concepts they want their hearers
to get from their message. Whatever it takes to communicate concepts,
theology, or practical principles, they will do.

The first ministers I ever saw who used charts to preach the Word of
God were cholerics. It is not uncommon for them to use blackboards,
flipover charts, and graphs. The overhead projector is tailor-made for the
choleric. He readily accepts the educator's maxim that "you remember
10 percent of what you hear and 60 percent of what you see." So he
uses the overhead as if it was designed for him. While the melancholy is
afraid to use the overhead because he might not spell everything
perfectly and the sanguine can't be tied down by the visuals prepared in
advance, the phlegmatic just can't seem to get around to using one. But
the choleric thinks it is the finest educational tool ever invented. If
someone criticized his spelling or the fact he put too much on a visual,
he could care less. All he cares about is using it to communicate in ways
that people will remember. "Line upon line, precept upon precept, here
a little and there a little," is a way of life to this compulsive
communicator. Rarely do you attend his service without learning
something new from the Word of God that you can apply to your life.

3. *Positive and powerful.* One thing about choleric preachers is that
you never have to wonder what he is trying to say. He tells you the
same thing eight different ways and always with a positive emphasis. As
one choleric preacher told me, "You have to tell people the same thing
at least three times before they get it. I tell them what I'm going to say,
and then I teach it, then I tell them what I said."

They are so positive and enthusiastic of the gospel—you never
wonder what they believe about something. Melancholies may serve up
"smorgasbord theology"—that is, they may share with their audience
the five different interpretations of a passage. Not so the choleric; he
only gives one—his. His hearers are convinced that Christianity is not
just a popular way of life and salvation; it is the only way.

4. *Unemotional.* Cholerics, you may recall, only fluctuate about five

degrees emotionally each year. Their tear ducts are seldom, if ever, used; so they rarely "drill for water." Instead, they are more apt to use positive affirmation, pulpit pounding, and dogmatism in the pulpit to hammer home some truth than an emotionally moving story—unless someone shares with them the old truism that "logic makes people think, emotion makes people act." Once that principle burns its way into his head, the choleric is practical enough to make the observation that as a motivator of people, he has to use a little emotion; consequently he will learn to do so. But don't count on him ever becoming a sanguine storyteller, and don't watch for him to shed tears during a message.

That doesn't mean he doesn't *feel* the truths of God. Quite the contrary, his feelings run deep to the point of committing his life to Christ as long as he lives. And he preaches to accomplish the same thing in the lives of his hearers.

5. *Long, long sermons.* If you like "sermonettes from preacherettes" (in the words of Dr. Vance Havner), you won't enjoy Pastor Choleric's sermons. He isn't too much into music and worship; so when you go to his church expect to get a forty-five to seventy minute sermon. Take your pen and paper and take notes or you will miss something, but don't expect him to be brief. He thinks the truths of God are so essential to know that he takes ample time to preach them.

A humorous illustration of that happened to me one Sunday evening when I preached a Father's Day message. I've already confessed to being predominantly a choleric temperament. So you won't be too surprised when I say I had studied every message to fathers in the book of Proverbs, and tried to cram too much into one sermon. We had two locations for our church; so I preached my first message at 5:00 p.m. at Scott West and then sped out to Scott East where I preached the same sermon the second time. Somehow the clock was stopped at Scott East, and I had forgotten my watch. So I preached until I got tired. As I got into the car fully exhausted, my wife turned to me and asked, "Do you know how long you preached tonight?" I replied, "About fifty minutes to an hour." She said, "you spoke one hour and twenty-five minutes by my watch!"

The next night I picked up the Chairman of the Board of Trustees en route to our monthly meeting, and as he got into the car he said, "Pastor, do you know how long you preached last night?" "Yes," I replied. "My wife told me. But don't worry. Ralph. I've never preached as long as the Apostle Paul, who preached until a man fell out of the third-story window and killed himself." To which my friend replied,

"Pastor, when you can do what Paul did after that, then go ahead and preach that long." The perfect squelch for any choleric preacher!

6. *Practical illustrator.* Most cholerics need the advice of the great preacher, Charles Haddon Spurgeon, that sermons are like buildings— they need windows to let the light in. Illustrations are windows for conveying truth. But the choleric usually doesn't like canned or emotional success-story illustrations. He likes to use practical everyday life experiences to use as windows for his sermon buildings. One veteran choleric preacher told me, "if you use three life illustrations of real people, you will hit everyone in your audience at least once and sometimes twice." I think his point is well taken.

7. *Outspoken crusader.* Trafficking in unlived truth is not for the choleric. He is not content to preach against sin—he has to name it. He is more apt to speak out on the moral issues that are destroying our society than any of the other temperaments. His choleric voice is often raised against abortion, homosexuality, permissiveness, and other cultural expressions of secular humanism than any other temperament. That may be one reason choleric ministers are attracting larger crowds than other temperaments and why their churches are booming. People respond to a man of conviction who is not afraid to preach what he believes—so long as he can support his beliefs and prejudices by the Word of God.

But cholerics are seldom content to just speak out on the issues, they want to do something about them. It is often the choleric pastor who organizes other pastors to give a united voice in opposition to pornography, the violation of parental rights, and the humanists' usurption of the taxpayer's right to have his values taught to his children in our tax-supported public schools. If the church can produce enough choleric pastors for our country, it just may be that the humanist onslaught of destruction to the religious values of this nation before the twenty-first century may well be averted. Fortunately, the issues are becoming clearer and easier for people of every temperament to see. Hopefully, the Church of Jesus Christ, whatever its denomination, will wake up to the fact that we are the only army in the nation large enough to go to the ballot box and vote the humanists out of office and replace them with elected leaders committed to traditional moral values. The cholerics can't do it alone. They need the votes and the help of all the temperaments; together we can change the moral climate of our nation. We owe our children and our grandchildren at least that much. The next time you hear a choleric man speaking out on these issues, encourage him and volunteer to help him. It won't be hard. All we have to do is motivate the fifteen million unregistered Christians in this country to become registered, informed voters. Any temperament can do that.

POTENTIAL WEAKNESSES OF THE CHOLERIC PREACHER

It is almost impossible for a choleric minister to hide his potential preaching weaknesses. Like the sanguine preacher, he is an extrovert. Consequently, his weaknesses are given equal exposure with his strengths. His positive, contagious spirit can be a thing of beauty—if his potential weaknesses do not become dominant. Where choleric ministers have been successful over long years in the ministry, it is because they learned to overcome some of the following potential excesses or weaknesses.

1. *Bulldogmatic and opinionated.* You will rarely find a choleric who does not have a strong opinion on any subject of importance. He probably won't care what color curtains his wife hangs in their home, but you can be sure he has an opinion on anything that pertains to his church, denomination, city, and neighborhood that has a bearing on his ministry. This opinionism comes out strong in his preaching. Hopefully his opinions are not just the result of his intuitive prejudices, but are based on Scripture or biblical principles.

Everyone likes a minister who has strong convictions. The day of the wishy-washy minister is long gone. In the day of pending nuclear disaster, people want to hear a man share "what saith the Lord God." The problem is, cholerics are so dogmatic by nature that it is often hard to tell where God's message leaves off and the choleric pastor's misguided dogmatism begins. The pulpit itself is dogmatic. Cholerics make it even more so—which is fine as long as they are right. Their people need to test their teachings by the Word of God. But then, all believers should do this (1 John 4:1-4). If a choleric is a Spirit-controlled preacher, he won't mind having his teaching tested by God's Word. He knows it is necessary.

2. *Self-sufficient and cold.* Rarely will you hear a choleric minister let down his hair and reveal his needs, shortcomings, and failures—unless he is truly humbled by the ministry of the Holy Spirit. Instead, he is prone to exude a cold, self-sufficiency through his message. The response of one of the great evangelists of a past generation is typical of the choleric thinking pattern. He had been campaigning hard in his sermon against "demon rum." The pastor of one of the cooperating

churches said, "Brother, you're rubbing the fur the wrong way." To
which Billy Sunday said, "Then turn the cat around!" That illustrates the
mental attitude of most choleric speakers.

3. *Sarcastic, caustic, and often cruel.* No one can be more verbally
cruel than the choleric. And going into the ministry does not
automatically cure that problem. Instead, it often provides greater
exposure of his problem. When controlled by the Holy Spirit, he will
recognize this tendency and make sure his criticism is reserved for those
who violate the Word of God. Even then, his condemnation can come
across more cruel than God ever intended. Compassion, a fruit of the
Spirit, will offset this tendency.

4. *Crusading hobby horse.* The Apostle Paul said, "Let your
moderation be known to all men, the Lord is at hand." The choleric
preacher needs to recognize that in his preaching. As we have seen, he
is a crusader by nature and the easiest of all temperaments to motivate
to some form of activism. But you don't build a congregation's spiritual
life on a steady diet of opposition to the social and moral ills of our day.
While some ministers put their head in the sand and like an ostrich
refuse to get involved, the choleric tendency is to get too involved. His
commission is to preach the gospel, teach the Word, build up the saints,
etc.—and to "expose the unfruitful works of darkness." But balance is
needed.

Doubtless I was far from perfect in this area during my twenty-five
pastoral years in San Diego. I was often found opposing and exposing
the antibiblical ills of our day. But I tried to keep it in balance. The
thought that often sobered me into speaking out on the issues as only
part of my message was the realistic fact that on any given Sunday in an
audience of 2,500 or so people, there was bound to be someone there
for the first time who desperately needed Christ or spiritual food.
Sixteen million abortions is undoubtedly a sin that must be spoken
against by a true man of God. But the couple who just the night before
were confronted with the sin of infidelity in their marriage needs help—
as do the many other needy souls who attend the average church
service. There is a place for pulpit crusading, but rarely will it deserve
the major place in a message, and certainly not at the expense of a
suggested solution. Problem-solving is one of the fortes of the choleric
preacher. He needs to apply that gift to his crusading messages. I found
that five minutes of crusading every Sunday was better most of the time
than a whole sermon on the issues.

5. *Demagoguery.* The power of the pulpit can make a leader out of

anyone, because the preacher is a spokesman for God. To the choleric, this can become an opportunity for demagoguery. And it doesn't matter how much the traditions of the church and its stated beliefs oppose this practice; a preacher with a god complex can develop a congregational dependence on him instead of God.

The preacher, whatever his temperament, should never lose sight of the fact that he is an instrument in the hand of God. He is not the source of truth; he is its conduit. If he isn't careful, he can begin taking credit for the concepts, precepts, and revelation instead of humbly conveying the truth.

People have always had tendency to worship leaders. History is filled with their resultant tragedies. The choleric minister needs to carefully and consistently build his preaching and ministry on the Lord and his Word, not on the power of his own person and leadership. The true test of a man's ministry is not always how things go while he is there. The real test comes when he leaves. In his absence you will be able to tell whether he has built his people on the Lord or on himself. The ideal minister will find his successor building on the foundation which he has laid.

Meet Pastor Melancholy

The melancholy minister is most likely of all the temperaments to fulfill the academic requirements for the ministry. If a doctoral degree is the ideal in his denomination, that is his goal as soon as he feels the call of God to preach. Melancholies can't shortcut anything. Besides, he has the gifted intelligence to come to grips mentally with the most complex thinkers; he is creative and thorough. In fact, I have noticed the higher the academic requirements, the greater the number of melancholies that go into that field. Consider, for instance, the medical field. It is overwhelmingly populated by melancholies. I don't think you could get through medical school without a high degree of melancholy temperament, either as your primary temperament or your secondary one.

Many great pastors, preachers, theologians, and seminary professors have been melancholies, both in the Bible and throughout church history. Given an equal call of God to all four temperaments, it seems the melancholy temperament is more willing to respond to God than any of the other temperament types. And usually just earning a good income or being successful in life is not adequate for a melancholy; he wants to invest his life in something eternal.

I am reminded of the veteran missionary to China in the thirties who was approached by the Standard Oil Company to be their representative to that vast country. He knew the language and was acclimated but refused their offer. The oil company representative increased his financial offer four times, but the missionary still refused. Finally the man from Standard Oil said, "What's wrong? Is the salary too small?" "Oh no," replied the missionary with a laugh. "It's already three times more than I receive now. The problem is, the job is too small." I don't know if that missionary was a melancholy, but I do know missionary service is very appealing to melancholies and that is something a melancholy would do. When my wife and I ministered in 1977 in forty-two countries to one-sixth of the world's population of missionaries, we observed that a high percentage were of the melancholy temperament.

Another thing about the melancholy temperament—if he walks with God, he has an incredible capacity to commune with God. Now it is true that God can become personal to any of us, but it has been my experience in talking with melancholies that more of them seem to have a vital prayer life and are more faithful in having daily devotions than the other temperaments. This capacity for God may explain why all the prophets were melancholies. Name a prophet—any prophet—and you have just named a melancholy. From Elijah to Jeremiah to Jonah to Daniel and John the Baptist—all were melancholies. They were not all of the same intensity in their possession of the melancholy temperament, for some were more melancholy than others, but I cannot think of a prophet whose primary temperament was not melancholy. I cannot think of a single sanguine or choleric prophet.

The one problem with a melancholy temperament that may keep them from answering the call of God is their tendency to put themselves down—like melancholy Moses, who said, "Who am I that I should lead the children of Israel?" That is the patented melancholy response to the call of God. Once he gets beyond that to the fact that it is God working in us, not our own clever ways, he can have a productive lifetime ministry.

Now let's take a look at his preaching style. Most melancholy preachers will have some or all of these characteristics.

1. *Dramatic and moving.* Melancholies have a flair for the dramatic. They feel deeply themselves and move their audience with their depth of feeling. The things they preach have rich meaning to them, and they have the capacity to communicate that to their audience. Melancholy people often have the ability to be great actors. They seem to submerge themselves in a role or character and can impersonate other people. The melancholy preacher may subconsciously assume some role from his boyhood that for him has become the norm for the way a godly preacher of the Word conducts himself in the pulpit. I well remember my first visit to the Hollywood Presbyterian Church. After the worship of music and Scripture, the organist played a dramatic introduction, the spotlight came on, and the tall handsome minister dramatically walked to the steps that led to the pulpit. Every movement was dramatic. He reverently bowed his head for silent prayer, his hands held in a gripping pose of prayer. When he finally assumed the pulpit, he proceeded to deliver a masterful oration. The whole scene was dramatic.

One of the things I have noticed about some ministers perplexed me for many years—how could they act so sanguine on the platform and yet have so little personality off the platform? A real sanguine is an exuberant personality both on and off the platform. Preaching may intensify it, but he is just a bubbly person by nature. Not the melancholy who assumes the sanguine role for the pulpit. Finally it dawned on me what caused some men to appear outgoing and extrovertish in the pulpit, but introverts in real life. Somehow in their past they saw a sanguine in the pulpit and assumed that his style was the way a preacher preaches. So they made a habit of assuming the role of a sanguine in the pulpit. You can see how easily this could entrench itself in a youthful melancholy boy's heart and mind. If as a child he grew up in a church under a sanguine minister, that became his role model. Incidentally, that is not lack of sincerity—that is true sincerity. He wants to be the best preacher he can be, so he learns to preach according to what he thinks is the proper style.

I know two great preachers that make good examples. In the pulpit they are powerful, positive, and fiery. But once they step off the platform, they turn into personality pumpkins. Fortunately for both, they have wives who step in and take over the social graces necessary to life in the ministry.

2. *Great orators.* No one is a better pulpit orator than a melancholy. They have sharp memories and can quickly learn long portions of their sermons. One Baptist minister with a predominant melancholy

temperament visited our church and spoke to me afterward. He said, "I counted in your bulletin five different messages you will give this week. How do you find time to memorize so many sermons?" I blurted out, "I've never memorized a sermon in my life!" He couldn't believe it. To a melancholy preacher, words, phrases, and dramatic pauses are extremely important; that's his style. And his sermons are usually punctuated with poetry. He also loves poetry. Many melancholy preachers build to a dramatic climax in their oratorical message and cap it off with a beautiful poem that hammers home the truth they are trying to convey.

3. *Homiletical.* All preachers are influenced by their training and role models. But more than any others, the melancholy pastor will be addicted to a preaching form or homiletics. If he was taught that three points, six stories, and two poems make a good sermon, that becomes his style. All of his messages will be marked by method and planning. His preaching may look spontaneous, but rarely is it. His spontaneity usually comes to him in the quiet of his study.

4. *Creative.* The melancholy pastor is a creative thinker. That is important for the church member who has attended services faithfully for thirty years. The melancholy mind has the ability to present familiar truth in a unique and different manner every week. You will often find yourself impressed by the sermon quality of Pastor Melancholy.

5. *Stimulating mentally.* Most melancholy preachers are intellectually gifted and attract people of intelligence and education. His sermons make you think. He will never preach what I call "a teacup sermon"—shallow as a teacup. His sermons have substance and depth. He never comes to the pulpit unprepared—although personally he never feels his preparation is adequate. Left to his own choosing, he would study all the time. He has the capacity to lose himself in books.

If he is a biblical conservative, you will find him using much Scripture because his gifted memory helps him compare Scripture with Scripture. And he will probably love to use Old Testament stories to illustrate his message. As one melancholy preacher told me, "For me, the best preaching is to use the Old Testament as God's picturebook to illustrate New Testament truth."

6. *Theological and philosophical.* The complex analytical mind of the melancholy individual makes him a lover of philosophy. The world's great theologians—Calvin, Luther, Melancthon, Henry, Smith, and others—were predominantly melancholy temperaments. The melancholy mind sees more than the free gift of God's grace in John

3:16. He sees the sovereignty of God, his attributes, the fall of sinful man, and eternity. His most difficult task in sermonizing is to see the simple.

7. *Socially conscious.* No minister is more apt to get involved in the social problems of the day. He is one person who has a genuine concern for the poor. It is Pastor Melancholy who often calls the affluent church to task for remanding to the federal government through welfare, food stamps, and Social Security the responsibility of caring for the poor, the handicapped, and the elderly. His sermons will stir your conscience and make you evaluate your "true religion" in the light of biblical priorities.

The direction of his social consciousness will usually be the result of his theology. If he is a liberal, he may march or sit in or go on a hunger strike in behalf of racial rights, homosexual discrimination, social reform, or other evils he associates with a free enterprise system which he considers to be a cause of greed, selfishness, and social inequities.

If he is a conservative, he may campaign for "true godliness," "prayer and fasting for national repentance," "a moral revival," or preach against "the holocaust of abortion." He tends toward legalism, and any deviation from his denominational, theological, religious standards will become the target of his criticism. He is the voice that constantly calls us back to the place of true religion undefiled before God and man. He is a purist, and it comes out loud and clear in his sermons. His is a voice that is sorely needed in the modern pulpit.

POTENTIAL WEAKNESSES OF THE MELANCHOLY PREACHER

It would be ideal if I didn't have to bring up the weaknesses of this temperament, because he is usually critical enough of himself. He doesn't need someone else picking on him. Because of unrealistically high standards, most melancholy preachers never go to bed with a sense of well-being or accomplishment at a job well done or the feeling he preached a good sermon. Everyone in the church may have received a rich blessing from his message, but he is troubled by the point he omitted or the word he mispronounced. Not so with the sanguine preacher. He may have preached the world's worst sermon, but because during his twenty-five minute invitation ten people came forward, he goes to bed with a spirit of exhilaration. Pastor Melancholy often retires depressed because "I didn't do better." The following are some areas the melancholy minister needs to watch for to be the best tool for God that he can be.

1. *Too complex.* If any minister is prone to preach over the heads of

his congregation, it is Pastor Melancholy. He is a deep thinker himself and assumes that everyone else is. Melancholies are often very self-centered people; so they usually preach to their needs instead of those of their congregations. The melancholy's vocabulary is often too heavy for the carpenters and plumbers in his congregation, because he uses theological terms that only the theologically trained can understand. Academia will do that for you, and the melancholy, as we have seen, has a lust for higher education.

Dr. Henry Brandt, a Christian psychologist who has been a dear friend for years, told me this story. After backing into the counseling profession by counseling his work associates while an engineer at the Chrysler Corporation, he succumbed to the advice of others to go to school (Cornell University Graduate School). Between September and December he busied himself learning all the psychological jargon and vocabulary of his profession. (It's a form of educationese known only to the enlightened.) During the Christmas break he returned to Detroit and visited some of his friends at the factory. As he was leaving, one of them candidly said, "Henry, I don't know what they're teaching you at that university, but I can't understand you anymore." Dr. Brandt said he walked to his car thinking about his old friend's comment and made a lifetime decision. "Never again will I use a two-syllable word when a one-syllable word will suffice." That may be why Dr. Brandt never lacks for a hearing while many psychologists are still talking to each other.

Unfortunately, seminaries are like that, taught mostly by melancholy scholars who may give in to the temptation to try to impress their students by employing a complex vocabulary and thinking-pattern. Consequently, their students graduate with a vocabulary that sounds almost foreign to the congregation. Preaching is not just speaking; it must be understood by its hearers. One of my sons in the ministry asked me to attend chapel at his seminary where he and two other seminarians preached 10-minute sermons. I could not understand what these young men were saying. How could the untrained layman be expected to understand them? Such preaching does not build great churches.

2. *Theoretical and idealistic.* Theory is good—if it works. But the best theory in the world is worthless if it doesn't work. And idealistic theories can often be unrelated to life in the real world. Extolling the holy lives of Jeremiah, Daniel, Paul, and some others who were single and could give 100 percent of their time to serving God may not be a relevant illustration to use in challenging family heads to an everyday

standard of behavior, particularly when they have small children living at home.

One of the most popular things I have done to help families on a consistent basis has been the writing of a Daily Devotional Guide for our television audience. (For a free copy just write to me, Box 16000, San Diego, CA 92116.) In it I combine Saturday and Sunday, assuming that people attend worship on the Lord's day. Then I challenge them to use it either personally or with their family four or five of the six days a week. A melancholy pastor has a problem with that thought process. He knows *ideally* they should have devotions everyday. What he doesn't realize is that many people get discouraged by the perfect ideal and give up altogether. To the choleric pastor, even three days a week is better than none. That reasoning is hard for a melancholy to handle.

3. *Impractical.* Christianity is practical. In 2 Timothy 3:16 the Apostle Paul tells us: "All Scripture is God-breathed and is useful for teaching, rebuking, correcting and training in righteousness" (NIV). All scripture is "useful" or practical. God wrote his Bible not only to help people prepare for the next life but to live in this one. True Christianity will help you live a better life. That should be reflected in preaching.

At the risk of sounding like I'm picking on seminaries, which I'm not, I do want to point out that a greater emphasis needs to be placed on practicality. Theological validity is essential, but truth should affect the way we live; and the sermon that does not make better men, fathers, husbands, workers, and people is too impractical. Our seminaries need to be more practical in their preparation of future ministers.

4. *Too involved.* Details are important to the melancholy mind, but they may not be of interest to the average churchgoer. Pastor Melancholy has a difficult time resisting the temptation to prove everything he says with ten different reasons why his point is true. By the time he goes on to the next point, his congregation has lost the first one. As we shall see, he needs to develop the gift of simplicity. Someone has said of the melancholy preacher, "He can go down deeper, stay down longer, and come up drier than any preacher I know." Preachers like that don't have much of a congregation for very long.

5. *Legalistic.* Perfectionists usually have a problem with legalism. They find it difficult to preach mercy and grace, but love to preach judgment, repentance, and restitution. The obvious "thou shalt nots" of Scripture *are* the basis for moral values, but the melancholy is inclined to raise his thinking and his philosophical reasonings to the same level as

God's explicit commands and also tends to produce a lengthy list of do's and don'ts that are fundamental to his belief system. Such preaching puts people under bondage to the court of public opinion and makes their victory in Christ the result of what others think of them. When a Christian's first thought is, "What will people think?" he is a legalist. Our first thought should always be, "Does it please the Lord?"

Legalists often find it difficult to forgive and even more difficult to accept the forgiveness of God. "Love, joy, and peace," the fruit of the Spirit, are not the fruit of legalism.

6. *Pessimistic and negative.* Melancholies by nature are not born optimists. Quite contrary, they seem endowed with an ability to expect the worst in any given situation. Pastor Melancholy tends to take that pessimistic trait into the pulpit, and if not careful will present a negative message. He finds it easier to criticize the bad than to commend the good. This can have a demoralizing effect on a congregation. The tendency of most people is, "I'm a sinner anyway. There's no good in me, so what's the use—I'll just give in to my baser appetites."

Christianity is a positive message and offers hope to a dying world. For example, when my optimist friend Bill Bright was led of God to create the "Four Spiritual Laws" as an incredibly successful tool for personal soul-winning, he had to alter the time-honored pessimistic pattern of his day. Thirty years ago the soul-winning procedure we were taught began with the point, All have sinned and come short of the glory of God. Bill included that point in his four laws, but he saved it for point *two,* after he had confronted his hearer with the good news of the first spiritual law that "God loves you and has a wonderful plan for your life." Both points are essential, but by using God's love first, the message comes through positively, whereas the old message was negative and pessimistic at the outset. Yet both presentations are the gospel—it is all in the way it is presented.

This positive principle needs to be incorporated into the whole preaching style of the melancholy preacher. A diet of pessimism, negativism, and legalism is a self-defeating message that puts the individual in the congregation under a heavy pile of guilt. Admittedly there are times when we need to extol the holiness, justice, and magnitude of God. But God's love is a positive message and has created an attitude of hope within the child of God. Every sermon should hold out a message of hope to God's children.

Melancholy preachers have unlimited potential, and with the power of the Spirit of God in their lives they can be a rich source of blessing to the Kingdom of God. But they must resist all through their active ministry the temptation to give in to the above weaknesses.

Meet Pastor Phlegmatic

Phlegmatic people are not *usually* gifted public speakers. That does not mean that God cannot or has never used phlegmatics to pastor churches or serve in his vineyard. But it does suggest that it is the exception not the rule. We have already seen that Barnabas, one of the pastors of the church at Antioch, was a phlegmatic, as were Andrew, Philip, Bartholomew, Matthew, and others. Obviously God has used them in the past and will yet use them. I have known many phlegmatic pastors, for they have many traits that commend them to the ministry. And when filled with the Spirit they can be a significant tool in the hand of God for advancing his Kingdom. When called to preach, here are some of a phlegmatic's preaching styles.

1. *Calm and unexcited.* Don't expect the phlegmatic preacher to be dynamic and powerful. Rarely, if ever, does he pound the pulpit to drive home a point. He is not a "screamer" or a threatener; instead, he calmly and with logic presents his message. He is unexcitable by nature and often is not an exciting preacher unless he has good training and works hard on his delivery. Anyone can learn to use vocal force and body language to communicate a message about which he is truly enthused. But it takes training; it does not come naturally to Pastor Phlegmatic.

2. *Well organized and systematic.* The phlegmatic has a well-organized mind. That is why so many phlegmatics go into engineering, math, teaching, and accounting. This trait goes with him into the ministry and will provide a hallmark to his teaching and preaching. You can be sure he will not begin a point and flit off to another subject. Each point will be based on the initial premise and work toward a logical conclusion. While he will not convince you with emotion or rhetoric, he will attempt to convince you with logic.

Neither will he leave any dangling parts to his sermon; all are a part of the systematic whole. One observation I have made is he loves alliterated sermons. Phlegmatic preachers are not sure a sermon is inspired unless it is alliterated. One thing about their teaching—they won't talk you to death. They say what they want to and expect you to apply the point to your life. Rarely do phlegmatics preach long sermons.

3. *Quality Bible study.* Another observation I've made about phlegmatic Bible teachers is they give quality material. It may not be presented in the most inspiring or gripping manner, but it will be thorough. The average sanguine or choleric could make two forty-five-minute sermons out of one good thirty-minute message by Pastor Phlegmatic. If he can maintain their attention, this pastor has a congregation that knows its Bible.

4. *Dry humor and ready wit.* No one has a better sense of humor than a phlegmatic, unless it is a sanguine-phlegmatic. Both of these temperaments have a sense of humor, but phlegmatic temperaments by themselves don't often verbalize it. The ministry provides a phlegmatic ample opportunity to use his dry wit. He sees humor in almost any situation. Most of the great cartoonists are phlegmatics. It is a marvelous asset to a preacher to see humor, wherever it is appropriate. Humor helps people visualize truth and probably helps them remember it.

5. *A slave to notes.* The sermon notes of both the melancholy and the phlegmatic are usually good enough to publish. And because the phlegmatic lacks the gifted memory of the melancholy, he frequently resorts to reading his message. This is not bad if he will do three things: (1) Print big notes. Most phlegmatics write very small. Too small to read in the pulpit. It is a wise church that provides their phlegmatic pastor with a large print typewriter. It will be a great boost to his preaching. Otherwise, his congregation gets used to seeing only the top of his head as he becomes a slave to his notes. (2) Memorize the major points, poems and illustrations and only use your notes at these points for referral. (3) Familiarize yourself with the text you're going to read. It is a temptation to the phlegmatic preacher to assume his sermon is complete once it is written out on paper. That is only half true. The other 50 percent of his sermon preparation is practice on the delivery.

When a phlegmatic preaches a weak sermon, it is rarely due to inadequate study. It is because he failed to practice delivering it to its most interesting and compelling advantage.

A preacher who reads his sermon will invariably give a much more quality message than the man who speaks extemporaneously. But the extemporaneous speaker may convey more message than the man rigidly bound by superior notes. The difference is lack of attention. The best message in the world will not accomplish much unless the hearers are awake to receive it.

6. *Well substantiated.* The phlegmatic preacher finds it very difficult to make a point without thoroughly substantiating it to his hearers. In his

personal life, he is devoted to minutia and trivia. As a preacher he will have a strong tendency to do the same. He needs to explain some truth, but some just needs to be stated. If God said it, it is true. Pastor Phlegmatic needs to discern between what material needs to be included and where is the surrendering of his creativity to his self-indulgent inclination to explore trivia.

7. *Proper and noncontroversial.* What people think of him is very important to a phlegmatic. For that reason, he rarely embarrasses his congregation or engages in anything controversial. He "goes along" with his denomination and seldom speaks out against the social or moral ills of our day. He is not a fighter by nature, but a peacemaker. He and the melancholies are usually the first in line to campaign against nuclear disarmament. As one phlegmatic speaker (not a minister) said, "We must assume that the Russians will honor our gesture to disarm." It is totally impossible for a choleric to understand that kind of reasoning. He says, "How can we trust murderers who have destroyed millions of their own countrymen to treat us any differently?" The noncontroversial peacemaking phlegmatic sees the issues not as they are, but as he wishes them to be. This trait shows up in his preaching.

As a general rule, preachers who are predominantly phlegmatic with little or no sanguine or choleric temperament to go with it rarely build great churches. The reason is, phlegmatics do not usually make good preachers and good preaching is what builds great churches today. There are many places in the work of God where a phlegmatic's traits are valuable. Many make good pastors and are loved by their congregation. But unless they seek the Holy Spirit's filling for sufficient discipline to work on their procrastination and lack of forcefulness, they will not reach their potential.

Phlegmatic ministers make good associate pastors. They are loyal and dependable. They can become excellent counselors and are usually loved for their hospital visitation ministry. They function best when they have someone to whom they give account for their efforts on a regular basis.

THE WEAKNESSES OF THE PHLEGMATIC MINISTER'S PREACHING	Everyone should be evaluated in the light of his total person. It is really unfair to judge any minister in the light of his preaching style only. And in this book, I am not doing that. For we will evaluate each of the temperaments in the light of the two main phases of the minsitry,

preaching and pastoral duties. All ministers should be considered in both
areas. Incidentally, very few pastors shine in both these categories. The
average pastor usually shines in only one of them. As we shall see,
phlegmatic ministers have positive traits that are an asset to them in the
ministry, but preaching is not one of them—unless the Holy Spirit
chooses to do a very special job of temperament modification on him—
which, of course, can and has happened.

1. *Uninspiring, timid and punchless.* One of the chief weaknesses of a
phlegmatic preacher is that he is so timid in his presentation that he
lacks punch. He can make an incredibly powerful point in such a calm
and mild manner that its importance is all but overlooked by his hearers.
Such preaching obviously is not inspiring. To most people, if a minister
cannot get excited about what he is preaching, he will rarely excite his
congregation. That is not to say that phlegmatics do not have strong
convictions, they do indeed. But it rarely comes through in their
preaching style. If you examine his entire church service, you will find it
to be proper, orderly, the same every week—and colorless and
uninspiring. He doesn't like that any better than you do, but that's the
way he is.

2. *Unemotional.* Phlegmatics are very protective of their emotions,
particularly if they had their love rejected by a parent in their early
years. Such individuals come across as aloof or cold. That is a serious
negative in the pulpit. I am not saying that a phlegmatic minister should
pump up false emotions. What I am saying is that he should work
harder at exhibiting his true feelings when it is appropriate.

3. *Dry and uninteresting or light and humorous.* Phlegmatics can be
funnier than a rubber crutch. Most of the world's great stand-up comics
are phlegmatics. They excel at dry humor and ready wit. Phlegmatics
don't have to try to be humorous, they just are—if their inhibitions do
not stifle their spontaneous humor.

Pastor Phlegmatic takes this trait into the pulpit with him. Some will
overuse it to cover up their naturally dry and uninteresting style of
delivery. When it is used in conjunction with quality teaching, it can be a
great blessing, but the tendency of phlegmatics is to make people like
them or to please people. So if a young phlegmatic minister notices how
he can inject humor into his sermons to cover up his lack of emotion
and dry presentation, he may go heavy into humor at his peril.

There is a place for clean humor. I think God has a sense of humor.
Have you ever seen a little French poodle? Surely the poodle's designer
had a sense of humor. The problem is, teaching the revelation of God is

serious business. Not that humor cannot be injected in appropriate
spots. However, you cannot build a ministry on humor without
appearing light and frivolous. It is hard to take a comic seriously. And
when a pastor's humor is injected so frequently that his congregation
cannot take him seriously—both he and the church are in trouble. Like
anything else in the Christian life, moderation is the name of the game.
"Let your moderation be known to all men . . ." includes humor. A good
rule of thumb for any minister: It is appropriate to be known as having a
good sense of humor, but it is not acceptable for a minister to be
regarded as a comic.

However, the alternative is no solution for the phlegmatic pastor or he
will be so dry his congregation has a good "nodding acquaintance" with
him. Since I resigned from my church after twenty-five years to go into a
television ministry, I have a new appreciation for sermon listening. There
are times on Sunday mornings when the inclination to go back to sleep
is almost overpowering. Unless the minister's sermon is challenging and
inspiring, many hearers lose the battle and are overcome by heavy
eyelids. That does nothing for the parishioners or the preacher.

4. *Avoids issues.* We have already seen that phlegmatic ministers are
noncontroversial and lack punch. Consequently, he will often avoid the
issues. His congregation can be riddled with immorality, family
breakdown, worldliness and sin and he may announce a series of
messages on "the wilderness wanderings of the children of Israel." By
nature phlegmatics do not have the prophetic tone in their preaching
when the man of God cries out in condemnation at the wickedness of
the people of God. Melancholies are the prophet-preachers—John the
Baptist was typical. He raised his prophetic voice against the immorality
of King Herod even though it cost him his head—but that made no
difference. A melancholy preacher like John would do that if he knew
the cost in advance. Not so with the phlegmatic. He is such a
peacemaker he wouldn't name sin and demand Christian discipline for
fear of reprisal.

Unfortunately, there must be a lot of preachers who have more
phlegmatic temperament than they admit to because I have noticed that
many churches are extremely reluctant to invoke Christian discipline on
those who clearly violate God's standards of Christian behavior. I saw
that when our deacon board had to expel one of their own board
members from the membership of the church for leaving his wife to
marry another woman with whom he had fallen in love. After the
deacons' action I put the announcement in the church paper and was

criticized by some of my noncontroversial friends for "putting it on the front page" or "making the announcement too big." Condemning sin is never easy. But I have found that problems don't go away by themselves. If you don't deal with them when they are small, they will have to be dealt with when they are giants. It is hard for phlegmatic ministers to accept that.

5. *Unrelated to life.* Preaching should be relevant! The businessman needs good preaching to help him be a better Christian businessman. The housewife and mother needs to be challenged to the relevance of her role in life. The Word of God has much to say about such practical subjects, and preachers need to teach it. But phlegmatic ministers, much like their melancholy friends, have an absorbing interest in minutia. They can spend forever it seems, talking about something of no consequence. They can go to great lengths to describe trivia at the expense of the relevant.

Some phlegmatic ministers have a difficult time maintaining eye contact with their congregation. It is almost as if they are intimidated by their people. One phlegmatic pastor I know rarely looks at his congregation. He looks down at his notes, reads the Scripture, looks from side to side, glances at the floor, the ceiling, and the clock, but rarely looks at the people. Needless to say, he is presiding over a dying church. But such a practice cheats him out of preaching to real life people. When a pastor looks people straight in the eye, he is inspired by their needs, their hurts and their problems. God told the prophet Ezekiel, "Be not afraid of the faces of the people!" The phlegmatic minister needs to heed that advice because it is from the faces of the people that he gains the inspiration to preach to the needs of his flock.

CHAPTER
EIGHTEEN

Temperament and Pastoral Style

Preachers are a needy people, because they are human. We have seen that all temperaments go into the ministry, bringing both strengths and weaknesses with them. We have seen both of these demonstrated in their preaching style. Before we detail the needs of each of these pastoral temperaments, we should examine the other area of their ministry that is almost as important as their preaching. It is their pastoral ministry. You will find that those who inherited the best gifts for preaching may not have the best gifts for pastoring. Even at this stage of our study, it is good to point out that the God who calls such men to his work is more than adequate to outfit them for his ministry, whatever their temperament. But before we get into the resources available to ministers, we should explain their inherited pastoral traits according to their temperament.

It has been my observation that besides preaching there are six other important areas of pastoring a church. They are pastoral care, leadership, administration, counseling, social life and personal life. We shall examine each in the light of the pastor's predisposed temperament.

The Sanguine Pastor and His Pastoral Ministry

Sanguines are people-oriented people. For that reason, sanguine pastors often make good shepherds; they love the flock of God. It is easy for a sanguine to sincerely "weep with those that

weep and rejoice with those that do rejoice."
His contagious spirit infects his congregation,
which usually is effusively friendly.

The spirit of the man in the pulpit is often
reflected by the people in the congregation. He
is a hand-shaker and a back-slapper who
makes everyone feel at home. His people do
the same. It is almost impossible to attend his
church without feeling welcome.

1. *The pastoral care of the sanguine minister.* Sanguine pastors
genuinely care for the sheep of God. They usually have lots of energy;
so keeping up with the needs of a growing congregation is a challenge,
not a burden to them. They love hospital visitation; they are the only
temperament that wins the race with the stork to the hospital. A visit to
the sick by Pastor Sanguine is often more beneficial than a visit by the
patient's doctor, and Pastor Sanguine doesn't have medication to give.
As Solomon says, "A merry heart does a person good like a medicine."
Pastor Sanguine has a merry heart. His happy optimism can make
almost any patient feel better—as long as he is in the room. This man,
if he stays in the church any length of time, will eventually touch every
family in the church at a time of need. Long-term sanguine pastors are
usually the most loved by their people.

No one is a better funeral man than Pastor Sanguine. No other type
feels more at home in a funeral parlor than the sanguine. He weeps with
the grieving and comforts the broken-hearted. I once had a sanguine
associate pastor, the late Dr. Alan Smythe. Everyone loved him! And did
he ever shine in the funeral parlor. I always felt like I had three heads
and one hand at times of death. Not Alan. He moved right in—
comforting, encouraging, and lifting the spirits of the mourners. He
didn't have to try to be that way, and no one had to teach him; it was
natural. The morticians in our city would call Alan whenever they
needed a minister, which gave him lots of opportunities to preach the
gospel. Sanguines who walk with God make good pastors.

2. *Sanguine pastors as leaders.* Sanguines are too spontaneous to be
good leaders over the long haul. As we have seen, they look like such
good leaders in college they are voted "the man most likely to succeed."
But in my years at a Christian college three of the four sanguines we
elected failed in life. Sanguines just have a difficult time getting their act
together.

The sanguine pastor is forceful and often bluffs people into thinking

he is a good leader, but his inattention to detail will keep him from
succeeding unless some of the businessmen in the church who dearly
love him will take him on as a spiritual project to assist in his success.
They will do his long-range planning, of which he is incapable. They will
help with his staff selection because sanguines are very poor evaluators
of people—they love and want to hire everyone.

Without such a support group to hold up his hands and give strength
to his leadership, Pastor Sanguine is usually only good for a three to five
year ministry. Unless he is unusually gifted, his natural charisma can only
inspire a congregation to follow him just so long. It is difficult for his
people to follow as he launches new projects or campaigns when he has
a history of never finishing what he already has started. Sanguines can
be good front men, but by themselves they are not good leaders. The
trouble is, they think they are. Consequently, they won't accept help
even when it is offered.

3. *Sanguine administration.* A growing church is big business today.
When I left my congregation in 1981, we had a total minimum budget
for the church, college, school system, science center, retirement center,
and other related ministries of $10 million—and 337 employees. Just
the personnel selection eats up enormous amounts of time.

Sanguines are not born administrators! In fact, they are adminis-
trational disasters waiting to happen. They hate detail, can't keep
appointments, do not function according to plan, but respond to the
whim of the moment. They can't follow schedules and are all but fiscally
irresponsible. Most sanguines keep their church continually in debt. They
blame it on the Lord's leading, but in truth many times it is the result of
overspending and underplanning. If it weren't for the fact they are good
fund-raisers, many sanguines would be forced to take their church into
bankruptcy proceedings.

Growing debt doesn't seem to bother a sanguine. He can sleep at
night even though the ministry he heads may financially be like a
runaway truck going downhill without brakes. As I said earlier in the
book, "Sanguines never get ulcers; they give them to everyone else."
The sanguine minister's administrative policies often give ulcers to the
conscientious individuals associated with him. The sanguine pastor's
disorganized administrative style eventually brings him into conflict with
the sharp business types in his congregation. When he senses their
disapproval—particularly if they are board members—he knows he
must do something. His response is interesting. He invites them out for
coffee. He doesn't bring up the problems at hand; he just charms his

detractors, "fellowships" with them, and goes on his merry way thinking he has solved the problem. He has—for about three more weeks!

Never expect a sanguine to write you a letter. He is a telephone man, not a letter-writer. It isn't that he doesn't love you or doesn't think you are important; it's just that he can't be bothered with details like answering letters. Lack of discipline *can* influence everything in his life— unless he is filled with the Holy Spirit.

4. *Pastor Sanguine as a counselor.* All ministers do counseling, whether they are trained for it or not, or whether they are fitted for it by temperament. Sanguine pastors do not as a rule make good counselors—not because they don't love people, but because they are large-group-oriented. To them "all the world's a stage," and although they can function in front of a crowd of one, that is not their favorite pastime. Besides, to be a good counselor, you have to keep regular counseling hours, you have to be detailed in taking notes during an interview, you have to follow through and check up on the spiritual insights you give your counselee, and you have to listen long enough to diagnose the problem before giving your pearls of wisdom. All of these are next to impossible for an impatient, opinionated sanguine with a short interest span. It only takes him ninety seconds into an interview to size up the situation, decide who is at fault, and place the blame. Unfortunately, he is usually wrong. And if the counselee cries, he's gone. He is a sucker for tears and usually sheds some in return. Naturally to him the one who weeps is the innocent party.

Usually an hour interview with a sanguine counselor will consist of your talking five minutes while he talks fifty minutes or more. Everything you tell him reminds him of something that happened in his life or childhood. By the time your hour is up, you know more about him than he does about you. And he is such a people-person, it is difficult for him to confront people with the real cause of their difficulty even if he is successful in diagnosing it.

Sanguines mean well, and they sincerely want to help people. But counseling is not usually their best way of doing so, unless they have disciplined themselves sufficiently to get the proper training and learn the principles of God that people need to straighten out their lives. Generally he will not have the success in this phase of the ministry that he has in others.

5. *The sanguine pastor and the social life of the church.* A sanguine minister loves the social life of the church, and it is here where he really shines. Anywhere there are people and where he is at the center of

attention is exciting to him. He loves parties, meetings, or any excuse
for "fellowship." The fact that he may have to forfeit valuable study time
or administration time to attend a church social function never deters
him. He must go where the people are.

And his congregation usually loves him. He has that charming
capacity of looking into people's eyes and making them feel they are the
most important people in the world. He may not be a good counselor,
but he is certainly a good charmer; and in the impersonal cold age in
which we live, this is very important to many people.

Pastor Sanguine loves church dinners, fellowship suppers, potlucks, or
whatever they call them. He knows that if he can get the people
together where he can be with them, he can make most of them
happy—and he does. Being the master of the spontaneous speech, it is
a fun time that requires no preparation on his part, and yet he gets to
do the thing he does best—talk. And church picnics—that's where he
really shines. He is a happy man and tends to raise up a happy church.

There are a few dangers in the sanguine minister's style that can get
him into trouble as the church grows in numbers. If he shows too much
attention to the new people, he soon gets the reputation of "showing
favorites" or "not being interested in the old-time members of the
church." Sanguines are great baby kissers, and sometimes they get
careless about the ages of those babies. He is "a hugger" by nature, and
if he isn't careful he can get the reputation of being "a ladies' man."
When that happens, he will lose the confidence of many of the men in
his church. It is a wise pastor who cultivates a healthy love relationship
with his wife and makes it clear to his congregation that she is the
woman in his life. It keeps any unfulfilled women in the congregation
from making advances toward him, relaxes the husbands, and does a lot
for the self-image of his wife.

One of the most apparent areas of the church's social life that can
create an obvious problem for the sanguine pastor is eating. He loves
food, and church socials can collect the largest quantity of high-calorie
food on earth. Each lady tries to outdo her friends in preparing the most
delectable dish of high-calorie food that she can. And of course Pastor
Sanguine must sample something from every dish. So as the church
grows, he grows with it. Most sanguines have a weight problem. They
think it's "gland trouble," but it's not the glands that reach out for that
second helping of dessert. Sanguine preachers are often thirty pounds
overweight by the time they are thirty and gaining every year.

The social life of the church has been a headache ever since the days of the early church when in Acts 6 some thought certain widows were being overlooked when the food was passed out. But I don't know how to solve the problem. You can't stop social activities completely; Christians need fellowship, and we certainly don't need to leave it only to the world to provide this necessary need in their lives. But we do have to be careful that the tail doesn't wag the dog and let the social life of the church be number one. No good church has ever been built just on a strong social life.

6. *Pastor Sanguine's personal life.* Now we are really going to get into trouble with our sanguine minister friends. But it is my intent to balance the scales by writing a similar section on each of the other three temperaments. You cannot separate a person's personal life from his ministry life, because first and foremost a man of God should be "an example to the believers." Admittedly he is human, but God expects pastors and Christian workers to be examples of what they teach. I have found you cannot teach one thing and preach another without losing your self-respect. The minister who has lost that is on a slippery path that makes mounting the pulpit a very difficult task.

It's hard to know where to begin on the personal life of this lovable, friendly, outgoing minister with the contagious sanguine spirit. Everything he does is so apparent, it is impossible to overlook him. And as you read this portion, bear in mind that no sanguine is entirely like the one I am describing. This one is a composite of all the weaknesses of many sanguine ministers whom I have observed through the years. And both his background and training can have a powerful influence on his pastoral style.

By nature, sanguines live a flamboyant life-style that is difficult to support on a minister's salary; consequently he is always in debt. He has absolutely no sales resistance and wants everything whether he needs it or not. Credit buying is tailor-made for the sanguine who really needs to adopt the policy that except for a home and car he will pay cash for everything. This would be a help to any temperament. This weakness for things has ruined many a sanguine preacher. He is forced to "moonlight" or create other ways of increasing his income that are not always in the best interest of his church; or even worse, he just may not pay his bills.

One significant area of their personal lives that all sanguines need to be extremely watchful about is their morals. Nothing will wipe a minister out of the ministry faster than a moral breakdown, and rightly so. He should be exemplary in every area. But he has several problems others do not experience to the same degree. Because he is a representative of God who teaches others about spiritual matters, many good women tend to let down their guard around a minister. Most women know that in all dealings with men they must be the policeman of their relationship. It shouldn't be that way, but it is. But to her minister she defers this policing responsibility because she regards him as her spiritual leader. This could be dangerous to them both and to the entire church. Even the best sanguine minister is still a man. He should never permit himself to get into a compromising or tempting situation.

If good women are a temptation, what about the not-so-good? Even in church there can come a psychologically dependent woman who hero-worships the man in the pulpit and then consciously or subconsciously decides to seduce him. Or she may just fantasize about him, and this can have the same effect on her conduct. When such a woman comes in for counseling, Pastor Sanguine is usually unsuspecting. Being an "emoter" by nature, he emotes concern, compassion, and Christian love. Either purposely or unconsciously, the counselee begins to emote a response and the emotional magnetism begins.

Through the years I have only had a very few dealings with the moral transgressions of ministers. Fortunately, it isn't as common as one would think among sanguines. But even one surrender to this sin is too many, and I include it here because sanguines are more vulnerable than others, and because whenever it occurs it is a tragedy.

Another area of his personal life that a sanguine minister can lose his testimony over is gossip. Sanguines tend to love dirt or confidential information and can gain the reputation of breaking confidences. This can be fatal to his counseling ministry. I have actually heard church members say, "I would never go to our pastor for counseling for fear that our story would be exposed in a sermon illustration to the whole church or that he would tell others about it." No wonder many Christians go to secular counselors for help. Who wants their secret to become a major concern in the church?

Still another personal area where Pastor Sanguine can ruin his ministry is his temper. While he may never carry a grudge once he has exploded over a matter, his explosion does nothing for his testimony. Admittedly, there are many frustrations to his job. But churches aren't unique; any organization that has people in it is capable of producing frustration. The sanguine pastor who "gets livid with rage" and "blows his top" will soon be looking for another church, no matter how good a preacher he is.

The last personal area we shall consider is the pastor's family. It is here that the real man stands up. If he does not walk in the Spirit at home, he can eventually lose everything. His fun-loving, carefree, energetic ways can endear him to his children, as long as he hasn't spent himself so much in his work he has nothing left for his children. And his ego may not be conducive to cementing a lasting love relationship with his wife. It is tempting for him to bask in the adoration of a loving congregation that doesn't really know him and draw the cold look of criticism to the eye of his melancholy wife who does. (As we saw in our chapter on opposites attracting each other, sanguines often marry melancholies who can be very critical.) This spirit can contribute to his feeling "more comfortable" away from home than with his family and may be a subconscious reason he tends to neglect his family for his church.

Pastor Sanguine can be a very successful and effective minister. No one is better endowed with the ability to communicate the Word of God. However, no person is made up only of strengths. And unless he lets the Spirit of God modify his weaknesses, he will never live up to his potential.

Sanguine ministers, just like the other three temperaments, have many needs, all of which God has more than ample resources to meet. After we have examined the pastoral duties of the others, we shall look into those of the sanguine.

The Choleric Pastor and His Pastoral Ministry

Cholerics are the hard-driving, goal-oriented, activist temperaments. A choleric pastor brings all of that drive and a pile of weaknesses into the ministry with him. As a rule, his congregation admires and respects him while at the same time fears him. He is not known for indulging incompetence in himself or anyone else and is a tireless motivator of people. His congregation is never without campaigns, projects, or goals. As one choleric minister advised me when I was a young man, "Always keep a project going for your people. The minute you don't have them working on a project *you* become their project." There is little danger of that happening to the choleric pastor, for his life is a continual project.

If he grew up in a strong evangelistic church or went to a seminary that was, he will have a continual evangelism program going in his congregation. He knows that one way to build a church is to get at least 10 percent of his members effectively sharing their faith and winning souls. All visitors to his church are called on within a week or ten days, and he trains his people to get visitors signed up as members.

1. *Pastoral care.* Choleric ministers are not good pastors personally, although their organizational and leadership ability usually provides good pastoring of the flock by the members themselves. He won't tolerate "deacons who won't deac." He trains them and puts them up in shepherding groups assigning a reasonable number for each deacon to shepherd. But personally he is so cold that those in greatest need are afraid to approach him. They fear he is so "together" that he could not relate to those who have difficulties or problems they can't cope with. And cholerics, unless touched by the Spirit of God, do not emote a sense of compassion.

This does not mean that he doesn't care for the needs of his people, but his reaction is to organize something to solve it. He delegates responsibility, and that includes pastoral care. He is not the world's most sensitive person, so hospital visitation is not his forte. He does it because it is expected of him, but he doesn't really enjoy it because he doesn't feel comfortable in the sick room or the funeral parlor. If he had the power, he would "heal them all" the way our Lord did so he could get back to his work.

He soon burns out on baptisms and weddings, and tries to delegate these to other staff members. Baby dedications are hard for a pure choleric minister because that is one time when he is not in control of the situation—babies are unpredictable. Besides, I wonder sometimes if they don't catch his gruff manner, and it makes them cry.

In fairness to the choleric pastor, he will protect the spiritual life of the congregation better than any other. If he finds a Sunday school teacher dabbling in error, he doesn't wait for boards and committees to solve the problem—he does. That teacher receives walking papers today! If immorality creeps into the congregation, he calls on the individuals and confronts them with their sin. He usually gives them two options: "Repent here and now, or be expelled publicly from the church." I know one crafty sinner who knew what would happen if he left his wife. So he conned her into transferring their membership to another church and then, when safely out of the control of his choleric pastor, he left her. That, however, did not keep his former pastor from contacting his new minister and telling him what he should do with the man.

Choleric ministers do care for their people, but they provide public opportunities for them to grow, including classes, Bible studies, daily devotional materials, books, and other helps. But they are weak on personally touching the lives of the people.

2. *Leadership*. No one is a stronger leader than a choleric. That's why business calls them S.N.L.—"Strong Natural Leader." So when an S.N.L. is called into the ministry, he will take that leadership ability into the church. His favorite verse in this connection is Peter's command to "shepherds or elders" to take the "the oversight" of the flock of God. Be sure of this—he will be the overseer. And he loves the words of Paul that a good pastor is one who "rules well." So he rules in the name of the Lord, forgetting that even if the Lord hadn't said it, he would rule because he is a ruler.

The danger in exercising this gift is that a carnal choleric pastor can become very dictatorial. He knows that the most effective form of government is a dictatorship, and he loves that kind of efficiency. This can be a detriment in the selection of a staff, for he may indulge the choleric tendency to select people he can dominate. He not only surrounds himself with less competent people than he needs, but he tends to stifle their creativity. The best leader is one who appreciates talent in other people and gives them the freedom (within specified limits) to express their creativity. Every choleric will have his own version of those specified limits.

The problem with dictator-pastors is that they drive away potential leaders and limit the creative potential of the church to one person. This soon leads to a stereotyped church. Unfortunately, some choleric ministers are so incredibly gifted intellectually they can get by with it. But imitators, beware! I know one choleric minister who gives seminars and conferences to pastors on how to build a great church and uses himself as an example. Because it works for him, many young men go home and try to follow his dictatorial ways and get booted out of their church. What these men didn't realize was that it was his incredibly good preaching that built his church, not his dictatorial practices. His church grew in spite of his dictatorship.

The test of a good leader is whether he is also a good follower. Sooner or later we all have to follow someone. A good leader will at times accept and follow other people's suggestions. The ministry is so complex today that no one person has all the answers. A good leader recognizes that to be successful he needs to listen to and cooperate with other people. A demagogic-dictator type doesn't believe that.

The choleric minister's ability to motivate people can make him a real slavedriver. If he isn't careful, he will soon learn who the potential workers are in his church and so overassign them to his endless projects that they have no time for their family, career, or anything else. That is when Christian service ceases to be enjoyable and becomes church work.

Some of the success of the choleric pastor today is that he knows where he is going and what he wants to accomplish and has the ability to translate that vision to his people to motivate them. That is good leadership, and God is using that kind of man to advance the Kingdom of God in the twentieth century.

3. *Choleric pastors and administrators.* The choleric minister is usually a good administrator, particularly if he has the proper management training. Unfortunately, it has only been in the past few years that seminaries have included this in their curriculum. Perhaps one of the reasons that some of the largest churches in the country today are headed by a choleric pastor is because he would be the best able to cope with the process of administrating the church without proper management training. And today's growing church requires an enormous amount of administration.

Cholerics are not perfectionists, and for some administrators that can be an advantage, particularly if he has a few perfectionists working under him. His forte in administration is that he has a real knack at selecting the priority tasks to spend his time on. Cholerics, like everyone else, only have twenty-four hours in a day. Although they like people to think they work long and hard, they are not always the hardest working types. They do, however, have a knack for concentrating on the priority items of life, while perfectionists spend their time perfecting the unnecessary or at least the less important.

One success motivation speaker coined the phrase, "from production to perfection—you never go from perfection to production." It is easier for a choleric to follow that advice than others. He conceives a project, launches it before it is really ready, and then tries to improve it as he goes. I often think of that in the light of the twelve different Christian organizations I have founded while pastoring churches. In 1965, I became burdened to start a Christian high school. I decided in March it was time to do it. We planned it in the spring, the church voted on it in July, we advertised it in August, and started it in September. Today it is a school system of ten schools, including two accredited high schools that are probably the largest of their kind in the country. The same thing happened in 1970 when we started Christian Heritage College. We conceived it in January, planned it in May, launched it in July, and opened for classes in September. Today we have over five hundred students. Admittedly, had we waited another year we would have been much better prepared for classes; but on the other hand, we might have had more time to study the potential problems we would encounter and be afraid to start at all. Fortunately for me, God led some very able people my way to pick up loose balls and bouncing details to make my enterprises successful, so I could go off and start something else.

All choleric ministers need a superb secretary and as soon as the church is large enough to afford it, they should hire an associate pastor to help pick up the details Pastor Choleric creates with his many projects. One thing about his staff: they should all be more perfectionistic than he!

One of the questions I have been asked about choleric managers (and pastors would fall into that category) is, "Are they good at delegating some of their tasks to other people?" I have studied that considerably and have come to two conclusions: (1) Delegation is an art that must be learned either by training or experience; (2) his secondary temperament will determine how difficult it is for him to learn. The easiest temperament combination to learn to delegate is the ChlorSan pastor. He has enough of the people-orientation of the sanguine to enjoy their success. The ChlorSan pastor feels that part of his calling from God is to be a Christian entrepreneur who creates opportunities for other Christians to serve the Lord. He delights in turning his projects over to other people once he gets them started. He is one of the first to learn that "you get more done by working through other people."

The ChlorPhleg pastor is a very efficient administrator, but he finds it more difficult to learn delegation. It usually takes the pressure of unfinished assignments to reluctantly turn over some of his duties to others. And when he does, he will be a careful "checker-upper." On the other hand, there are very few loose ends in the projects he launches.

The ChlorMel pastor finds delegation extremely difficult. He enjoys the work he is doing and is certain no one else will do it the way he would. As we shall see, melancholies find it all but impossible to delegate because they are such perfectionists. Some of that afflicts the ChlorMel pastor.

One of my dear friends heads one of the largest missionary ministries in the world. If I mentioned his name you would recognize him immediately. At a time when he was experiencing administrative overload because his growing organization had reached a level that required some restructuring of his ministry, he hired two Christian management experts to study all that he was involved in and advise him what he should do to solve the problem. After interviewing all his department heads and studying his work carefully, they asked for an interview with my friend and said, "Experts have found that the largest number of people a manager can successfully have answering directly to him is nine. Most of your problem is that you have twenty-three people answering to you." To which he characteristically replied, "You don't understand; I am an exception!" Today he probably has thirty-three people answering to him. He is an incredible person—who will probably die early in life. He is a workaholic, or he would never get all he does accomplished. ChlorMel temperaments are like that.

4. *The choleric pastor as a counselor.* It is impossible to stereotype the counseling ability or style of the choleric minister. Much will depend on his training and experiences in the early formative stages of his ministry.

Some choleric ministers are so impatient that they refuse to do counseling at all and prefer to hire a specialist to be the full-time pastoral counselor. One famous choleric pastor was asked the question at a pastor's seminar, "With all you have going on, how do you ever get time to counsel your huge congregation?" He responded, "I don't counsel people. If they want to talk to me, they can come up after the evening service and I'll counsel them for a couple of minutes." Unless he knows some tricks I have never heard of, that won't do it for most churches. And it certainly won't help people when they are hurting.

Actually the choleric minister can learn to be a good counselor if he works at it. He has a practical outlook on life and can usually see through the clutter in a counselee's thinking and get right to the heart of the problem. But he is sometimes so analytical that he gets off on an endless series of rabbit trails that lead to nowhere.

One of his problems is that his mind wanders during the interview. His head is filled with goals, objectives, and projects, and whenever the counseling appointment comes it is at an inopportune time because there are eighty-nine other things he should be doing. Consequently, he has to fight the tendency of his mind to wander off to his unfinished work as the counselee shares his burden. I have found that taking notes during the interview is a great help in sharpening concentration.

Another problem he may have is impatience. Cholerics usually have their life "together" and can't understand why others don't. He tends to evaluate others in the light of himself. That can be a serious flaw. He is decisive and can't understand why others aren't. He can usually size up problems quickly and finds it difficult to wrestle with endless objectives. But if he learns patience and is willing to hear people out, he can do them a lot of good.

He also has a tendency to be intolerant of weakness and is turned off by tears. If he isn't careful, he can be quite dictatorial. Those who don't follow his advice are not welcomed back.

One of the good features of the choleric counseling minister is that he, more than the other temperaments, is apt to give spiritual assignments to a counselee. That speeds the cure. He assigns Scripture reading, memorization, church attendance, book reading, and cassette listening. And he has the strength to insist they do it before their next interview. This part of his counseling ministry can be very productive in effecting the desired change in a person's behavior and attitude.

5. *The choleric minister and the social life of the church.* To a choleric minister, the social life of the church is a necessary evil that must have some purpose or he is not interested in it. Personally he doesn't need fellowship with other people and may not see the need of it for others. After arriving at his church, he may not catch the original purpose of some group and work to kill it after arriving, either because it has left its original purpose or he disagrees with it. When he starts a social activity, he always finds someone to handle the details and attaches some spiritual significance to it. The dinner or event must either be to win the lost, train soul-winners, get new people acquainted with the church so they can become members, or raise money. Meetings without a purpose are an anathema to him. Unless they have objectives, he will not show up; or if he does, it will be because it provides an opportunity to promote some project he's working on.

One choleric pastor I know launched a very successful dinner program for his church which resulted in hundreds of people coming to Christ. The condition for attendance was that you had to invite at least one unsaved person to sit at your table. Not only were many strangers introduced to that church for the first time, but every unsaved man married to a Christian wife who attended that church got a personal invitation. Another minister I know uses such a dinner at Christmas time each year to raise over $100,000 for the church's education ministries.

6. *The personal life of the choleric pastor.* The personal spiritual life of any minister is going to have a vital influence on his ministry. The key to that life is his devotional practice, including regular Bible study and prayer. Cholerics are often strong on Bible study but weak on prayer. They believe in it, but it takes too much time out of their busy schedule.

Besides, every time they get down to pray, their overactive brain
conjures up all kinds of activities. With many cholerics, their prayer life
is little more than planning their day's activities. Or they may adopt
the policy of praying for the big things in their life and ministry and
planning the routine things themselves. As one choleric minister said
to another, "Why pray about that? It makes sense so just go ahead and
do it."

Emotionally, cholerics have a problem with anger. I've made that clear
in this and in other books on temperament. He can flash up almost as
fast as a sanguine; but unlike the sanguine, he seldom forgives and
almost never forgets an insult, injury, or rejection. He will clash with the
strong-willed members of the congregation and use his anger to whip
people into line. He is particularly vulnerable to choleric women in the
church who try to boss him. If you want to watch sparks fly, just keep
an eye on the choleric minister who is called to a new church where a
strong-willed choleric woman has "ruled the roost" for years. No church
has room for two dominant leaders, and he has the notion that he's paid
to dominate. She will be the first person in the congregation to turn
against the new minister.

Morally speaking, most choleric ministers live a straight-arrow life.
They keep their commitments, and that includes their wedding vows.
One advantage they have over the charming sanguine minister is that
the women of the congregation are often afraid of them rather than
physically attracted to them. Another advantage they have is they are
not "touchers" by nature, and that particularly includes the women in
the congregation. When, however, a choleric minister does go off the
deep end morally and commits adultery, it has been my observation he
will try to justify it. Either his wife "is cold and not interested in sex," or
he blames the pressures of the ministry, or like one man I know actually
blame's "the woman's husband." But I am happy to say such choleric
ministers are in the minority. The overwhelming number of choleric
ministers I know, and I know many, live a godly life. They aren't perfect
by a long ways, but they love the Lord, love serving him, and enjoy
their work so much they wouldn't do anything to jeopardize it.

The medium-sized church can't possibly offer the average choleric
minister enough challenge to command his attention full-time. For that
reason, he will invest his energies in outside activities. To him, "the field
is the world" and anything he can conceive for the Lord should be done
using the local church as his base. That's why he usually has eighty-nine
irons in the fire at the same time. Most of these are church-related or at
least Christian enterprises.

I will never forget the entrepreneurial choleric minister who picked me up at the airport one day. As we sped across town he said, "I want to stop by my travel agency on the way to the church." I assumed he meant by that what I mean. My travel agent is the lady who books my flying schedules. Not him! He owned the agency. Later I discovered he had six other corporations—all church-related—a construction company to build churches, an architectural firm for the same purpose, a church loan institution, and others. And he had the most flourishing church in town! When I asked how his travel agency related to the church, he replied, "I take a lot of trips to minister to missionaries, and the agency provides my travel free." Who but a choleric would think that way?

The most underdeveloped part of a choleric minister's life is his family life. He is a perennial workaholic whose church activities provide him the excuse to indulge his first love—work, and usually at the expense of his family. It doesn't take him long to intimidate his wife into silence and often into frigidity as a means of retaliation for his constant domination and absence. Most extrovert choleric ministers marry introvert fearful wives. Consequently, he tends to lose himself in his work while she invests herself in the home and children. Unless he learns something about the Spirit-filled life, they often are lonely strangers by the time their children graduate from the home.

It is not uncommon for a choleric's children to hate their father's profession—whatever it is—because it robs them of the father they should have had. That is the main reason such a small number of young people take up their father's chosen profession as their own today. This also includes the ministry, unless the young person has a deeply moving spiritual experience that renders him open to the call of God. Choleric fathers tend to be overdominant without the necessary love their children need to compensate for it, which tends to create rebellion in their hearts, first at their father and then at God. Unless he is Spirit-led at home, this can have a serious effect on his family life.

Even vacations do not give the choleric pastor pleasure. As a rule he doesn't like them but combines them with speaking opportunities. His idea of a month's vacation (if he will ever agree to take one) is two summer Bible conferences, three weekend church meetings, and a trip by car of six thousand miles. He usually brings his family home from vacation so worn out, they need a vacation to recuperate from their vacation.

The external part of a choleric minister's family life will rarely cause his church alarm. It is what goes on behind closed doors that *can be* dangerous. Fortunately, all ministers are different—even those of identical temperament. Like every other temperament, if he walks in the Spirit his family life will be a blessing to each family member. And usually he is blessed with a gentle loving wife who is a super mom who learns to put up with him for the Lord's sake.

The Melancholy Pastor and His Pastoral Ministry

Melancholies are more than gifted and creative; they have a compulsion to serve others, particularly if they have been released by the Holy Spirit from their self-contemplation. They are sensitive to the Spirit of God and, as we have seen, need a cause greater than themselves in which they can invest themselves for life. The call to pastor is usually a lifetime mission into which they plunge their total being. They can submerge their rich temperament into the ministry of advancing the Kingdom of God to such an extent that it is hard to separate the melancholy pastor and his ministry. To him the ministry is his very life.

1. *His pastoral care ministry.* If you wanted a role model of the ideal pastor who calls on the sick, comforts the broken-hearted, and yearns for the lost, it will be Pastor Melancholy. He is such a consistent visitor at the local hospital that all the administrators recognize him. He is deeply moved by the suffering souls of his congregation and has a special way of comforting them through the Word of God and prayer. There is something about seeing a church member lying helplessly on his back that draws out his sympathy and concern to such a degree that he reaches out to and touches them in their hours of despair.

He is a good funeral man—not as effusive and contagious as the sanguine and will never talk too much. He knows intuitively that you don't have to carry on a useless line of chatter to comfort people. He just senses that being there when people hurt communicates he cares. And he really does. He willingly sacrifices his personal time, vacation, and family to minister to the needy.

His church services are heavy with worship. He likes well-structured services, formal calls to worship, music interludes (Bach, Beethoven, and other seventeenth-century musicians). He has a great flair for the aesthetic. His services start promptly and end on time. Choir anthems, formal attire, and atmosphere are usually important to him. Rarely will he surrender his pulpit to another speaker for fear he will not adequately care for the needs of his people.

2. *His leadership style.* Unless his secondary temperament is choleric or he has had proper training, the melancholy pastor does not usually make a good leader. He is too easily defeated by the disapproval of other people. What the people in the church think of him is much too important to him to buck them when they resist his leadership—even when he is led of God and knows in his heart that what he is trying to do is for the good of the church. He needs to learn that "the door of opportunity always swings on the hinges of opposition" and that there will always be someone around to willingly offer the opposition. They are not naturally born strong leaders.

Having said that, it should also be pointed out that melancholy ministers can at times rise to the challenge of greatness if it is necessary to advance the Kingdom of God. They are a paradox, much like the melancholy prophet Elijah who did not shirk from publicly taking on all the prophets of Baal in the name of God but later shrank away from the wicked Queen Jezebel who hated him. (I'm not sure whether or not that suggests that the disapproval of women is more significant to him than that of men.)

One melancholy pastor I know, a great Bible teacher, has successfully pastored the same church for over twenty-five years. When he was called to the church, he knew of its history of splits and angry business meetings. He had heard stories of members shaking their fists in each other's faces. So he prayed earnestly, accepted the call, and while conducting the first business meeting made one thing clear at the outset. He said, "As moderator of this meeting and as pastor of this church, I know you want me to keep you from grieving the Holy Spirit of God. So if anyone speaks angrily in this meeting, I will be forced to adjourn the meeting until next month at this time when we will resume our business." It took four months for that church to catch on that he was serious. Finally he convinced them that even church business could be settled in the Spirit. It literally transformed the life of that old dying church and today it is one of the leading congregations in that denomination.

Delegation is the bugaboo that often limits the great potential of a melancholy minister. As we have seen, he is very reluctant to delegate to others that which he feels is his responsibility. As the ministry grows, there are increasing demands on his time; so he works harder rather

than allowing other trusted individuals to help him. Two of the reasons
delegation is difficult for him is because he is a perfectionist and is afraid
others won't do the work right and because he is afraid someone else
might steal the affection of his people.

Moses, as you may recall, had no small problem with this in the
wilderness. Long lines of people were coming to him, waiting for him to
adjudicate matters of civil justice. He was continually exhausted and
could get nothing else accomplished. That is when Jethro, his father-in-
law, came on the scene and suggested that he appoint seventy elders to
hear the people's grievances. Obviously the seventy were more help
than he could ever be, but it was hard for melancholy Moses to accept
that. And so it is with Pastor Melancholy. He has to learn you can
always "get more done through other people" than you can do by
yourself.

Temperament differences are so fascinating to me in this regard. The
choleric pastor would rather have ten people doing work even if it was
only 80 percent up to the standards he sets for himself. Not so the
melancholy. He would rather that each job perform 100 percent up to
expectations even if he has to do it all himself.

3. *The melancholy pastor's administrative style.* Melancholies are
interesting administrators. And again prior training will have a great deal
to do with his style. But remember, a melancholy is a perfectionist, so
expect that in his administration and management. No one can churn
out more paperwork than Pastor Melancholy. His staff is relieved when
the church copy machine breaks down. He is usually the first one at
work in the morning and the last to leave at night. He is regimented to a
schedule, with certain days for certain tasks. The choleric assigns each
staff member one day a week to hospital visitation until he has six on his
staff, then quits hospital calling altogether. Not the melancholy. Even if he
has twelve staff members and two visit people each day, he will still take
the time to call on as many as he can—and feel guilty because he can't
see everyone. He is prone to do that on everything.

As a manager of people, he is a "checker-upper." Close supervision is
his style. Not so the choleric who is results-oriented. The melancholy
minister-manager sits down with his pastoral staff or volunteer leaders,
goes over every detail, sets guidelines and goals, then checks up on
them regularly—and watches over their shoulder in the meantime. He
may not verbalize his criticism the way a choleric or sanguine would, but
he emotes his disapproval. And to many temperaments, that can be
even more devastating.

Personally, his desk is a disaster area. If you go into his office, his desk is piled with papers, reports, letters, schedules, etc. Yet in spite of it all, he knows where everything is. He meets his deadlines and is able to pull together an incredible amount of pertinent information from his piles and desk debris. I call his style "a messy organizer." But who cares what it looks like, as long as he gets the job done.

One of my friends is the president of an enormous company, and she continually keeps a cluttered desk. In fact, she has two offices—one to work in. When I came into her office, she looked at her desk piled high and said, "I'm suspicious of an executive with a neat desk. I don't think they have anything to do!" Melancholies have plenty to do, and they keep a messy desk to prove it. Yet somehow they find the time to keep up with their correspondence.

In recent years melancholy pastors have taught us all something about streamlining our time. They have classes for everything. In their quest to be thorough, they launch membership classes, baptismal instruction classes, premarital instruction classes, counseling classes, seminars for deacons, trustees, deaconesses or whatever lay offices are in the church. You can't get into their church, baptismal pool, or official board without going through classes. I'm not knocking it, you understand; I had classes like that myself when I was pastoring. It's just that we all borrowed the idea from our melancholy pastor friends. I know one melancholy pastor who requires eight premarital classes before a person can get married in his church. And with the divorce rate being what it is today, even among Christians, who can say that's not a pretty good idea?

4. *The counseling style of the melancholy pastor.* Melancholy pastors make good counselors. They are patient, caring, and give the counselee their undivided attention. Anything he does gets his undivided attention, and you need that to be a good counselor. He is slow to make moral judgments and is not abrasive when placing blame or offering therapeutic remedies. He listens carefully, evaluates everything with that retentive memory of his, and analyzes the entire situation carefully.

Counseling with Pastor Melancholy will take a long time. His first get-acquainted interview takes at least two hours. There are forms to fill out, details to plumb, and subjects to cover that you may not have thought of for thirty years. He has to know all about you before he can accurately diagnose your problem. Then he must see you regularly, check up on you carefully, and make sure you are following through on his advice and assignments.

In spite of the condition of his desk, he will keep accurate files; and if

you come back to see him in ten years, he will have all your records
available. The MelPhleg pastor, with his gentle spirit and patient ways,
may just be the best temperament for a lifetime ministry of counseling.
Of one thing you can be sure—he will take your problem seriously and
try diligently not to offend you.

One of the weaknesses of the melancholy counselor is that, like the
sanguine, he tends to sympathize with those who wallow in self-pity.
That is the last thing they need! They are already feeling sorry enough
for themselves; that's why they are often depressed. And when a
counselor sympathizes with them, their inclination is to think, "I was
right all along to feel sorry for myself; even my counselor feels sorry for
me." No matter what temperament a counselor is who communicates
that message, that is bad counseling. But confrontation is difficult for a
melancholy. Confronting a self-pitying counselee with the terrible sin of
self-pity and its harmful consequences is tough for anyone. I should
know; I've had to do it over one thousand times. But if you want to help
depressed people, that is what it takes. And melancholies find that so
hard they often resort to more and longer counseling sessions to ease
the problem and then end up doing what they should have done in the
first place—the difficult task of confrontation.

A personal problem many melancholy counselors encounter is the
difficulty of leaving the problems of their counselees in the counseling
room. No family needs to live with the emotional accumulation of
seven or eight counseling experiences a day. Not only will his
superconscientious spirit make him share the burden of those he
counsels even when he goes home at night, but he can't handle the guilt
of failure. I don't care how super a counselor you are, you are going to
encounter human failure. Marriages you patch together may later come
apart. Young people you've helped overcome drugs may return to them
and overdose. Self-pitiers may return to their old thought patterns and
have to be committed or even commit suicide. Counseling is a heavy
business, and a melancholy pastor takes those failures very personally.
His first thought is, "What did I do wrong?" or "What clues did I miss?"
or "What should I have done differently?" And although he gets guilt-
ridden and depressed for his failure, he may have done everything
exactly as he should; no one can predict how another person will
exercise his free will. That's God's department!

One final note lest I discourage anyone from taking up a ministry in
counseling. There is an unadvertised blessing in being a counselor. I
think it makes you a better person, husband, and father. As you listen to

the hurts and complaints of others, it is impossible to be so impersonal you do not think at times, "I've been guilty of saying similar things to my wife" or "I wonder if I come across that way to the children." A conscientious man of God will be a better person by spending time in the counseling room with others.

5. *The melancholy pastor and the social life of his church.* The melancholy pastor doesn't fight the social life of his church. He may be a loner by nature and think he doesn't need social times (although he really does), but he is so into the church being used of God to minister to others that he will encourage an active social life. He recognizes that people who spend time together get along better with one another, and he tries to inspire as many opportunities for such activities as he can.

Personally he may not feel comfortable at church socials, parties, or gatherings because he is not an avid conversationalist; but once he assumes the role of the pastor he can rise to the occasion. To him, all social meetings must have some spiritual significance too and must provide some time for Bible study and prayer. But he will almost never disrupt the tradition of his congregation on this subject, unless he has strong biblical or other convictions against them.

6. *The personal life of the melancholy pastor.* One thing everyone expects from their pastor is that he live a godly life, and that is probably more likely for the melancholy pastor than any other. He has an enormous capacity to walk with God. He can learn to commune with him on a most intimate level and usually has a full, rich prayer life, while continually feeling inadequate—too worldly or carnal. He will probably be more consistent in daily devotions than any other temperament type.

He has a high standard of morality both for himself and for his congregation. His thought-life is generally considered pure, and he would legalistically guard against anything that would artificially inflame his carnal passions. He could not handle the guilt of moral infidelity, which tends to safeguard him when faced with such temptations.

Like his phlegmatic cousin, he has a fear or worry problem and rarely feels secure in his congregation. If a visiting minister is used of God in a moving way among the people, he tends to feel threatened. He may think more about his inadequacies than his talent, which does nothing for his self-confidence. He takes the lows of the congregation (and every church has some) personally and rarely takes credit for the highs, because he knows it should be better. If bickering, gossip, or feuding occurs in his congregation, he takes that personally, as he does broken marriages or any form of worldliness on the part of his members.

He can be easily discouraged by the opposition of others, particularly those in leadership. He cannot handle defeat and almost never leaves his church when things are going badly. His strong sense of loyalty would tie him to a sinking ship, so that if a dynamic church with a beautiful auditorium in a booming neighborhood were to extend him a call, he would be almost certain it could not be of God. Except for his sanguine wife, who urges him to "pray about it while I start packing," he would stay in the discouraging work the rest of his life. Melancholy pastors often overstay their ministry in a church. Cholerics by contrast are just the opposite. If a call doesn't come from a bigger and better opportunity that pays them a higher salary, he is sure it is not of God. The sanguine pastor, however, usually jumps at the next opportunity no matter where it comes from. His melancholy wife is usually a good packer—she gets lots of practice.

Mondays are usually wipe-out days for the melancholy pastor. That is why ministers for years got into the habit of taking Monday off. Melancholy ministers so instructed us in seminary. It's all quite simple. Every Sunday is the goal any pastor works for all week long. It's his primary job to feed the flock of God. The melancholy tends to let down after a project, so Monday he is emotionally and physically spent. The sanguine is so spent he is out on the golf course at 7:00 a.m. Monday morning, while the choleric is flying to some Bible college where he is scheduled to give a series of lectures. Not the melancholy; he is "shot!"

Personally, I think it's 99 percent in your mind. If you think you're going to be shot on Monday, you will be. If you plan to work on Monday, you will be able to. I think ministers should take Saturday off to be home with their children when they are out of school. But it's easy for me to say that—I'm not a melancholy.

One area a melancholy pastor has to watch out for is the neglect of his family. All relationships take time to cultivate. Melancholies can make good husbands (if they are not too everlastingly critical), but it takes time. Wives of workaholic melancholy ministers sometimes resent the church because he is such a worker; but he feels guilty if he is free to spend time at home some evening.

The pastorate is so structured that you never go home with your work complete. Every night for twenty-five years, when I went home there were things in that church I could and in some cases should have done. But sleep is a necessity for every temperament, and so is time spent as a husband and father. And that includes study. A melancholy has the ability to lose himself in books and enjoy it. He loves reading, research, and digging out information. But he needs to save that for an appropriate time and place.

Melancholy ministers have great potential as pastors if, like all the others, they refuse to give in to their weaknesses and walk in the Spirit.

The Phlegmatic Pastor and His Pastoral Ministry

Phlegmatics are the calm, quiet, never-get-excited superintrovert people who wear well and are known for patience, diplomacy, and a good sense of humor. Not many strong phlegmatics go into the preaching ministry because the very nature of the work requires an extrovert. (Percentages of temperament play an important part here. If for example, a person is 55 percent or 60 percent phlegmatic, he could learn to be a good public speaker. If he is 85 or 95 percent, it is doubtful.) However, there are many places for phlegmatics in the Lord's work. A high percentage of missionaries are phlegmatics. And many become associate or assistant pastors. The missionaries we shall explore later. Here we shall consider our gentle diplomatic friends, as we did the other three temperaments, in the light of the pastoral ministry. Many a church, after a tempest-tossed ministry under the direction of a carnal choleric or sanguine minister, could benefit by the soothing ministry of a Spirit-filled phlegmatic pastor.

1. *His pastoral ministry.* Like the melancholy, the phlegmatic has the gift of serving high on his priority list of spiritual gifts, often making him a much better pastor than he is a preacher. He is a diplomatic peacemaker who can somehow turn the most cantankerous church or board into a harmonious group. He doesn't do it with fanfare or crisis but very gently.

Phlegmatics shine in the hospital. They can put everything out of their mind and spend a whole day going from hospital to hospital and bedside to bedside and enjoy it. Even more important, they make the person they are visiting know they enjoy reaching out to them. The choleric pastor makes the person feel guilty for taking up his precious time. The phlegmatic pastor somehow makes the person feel he has been happy to have this opportunity to visit him in his hour of need.

The phlegmatic pastor almost never offends people. He never

embarrasses his congregation and will always do what is considered "proper." He is a great one to mend fences and will go quickly to the person he thinks may be upset.

Unless, however, his church has several aggressive adult Bible studies, don't expect the church to experience its all-time growth records under his leadership. Fanfare, promotional campaigns, and attendance contests are not his style. Unless the church has an advertising committee, they won't even put an ad in the church page of the paper, and putting his picture in the ad would not even occur to him. He is an under-advertiser. This is where thoughtful laymen can be of great help.

He is not a driver or a pusher; it's just not his way. The advantage to that is that members in the congregation will have a greater opportunity of using their spiritual gifts under his leadership. He doesn't seem threatened by those who want to lead in some area so long as they are spiritually motivated individuals. And when someone tries to push him into some scheme or program he doesn't want to do, he doesn't openly fight them or explode all over them the way a choleric or sanguine would. He just doesn't do it! But he doesn't do it nicely.

Many think because he goes along with certain strong-willed people that he is an easy mark or a pushover. That is not true; he is a peacemaker who only fights if it is absolutely necessary. He has learned that diplomacy can save wars, and he definitely does not like a fight. He will fight as a last resort, but only over significant issues.

One of his biggest problems is keeping the spirit of evangelism alive in his church. Sustaining a church calling program is a fight for any pastor regardless of temperament. Cholerics succeed just because of their dogged determination. But after a few attempts the phlegmatic pastor buries the whole program much to the delight of 97 percent of the congregation who never participated anyway. He feels a sense of guilt for this deficiency, but rarely succeeds in doing anything about it.

Many churches have benefited by the ministry of the phlegmatic pastor. And many a successor has reaped the harvest from their labors. I know I did. Rev. Homer Grimes was like that. Everyone loved him; he had almost no enemies before I began my twenty-five-year pastorate in San Diego. He pastored the church for six years. The church had not grown particularly during that time, for in examining old records I discovered that for four years before I came, the income had run between $46,000 and $47,000 a year. In fairness to him, he had been quite ill during that time. But oh, was he loved!

In fact, he was exactly what that church needed. They had

experienced a most tragic split and church fight before calling Homer.
He came to them and loved them. His ministry was putting oil on
troubled waters. When I came along six years later, the congregation was
in perfect condition to explode in new growth. Much of what God did in
the years that followed were a tribute to the faithful service of that
loving man.

As an aside here, I would like to insert a personal testimony. When I
was twenty-one years of age I was wrestling with the Spirit of God about
what to do with my life. I had been called to preach at fifteen, but at
twenty-one I decided I wanted to be a lawyer. I remember telling the
Lord, "If you let me go to law school, I'll come back and run for District
Attorney of Detroit and clean this town up." But God had different plans
for my life. One Sunday morning I attended the home church of my
young bride. During the invitation Dr. William Coltman, the pastor, led
with the song, "What Shall I Give Thee, Master?"—"Thou has given all
for me, not just a part but *all* of my heart. I will give *all* to thee." Sitting
there in the balcony I heard the Spirit call me again, and I gave *all* my
heart to him for the ministry. It was a deep moving experience that
righted my course and affected the rest of my life. Rev. Homer Grimes
wrote that song! Who would have dreamed that in the providence of
God we would both someday pastor the same church?

2. *The phlegmatic pastor's leadership style.* Phlegmatics are reluctant
leaders. They can be capable leaders if called upon, but they don't apply
for leadership. In their heart they wish someone else would do it. So
when they go into the ministry, they do not become aggressive leaders
because phlegmatics are not aggressive about anything.

One of the problems phlegmatics have is they are not very decisive.
Particularly is that true of major issues that must be confronted. The
most consistent criticism of phlegmatic pastors by people who really love
them is, "He is too noncommittal; we just can't get a decision out of
him." Part of the problem is his reluctance to offend anyone. Whenever
a big decision has to be made, someone doesn't like it. That never
bothers a choleric, but it bothers a phlegmatic. He doesn't like to have
anyone upset at him.

That does not mean phlegmatics cannot be good leaders. With the
proper training and the courage from God to do the unpleasant task in
making the unpleasant decision when it is necessary, they can be very
effective leaders. In fact, one of the side benefits of phlegmatics'
reluctant leadership style is that it tends to draw some of the natural
leadership within the church into service, while the more aggressive

temperaments tend to squelch natural leadership.

Probably one of the most serious drawbacks to phlegmatic leadership, and even this can be overcome, is his lack of vision. He is a status quo person. He is a routine person; launching new venturesome projects and bold new schemes that have never been tried before is not his style. Yet, it should be pointed out that many fine churches today enjoy the leadership of a phlegmatic pastor. I have preached in beautiful churches that were built during the ministry of phlegmatic pastors. And the neat thing about their leadership is that while they may not set world records, neither do they leave wounded Christians, damaged psyches, and broken spirits in their wake.

3. *The administrative style of the phlegmatic pastor.* Phlegmatics are usually efficient people and good organizers. As one church member said, "Our pastor has the dust on his desk organized." As we have seen, he works well with people, diplomatically solves personality conflicts, and never comes to a board meeting unprepared. He seems to anticipate what areas will come up or should, and usually brings the facts and figures he needs to make decisions. Board members love him because he rarely lets meetings he chairs wander and usually lets out on time. One phlegmatic chairman I know made up an agenda for each deacon's meeting and assigned a certain number of minutes for discussion of each item.

Probably the most difficult drawbacks to his administrative style are his reluctance to make decisions and his reticence to confront people when they need it. He will sometimes let a personality problem on his staff or in his church get out of hand because he doesn't like confrontation. There are times in a Christian's life when firing an employee is the only possible solution. That is very difficult for a phlegmatic pastor. He will often keep such a person on the payroll and make others work around them. Rarely does that solve anything. I have a phlegmatic minister friend who fired his custodian. We visited their home a few hours later, and my friend was in tears. Later I learned he felt so bad about it, he went to the man's home and apologized and gave him his job back. Six months later he had to go through that whole experience again. Now that is bad management! However, there are times when you reach an impasse with an employee and must fire him. When such a time comes, the best way to do it is call them in at 4:00 P.M., talk it over, explain what you have to do, pray with them, and then dismiss them. We always give them a check for their accumulated vacation, benefits, and two weeks pay. But I want them to clean out

their desk and be gone by the end of the day. It never works to keep a
person on after you have given notice—they poison everyone around
them. Phlegmatics can learn to do that if it ever becomes necessary. But
it will never be easy for them (it's never easy for any temperament).

4. *The counseling style of the phlegmatic pastor.* Phlegmatic pastors
have a real gift for counseling. They are nonthreatening, gentle people
who will listen patiently to the heartaches of others. No other
temperament is so apt to follow the Rogerian techniques of counseling
(nondirective). The danger of that kind of counseling is that it doesn't
work unless ultimately the counselor confronts the individual with the
mirror of the Word of God and challenges him to change his behavior.
Phlegmatic counselors enjoy the listening but not the confronting.
However, to their credit, they can learn.

Like the rest of his efficient life, the counseling program of a
phlegmatic minister will be very orderly. You usually get fifty-five minutes
in his counseling room. You talk forty-five minutes; he talks ten, gives
you literature and a spiritual prescription on which to base your change.
Then he takes a five-minute break before seeing the next client.

His unthreatening and noninterruptive style often allows the more
timid counselee to open his heart and reveal things to him he has never
shared with others. A phlegmatic minister committed to the Word of
God as the ultimate guide for human life and practice can be a good
counselor. You don't build a great church through counseling, but you
can certainly help lots of people. Many of the pastors now on the staff of
churches as associate pastors engaged as full-time counselors are
phlegmatics.

5. *The phlegmatic minister and the social life of the church.* The social
life of the church does not take a high position on the phlegmatic
minister's priority list. He can take it or leave it. If, however, it is a
tradition of the congregation, he will continue it and make an appearance
at all socials. He always does what is expected of him and if his
predecessor attended all social activities, so will he.

He may not say anything, nor will he try to change any time-honored
pattern. And even if it serves no real purpose, he will not kill it. Doing
the accepted thing is often too important to him. This, of course, is
where boards and committees are a help to him.

6. *The personal life of the phlegmatic minister.* Phlegmatics are not
too disciplined by nature, although a phlegmatic minister may be more
spiritually motivated to discipline than others. He is never an
embarrassment to his church in his public or personal life. He always

pays his debts, is not a flamboyant overspender. In fact, he is a saver. He
is the one temperament who when he makes out a budget will include
$50 or more a month for savings. He is security-conscious.

One area of concern could be his family. While many phlegmatics
have raised exemplary children, many others have been such weak
disciplinarians their children are wild and unruly. This can be both a
heartache to the pastor and his wife and an embarrassment to their
congregation, particularly when they are teenagers.

Morally speaking, the phlegmatic minister almost never disgraces his
family or his church. He is not aggressive about anything and that
includes his sexual activity. Besides, being proper is one of the most
important things in his life.

His lack of vision for his church will affect his family, except that his
more aggressive wife may motivate him and the family in their personal
pursuits. By nature he is a worrier whose fears keep him from venturing
very far. He is not the kind of minister who allows outside demands to
take him out of the congregation for large parts of the year. His church
often wishes he would accept other speaking engagements. But his fears
of comparison or his insecurities at having other ministers fill in for him
when he's gone keep him at home most of the time. Even when he goes
on vacation or speaks in some other church, he will rarely select a
dynamic preacher to fill his pulpit.

When he learns to walk in the Spirit and overcome his fears, timidity,
and insecurities, he can have a very positive ministry.

Rarely does a phlegmatic minister neglect his family. He is not one to
flit off in several directions at the same time. Instead, he lives a more
structured and routine life. He doesn't usually schedule extra night
meetings; consequently, he is at home with his family more than other
types. Because he is a happy, witty, unthreatening person, his children
relate well to him. He usually is a good father who spends lots of time
with his children. And once he learns a proper balance between
discipline and love, his children grow up and are a credit to him, his
church, and his Lord.

Temperament and Missionary Service

It probably will not surprise anyone to learn
that most of the missionaries of the world have been phlegmatics and
melancholies. Very few are cholerics or sanguines. If you know the
mission fields of the world and if you know the four temperaments, then

you will soon understand why. The Western world is predominantly
choleric/sanguine. Cholerics and sanguines create the pace and
contribute much to the life-style; and because of their Nordic-European
ancestry they tend to predominate. Or at least the more passive
temperaments tend to stand back and let them lead.

Not so in the mission fields of the world. In India, Africa, much of the
Orient, and in many Third World countries, the culture is much more
passive and "laid back." Sanguines and cholerics are often misfits in
such cultures, except in specific situations which call for their unique
talents.

I don't pretend to be an authority on missions, but I have been a
missionary-minded pastor for many years. God has used my ministry to
raise up over 200 missionary candidates, I have raised several million
dollars for missions, and I have taken two lengthy missionary tours when
I tried to minister to these very dedicated people. On one such tour, my
wife and I spoke to over eight thousand missionaries and I took a
voluntary temperament survey on over one thousand which I used in my
doctoral thesis in graduate school. In addition, I have talked at great
length with my brother-in-law, Rev. Bill Lyons, whom I brought on staff as
Paster of Missions in our church and who also functions as Director of
the Department of Missions at Christian Heritage College. He and his
wife were successful missionaries in Taiwan for over twenty years.

The reason I say all of this is not to impress you, but to point out that
I am a friend of missionaries and have checked what I am about to say
with others who know the mission field. However, that is not to say that
our sovereign God cannot or will not call whom he will, regardless of
temperament, into his vineyard. But I have noticed that God rarely puts
round pegs in square holes.

When we spent nine months of our lives speaking in forty-two
countries of the world in 1977, my wife and I only found two sanguine
male missionaries. We found several sanguine female missionaries,
married to melancholy men—that's why they were there. The one
sanguine man was located in Hong Kong, the son of missionary parents.
He was a godly man, a credit to his mission and the life of the party. He
was a delight to the other missionaries who elected him Field Chairman.
He wasn't the best leader, but because of his rich spiritual life and his
personal magnetism he was a blessing to the work of the others in his
mission. The other was in La Paz, Bolivia, where the mission chairman
was the charmer who kept the changing governments at peace with the
many missionaires operating out of La Paz. He was one of the most
personable Spirit-led men I met on that entire trip.

We met a few cholerics, like the young man in Singapore who mustered over six hundred people (mostly Asian couples) to our seminar. What vision! He told me, "If you draw a circle within two thousand miles of Singapore, you will encompass over 50 percent of the world's population. If we are ever going to reach the world for Christ, we will have to do it from Singapore!" And he had a battle plan. Most of his young converts spoke three languages—English, Malaysian, and their mother tongue (Chinese, Japanese, Indonesian, or wherever their parents came from). My choleric minister friend had not learned any foreign language, yet was having a very powerful ministry with the college students and college graduates, almost all of whom spoke English. He discipled them in the Word and trained them in evangelism to communicate in all three of those languages. And he had already seen 127 of those young people go back to the land of their origin to share the Good News of God's love.

Another choleric I recall in Korea was involved in church planting, summer camps for youth, a Christian school for missionary kids, radio, publishing, printing, and book sales. The last I heard he was trying to get into video work.

In all, we met two sanguines and about ten cholerics—all the rest seemed to favor the melancholy and phlegmatic temperaments. Why so few sanguines and cholerics? I asked my brother-in-law. Bill said, "Most of the time sanguines and cholerics are misfits on the mission field. There are some positions they can hold but not many. I have never seen any sanguine men in our part of the Orient, and all the cholerics I've seen have burned themselves out with the Orientals within eight to ten years."

At first I thought perhaps the problem is that we extroverts lack the dedication to go to the mission field, but then I remembered a spiritual climax in my life during my college years when I yielded myself to God to go out as a missionary only to discover he didn't want me to be a missionary. He just wanted me to be *willing* to be a missionary. As soon as I gave him a lifetime "yes," he quit speaking to me on that subject. And I find that my experience is not rare; most successful pastors can relate a similar experience.

What then is the reason? I don't know the complete story but I'm sure Bill is right. We of the ChlorSan or SanChlor temperament are not suited for missionary work in most cultures, particularly in the more passive societies. (South America and other Latin countries may be different.) Most of us get discouraged if we don't see tangible results in a reasonable period of time.

I'm not sure my temperament type could go for five months in Venezuela preaching every Sunday morning and every Sunday evening, plus Wednesday night before *anyone* came to church except my wife and two small children. Or another eighteen months before the first convert. I could never spend twenty-five years learning a language to preach to two hundred people because that's all that are left of one tribe. I know I could never spend many tedious years learning how to translate the Bible for a tribe that had no written language, when you have to invent one, translate into it, and then teach the people to read. Or risk your life for years among the Chamula Indians whose fifty thousand member tribe kills white male intruders. The list goes on, over two thousand tribes long. Yet someone must tell these people about Jesus! The Bible promises that there will be converts from every tongue and tribe and nation (Rev. 7:9) in Heaven. Thank God for the dedicated missionaries God has raised up in the past three centuries to reach out to the peoples of the world, and most of them seem to be melancholy and phlegmatic temperaments.

Naturally, their secondary temperament will have an influence on them also, but depending on the specific work, melancholies and phlegmatics have the best aptitude for mission work.

Early in my ministry I became vitally interested in the work of Wycliffe Bible Translators. Many of the over ninety missionaries our church supported were Wycliffe people. Have you ever met a translator that wasn't a melancholy temperament or phlegmatic or both? I'm not sure you could get through the translation school without a high degree of melancholy or phlegmatic temperament. And then you must patiently win the confidence of the tribe, learn to talk to them, and over a period of ten to twenty years translate the New Testament for them. During that time you have the dangers of dysentery, malaria, snake bite, drowning, bad weather while flying in small planes, and even the possibility of being run over on an American freeway while here on furlough. Who but melancholies and phlegmatics could or would go through all that?

CHAPTER
NINETEEN

The Minister's Resources

The main purpose of this whole study of temperaments is to discover our weaknesses, so we can go to the Holy Spirit of God for his strengths. In a practical way I believe that's what God means when he says, "Walk in the Spirit" or "Live in the Spirit." When we live in the Spirit, we are not continually overcome with our natural weaknesses, but instead overcome them with his strengths. But we have to be willing to let God's Spirit control our lives and work directly on those areas that displease him. His resources are more than adequate—even for ministers!

The Sanguine Minister's Basic Needs

Any appraisal of the sanguine needs will have to start with self-discipline. That is the one bugaboo that plagues him all through life, and unless he gains victory over it this fault will keep him from reaching his full potential for God. Very honestly, self-discipline is more important in the life of a servant of God than intelligence, creativity, or talent.

When I taught the San Diego Chargers football players' Bible study for three years, I made an observation. All of the players on that team were gifted athletes or they would not be there. But the best athletes were not always the ones who got to play. The successful athletes were those who learned how to discipline themselves consistently.

So it is with successful sanguine ministers. The reason they are used mightily by God while their friends fail is simply a matter of self-discipline. Pastor Sanguine needs to discipline himself in every area of his life. If he is overweight, that is a good place to start because it can slow him down, shorten his life, rob his health, and hinder his testimony. When he brings his body under control, his friends and church members can see it. He may never be trim like his melancholy or phlegmatic friends, but neither does he have to indulge fifty to a hundred pounds more than his body was designed to carry. He can succeed here by dropping sweets, starch, and second helpings from his diet and by jogging two or more miles a day—a small price to pay for lengthening his ministry and increasing its effectiveness.

Sanguines also have a need to discipline themselves in regard to daily meeting God in his Word. Regular devotions are on everyone's list as a daily requirement to be a man of God, and no Sanguine would disagree. Doing it regularly is another matter. But if he does, it will help him be more disciplined in other areas of his life. And there is a simple way to accomplish that requirement that works every time with sanguines. I've shared it with many. All he has to do is pass a resolution from which he will not vary—"no Bible, no breakfast." If he gets up too late or is too busy to feed his spiritual life that day, all he has to do is skip breakfast. He'll get up earlier the next day and do both.

He also needs to discipline himself with the ladies. More than any other temperament, he needs to avoid being alone with women other than his wife, and he needs to avoid touching them, flirting with them or being overly complimentary to them. Many of the temptations a sanguine falls into are of his own doing.

STUDY! STUDY! STUDY!

One of the most ministry-transforming areas of his life that must be disciplined is his study habits. We have already seen how sanguines are usually short-term pastors. Any sanguine could lengthen his ministry and make it far more effective if he would discipline himself to study, study, study. And professionally he would like himself a lot better if he did.

In recent years ministers themselves have advertised to their congregations that to be effective, he needs time to study. I am convinced it is the second most important thing he does, and it may even be the first. A minister's preaching is his Number One responsibility when called to pastor a church. It is through the pulpit that he makes his biggest investment in the lives of his congregation. But he must study in order to have something meaningful to preach.

I believe every minister should spend from 8:00 A.M. to at least 11:45 in his study *uninterrupted*, five days a week. He should train his congregation not to call him until the afternoon. Very few things must be handled "right now," the way some choleric church members think. He should then work at training his wife and secretary to protect those three and three-quarter hours from *any* interruption unless it is a matter of life or death. He needs to learn to stop reaching for the phone like a boxer answering the bell every time it rings. Either unplug it or put a pillow over it. His most important responsibility each morning is *not* talking to other people, but redeeming the time in his study with God, God's Word, and his sermons. The early apostles were successful because they said, we "will give our attention to prayer and the ministry of the Word" (Acts 6:4, NIV).

This kind of disciplined study can be habitual. At first a sanguine has to force himself to stay in his study and read, study, and work. He is so restless and inquisitive, he gets the urge to go somewhere and do something instead of study. As he resists that temptation, even the most sanguine pastor will gradually learn some good study habits. Until he gets to the point that he feels unprepared if he doesn't spend four to eight hours on each message, he has not learned good study habits. One trick I like to pass on to sanguines is to study in a bare room. No pictures, slogans—nothing! And don't keep anything on your desk that doesn't have a bearing on the subject. You don't need any distractions! The sanguine mind is so responsive and quick that a picture of last year's vacation on the wall can rob him of thirty minutes of valuable study time. And he should keep a time clock—that is, look at his watch and write down the time he begins the study and when he quits. I do that with writing. I time myself with each page. It takes me an average of thirty minutes to write one page of first-draft writing. I find timing each page speeds up my concentration and spurs me on.

Every temperament has its own problem with study, but the above suggestions will benefit any person. One observation I have made is that the pastors of the great churches today that are known as outstanding preachers of the Word follow a program similar to the above. They are unavailable in the morning and then do their pastoring, administration, and leadership in the afternoon. Rarely will a man of that calling sacrifice his morning study time for even long-distance phone calls. And a church member will be an asset to their pastor by protecting his early hours whenever possible.

**FINISH
WHAT YOU START**   Another thing a sanguine needs to work on is finishing what he starts before taking on something new. He is delightfully enthusiastic and will want to get involved with more than any human can do. He needs to take time to pray about the many challenges that come his way. As he "commits his way" to the Lord, God will give him the signal of what he wants him to spend his time on. It takes the average sanguine quite a while to realize that not every door that opens before him was opened by the Lord.

He also needs to learn to trust God and not his own natural ability. That is where that disciplined devotional life will help him. And he needs to work on "speaking the truth in love"—that is, to avoid hyperbole, exaggeration, and even excessive praise.

Last but not least, Pastor Sanguine needs to "walk in the Spirit" to overcome his tendency to be hot-headed and instantly angry. He is a responsive outgoing person who telegraphs his anger every time it rises. The Bible teaches us to avoid it, to "cease from anger," or to "forsake wrath." The "love, joy, peace, and self-control" of the Spirit will take care of that for him.

The Choleric Minister's Basic Needs

No one is perfect (I hope that message is coming through loud and clear in this analysis of temperament), and that includes ministers. They all have their individual talents and their varying needs according to their temperament.

One of the problems with the choleric temperament, no matter what his profession, is that he thinks he doesn't have any needs. He is the person who thinks, "Others have needs, but not me!" He is the "I'm OK, but you're not OK" person. And choleric ministers are no different. They may appear outwardly to have it together, but believe me, they have their problems too.

Like the sanguine and all the other temperaments, the choleric minister needs a regular devotional time to let God speak to him. Being self-disciplined by nature (or temperament), he and the melancholy are most likely to be consistent in having a daily Bible study time. Unlike the melancholy, he does not naturally develop a vital prayer life; that he must be taught. But his problem is that his regular Bible reading and study does not benefit him as much as others because he doesn't internalize or apply it to himself. When he finds something challenging in the Word, it is usually something he wants to use in preaching to others, when in reality he needs to apply it to his own life first.

He needs to let God put compassion in his life. A minister without compassion is like a robot or machine. Push the button or wind the clock and out comes the impersonal message for the day. A message from Buddha or Mohammed would be almost as challenging. He needs to develop a compassion like Paul, who went from house to house warning people with tears to turn to Christ. He needs to realize he is an ambassador for Christ, communicating the thoughts of God, not creating new ones.

That is why the love of the Holy Spirit is so necessary in a choleric's life. He needs first to recognize that he lacks compassion (I'm sure his emotionally shell-shocked wife will acknowledge that) and make it a daily quest of the Holy Spirit. As the psalmist said, "He that goes forth and weeps bears precious souls!" It isn't the tears that do anything; it is the spirit of compassion that causes the tears that God uses.

As his spirit of compassion grows, the choleric minister will see the needs of his flock, attend to their hurts, and take the time to praise and encourage them. I have noticed, for reasons I don't know, that people involuntarily look to cholerics for approval. It may be because they usually assume a leadership role and people look up to them, or it may be they emote a spirit of self-confidence and togetherness. Whatever it is, most people need stroking and involuntarily look to a choleric leader for it. Children need their father's strokes, and adults are often just children grown taller with the same emotional needs. A Spirit-filled choleric will learn to be a back-patter. Church people need that from their pastor. They often get his condemnation from the pulpit. In person they need his encouragement and consolation—and not just when they are bleeding. Approval always is appropriate after a difficult task or after they fulfill a long-term goal. Choleric ministers need to realize that people need their encouragement not just because of who they are, but because of who they represent.

Another thing he needs is to trust God in everything. His natural tendency is to say, "I'll trust God for the major things in life, the things I can't work out for myself; but the everyday things I'll take care of myself." If you try to serve God with your ability, he will let you. But if you trust him for supernatural power, he will give that also. God seems to adapt his dealings with us according to our acknowledged needs. The choleric needs to learn to "acknowledge him in *all* his ways."

And last but by no means least important, Pastor Choleric needs to "walk in the Spirit" to gain victory from God over his lifetime problems with anger. Anger is so much a part of a choleric's temperament that anytime you see a choleric who does not respond to adversity in anger, you are watching a demonstration of the Holy Spirit-filled life in action. Just controlling the expression of his wrath by the power of his determined will is no answer. His thoughts turn to poison and eventually erupt into anger. He needs to memorize Ephesians 4:30-32 and put it into action.

A most revealing conversation occurred in bed one night just a few weeks after I was filled with the Spirit for the first time in my adult life. It was 12:30 A.M. Bev was already in bed, and she said, "How did your trustees' meeting go?" "Not very well," I replied. "They rejected my proposal of adding a new staff member, they delayed starting my summer visitation program, and really didn't want me to start a Christian school." Gradually my breathing became heavy and I was almost asleep when her voice shattered the silence by asking, "What are you doing?" "I'm trying to go to sleep!" And then she asked what she was really trying to say, "You mean you're not mad and upset about it?" And we both burst out laughing. For the first time in my ministry I was not mad or upset by the rejection of a board. For me that was the work of the Holy Spirit. I didn't give up on those projects, but I was not upset by their rejection either. I wish that experience for *every* choleric minister.

The Melancholy Minister's Basic Needs

The melancholy is a perfectionist, but like all the rest of us he is far from perfect. He too needs a touch of the Spirit of God to overcome his weaknesses.

Like all other temperaments, Pastor Melancholy needs to discipline himself in his devotional life. Like his choleric counterpart, Pastor Melancholy is apt to be consistent in conducting his devotions or Bible study, but he has a difficult time applying it positively. Everything he sees in the Word only convinces him he has fallen below the standards of God. So instead of gaining new and uplifting insights from the Word, he is apt to be triggered by an introspection process that causes him to pick himself apart layer by layer. He can come away from his devotions more out of fellowship than when he started because he feeds his inferiority complex. Or he may sit down to do his devotions and be triggered off into some intricate hair-splitting doctrinal or legalistic subject that feeds his already overactive spirit of criticism. That only poisons him rather than communicates "love, peace, and joy."

No one is apt to have a greater prayer life than the melancholy minister. He is the person who tells you he will put you on his prayer list and does. He usually has the longest prayer list in town. But if he indulges his temperament tendency, he will get up from his knees in worse condition than when he started. For if he isn't careful, his prayer life can become a spiritual gripe session. He can spend most of his time griping at God for the things people do, the circumstances of his church or life, or even at the way God is running things. To such people, prayer can be a hazard that leaves them depressed.

What he needs to do is to learn the art of thankful praying. Many passages in the New Testament make it clear that all prayer should be made with thanksgiving. And anyone who knows the Bible knows that there is in every circumstance of life something for which we can give thanks—even if it is only the fact that God loves us and is able to do something about the situation. But prayer without thanksgiving can be detrimental.

He also needs to cultivate the practice of "rejoicing evermore." He is not a joyful person by nature and will get morose if left to follow his own natural pattern. He definitely needs to obey the command, "Rejoice evermore, and again I say rejoice."

This will have a bearing on another of his needs—that of learning to accept people as they are, sinful fallen creatures of the Adamic race. He takes the failures of people too seriously and too personally. He is prone to criticize people in his mind, and that is almost as devastating as criticizing them verbally.

We all emote messages to other people. What you think, you will emote as a message to others. One of the reasons Sanguines are such good salesmen is they emote well-being, success, and an interest in you. Melancholies are prone to emote negativism, pessimism, and criticism, which turns people against them. The way to change the message you emote is to change what you think. You are what you think.

Another thing Pastor Melancholy needs to develop is rhinoceros hide. I remember when I came to the church in San Diego, a lady said to me,

"One of our old pastors, Dr. Culver, used to say, 'If you are going to pastor this church, you had better develop a rhinoceros' hide.' " It took me just six weeks to discover what she meant. The ministry is a difficult place for a thin-skinned preacher, and melancholies are usually thin-skinned. The pastor by the very nature of his position is a perfect target for the criticism, sarcasm, and sometimes cruelty of carnal church members. He needs to expect it, and to evaluate his critics. When a spiritual person criticizes him, that's one thing he should listen to. When a carnal Christian vents his spleen, it is usually sour grapes and should be ignored.

Pastor Melancholy is the only temperament I know that needs to develop the gift of simplicity. His natural gifts, as we have seen, lean toward complexity. He needs to stop thinking and pleasing the college professor's mind as he did in college and seminary when preparing messages or papers. Now he must develop the ability to speak to the common man, as Jesus did. Besides, there are about 225 million more of the common folk in this country alone. I find it helpful to pick out a good stable working man in your congregation with at least an eleventh grade education and preach to him. Such preaching is understood by almost everyone in the house. And you will be surprised, God will use your message to touch the highly educated too. I have found that the Word of God can speak to anyone's needs. But it must be related to life in a practical way.

And, of course, the melancholy preacher must also learn to walk in the Spirit to gain victory over his three main emotional problems—anger, fear, and depression. We covered that more in depth in an earlier chapter. But here I just want to point out that you cannot walk in the Spirit with mental attitudes of anger, worry, or self-pity, and love, joy, and peace at the same time. Melancholy ministers can be great men of God if they "walk in the Spirit."

The Phlegmatic Minister's Basic Needs

It is impossible to cover all the needs of all the temperaments. I have only tried to touch on what I think are the most significant. This we will also do with the phlegmatic minister.

Self-discipline is not a hallmark of the phlegmatic temperament, as we have already seen. So when he goes into the ministry, it becomes crucial

to develop a disciplined devotional life to help discipline the other areas
of his life and to help him gain the courage and faith he needs from God
to face the situations he will face in his church. The Word of God gives
faith, and that alone will help overcome his worries, fears, doubts, and
anxieties. Actually phlegmatics have a practical bent to their mind and
do not have some of the complicated tendencies of the melancholy that
would offset the benefits of a good devotional life. His problem is just
getting around to doing it. He can be the world's best procrastinator, and
daily devotions are one thing he puts off at his spiritual peril.

Pastor Phlegmatic needs to forget what people think and say. He
should look them right in the eye and remember they have a right to
their opinion just as he does to his; but he is, under God, the pastor of
the church, and he will stay there until God is finished with him. When it
comes to making decisions, he should stop thinking so much about the
consequences, do what is right, and trust God to take care of the
consequences.

If things go wrong or if people get on his case, he needs to look them
straight in the eye and take full responsibility for his decision. One
tendency some phlegmatics have is to make excuses for their mistakes
or blame others. A good leader is not always right, but he never blames
others for what he considers his own failures.

A habit I could wish for every phlegmatic minister is to think big and
set high goals for himself and his ministry. Sometimes he seems so afraid
of failure, he only attempts such easy things that if God fails him he
can still reach them some other way. That isn't faith; that is limiting
God by unbelief. It is a wise phlegmatic who understands that one of his
weaknesses is to think small; so he should double everything he
attempts. Gradually he will increase his vision even over that, because
God leads us "from faith to faith." Each time he sees God's faithfulness
accomplishing more than he originally envisioned because he claimed it
by faith, it will give him courage to attempt even more the next time.

And finally, Pastor Phlegmatic should "walk in the Spirit" daily, and so
overcome his self-limiting tendency to worry about everything and limit
God through unbelief. "God hath not given us the spirit of fear; but of
power, and of love, and of a sound mind" (2 Tim. 1:7). If God didn't
give it, where did it come from? There are only two possibilities—the
spirit of man or Satan. With most phlegmatics, it is the spirit of man
working through their temperament. Then each time they give in to the
temptation to limit God through fear or unbelief, it becomes easier to do

it again. That is the way we develop habits—good and bad. It is time to begin trusting God on a day by day basis and let God prove that he is abundantly able to do *more* than we can ask or think.

The Common Thread

Hopefully you noticed the two common threads that all four of these ministers need. They need them because they are the two major spiritual needs of every temperament. And a minister's temperament is the most powerful single force in molding his ministry. The two needs are these: (1) Personal self-disciplined study of the Word; (2) Walking in the Spirit daily.

Any temperament or combination of temperaments will have its own set of weaknesses depending on background, education, childhood training, and its many life experiences. But the needs discussed in this chapter are the most common of the four basic temperaments. Each preacher will find his own pattern and particularly his own "besetting sin." But these are presented to convince you that whether it is your most powerful weakness or a common weakness, the Holy Spirit has a strength for it. That's why the Bible says that the greatest need for all of us is to "walk in the Spirit."

Any temperament combination can be an effective tool of God if a person incorporates the two ingredients above into his personal life and then finds and does the will of God. Never grumble at God about the temperament he gave you. There is no temperament that is better than another. God makes no mistakes; you are exactly the temperament combination he wants you to be. Now it's up to you to let him use you to the maximum of your potential.

PART Eight

HISTORY OF THE TEMPERAMENTS

CHAPTER
TWENTY

The Heritage of Temperament

It is particularly fascinating to me that the first mention in all of literature regarding four kinds of people is found in the Bible. When I began speaking and writing on the four temperaments, I found a few skeptics of the theory in the Christian community. The fact that the theory is so compatible with the biblical view of human nature, the fall, the flesh, "the sin that so easily besets us," and our human need of the external power of God working in us to strengthen our weaknesses was sufficient for me. But that didn't satisfy some of my friends. They wanted chapter and verse. Well, I've found it! And for the first time, I am putting it into print.

Keep in mind, however, that this biblical reference is embryonic; so don't expect too much. After all, since it was recorded over six hundred years *before* Hippocrates was born, it only represents that the ancients saw four kinds of people. The biblical writer I am about to cite does not even touch on the strengths of the four temperaments; he just deals with their weaknesses. But anyone familiar with the ancient theory of the four temperaments will recognize them immediately.

Solomon, the wisest man who ever lived, wrote most of the book of Proverbs. But the last two chapters are ascribed to a man named Agur. We are not certain who he is, though most Bible scholars assume he was a wise sage of Israel at about the same time as Solomon. He may have predated Solomon; hence his two chapters were edited into the proverbs of Solomon. Whoever he was, he saw that people fell into four basic divisions.

The wording as interpreted by the King James Version is not clear.

The *American Standard Version*, however, considered a very accurate translation of the Hebrew and Greek Scriptures, states that "there is a kind of man" and repeats that four times. The following is my analysis of what the inspired writer of Proverbs was saying—*long before* anyone had ever conceived of the four temperaments as developed by Hippocrates.

The melancholy temperament: "There is a kind of man who curses his father, and does not bless his mother" (Prov. 30:11, NASB).

How typical this is of the melancholy temperament—ungrateful and critical, probably their two most significant weaknesses. It is the melancholy child who does not bless or thank his parents. Instead he blames them for his very birth. If a melancholy can overcome his tendency to gripe, be critical, and find fault with everything and everyone, it will transform his whole personality and potential.

The phlegmatic temperament: "There is a kind who is pure in his own eyes, yet is not washed from his filthiness" (Prov. 30:12, NASB).

In the above verse, Agur is describing the phlegmatic person. The phlegmatic is generally emotionally detached from others around him. He is the "cool onlooker" who experiences neither highs or lows in his emotions. He is self-satisfied, and doesn't really feel hostile toward anyone. The problem with the phlegmatic is that he often can't see his own sins. He is one of the most difficult to reach for the Lord. He is literally "pure in his own eyes," yet "unwashed from his filthiness."

The phlegmatic is the nicest of all the temperaments. Rarely do they have to apologize for anything they have said or done because they are so quiet and passive. They are proper, gentle, and noncompetitive. But I have noticed that they too recognize how "nice" they are. How well I recall sharing the gospel of Christ with a medical doctor. Finally, we were able to answer his skepticism about the deity of our Lord, convincing him Jesus really did rise from the dead. But to my amazement he said, "But I don't need that like my wife and kids. I'm not that bad! I keep my word, I pay my bills, I don't think I have any sins to be forgiven." Needless to say, he was a phlegmatic. (Note: Fortunately he came to church regularly with his family, and one day he was convicted of his sin by the Holy Spirit and came forward to receive Christ. Now we both laugh at his former phlegmatic self-righteousness.)

The sanguine temperament: "There is a kind—oh, how lofty are his eyes! And his eyelids are raised in arrogance" (Prov. 30:13, NASB).

In verse 13 the writer is making an observation about those who have a sanguine temperament. He's talking about the person who is self-exalting. The sanguine is a cheerful person who genuinely enjoys life. But one of his weaknesses is that he thinks too highly of himself. He borders on being egocentric; he has "I" trouble.

The choleric temperament: "There is a kind of man whose teeth are like swords, and his jaw teeth like knives, to devour the afflicted from the earth" (Prov. 30:14, NASB).

Verse 14 describes the typical choleric—he has a sharp, caustic, sarcastic tongue, an angry disposition and a critical spirit. If you have ever been raked over by a choleric, you know what it is like to be set upon by a person whose teeth are like swords devouring the afflicted. But the Spirit of God can do much to improve the weaknesses of a choleric—as he can for any temperament.

To my knowledge, little else is known about the division of people into four different categories after the writing of Proverbs. During the silent years of the Hebrew prophets (Malachi to John the Baptist), it was the Greeks that started writing on their observations that people tended to fall into four basic categories.

The Greek Thinkers and Temperament Theory

When we look into the history of the theory of temperaments, we find the Greeks taking the lead in categorizing and describing the four temperaments.

Hippocrates (460-370 B.C.): Most historians credit Hippocrates, the father of medicine, with first detailing the four temperament types. Yet Hippocrates was simply building upon the theories of earlier Greek philosophers.

He was influenced by the theories of Empedocles (495-435 B.C.), who believed the universe was based on four elements: air, fire, water, and earth. Empedocles called them the "four roots of all things." Hippocrates took this idea and applied it to medical and psychological descriptions of man.

Hippocrates theorized that there were four basic fluids within the body of each person. These four fluids were the determining factors in how a person acted. The four fluids or "humors" were: blood (warm), black bile (humid), yellow bile (dry), and phlegm (cold or thick).

A person dominated by blood, for example, was a sanguine temperament. The melancholic was dominated by black bile, the choleric by yellow bile, and the phlegmatic person was slow and easy because of an abundance of phlegm in his system. This theory was often called "the four humors," because it was based on body fluids. This, of course, proved to be unscientific, and is one reason the theory was discarded over one hundred years ago. But when one realizes that Hippocrates wrote nearly 2,400 years ago, we can afford to be understanding. If he lived today he would be speaking about genes and chromosomes instead of humors, blood, and bile. But he probably would still believe in the existence of the four temperaments.

Aristotle (385-322 B.C.): Building upon Hippocrates' four-temperament theory were Aristotle and Theophrastus (372-287 B.C.). These men were both Greek philosophers and contemporaries who wrote extensively about the origins of the universe, politics, and human character. Theophrastus eventually succeeded Aristotle as head of the Peripatetic School. Aristotle modified Hippocrates' temperament theory to fit a more scientific approach, but he did not refute the theory.

Theophrastus (A.D. 372-287): Theophrastus was an avid student of temperament. He wrote Characters, a classic work containing thirty sketches of personality types.

Galen (A.D. 131-200): After Hippocrates, however, perhaps the most significant contributor to the four-temperament theory was Galen. He served as the personal physician of three Roman emperors, wrote more than 500 books, and did extensive research into the anatomical and physiological makeup of man.

Galen had adopted Hippocrates' four-temperament theory, but had expanded upon it, eventually listing nine temperaments. He listed the four basic ones, then described combinations of them. He combined wet and dry, warm and humid, cold and dry, and cold and humid. In his book On the Natural Faculties he observed, "It appears to me, then, that the vein, as well as each of the other parts, functions in such a way according to the manner in which the four qualities are mixed. There are, however, a considerable number of not undistinguished men— philosophers and physicians—who refer action to the Warm and the Cold, and who subordinate to these, as passive, the Dry and the Moist." Galen's temperament theory was accepted by the scientific world up until the seventeenth century.

Dr. Vindician (fourth century): In the fourth century A.D. the physician Vindician developed another theory about the four temperaments. He believed in the four humors and fluids, but he felt that each fluid ruled a different part of the body. The blood, for example, ruled the heart and the right side; yellow bile ruled the liver; black bile ruled the left side and the spleen; and phlegm ruled the head and bladder.

He also gave a "virtue" to each of the humors. Blood had the virtue of sweetness, warmth, and moistness; yellow bile was bitterness, dryness, and greenish fire; black bile was characterized as acidity, coldness, and dryness; phlegm was salty, cold, and moist.

He believed that whenever one of the fluids dominated the body, the person's behavior would change. Even though he could not scientifically prove his theories, modern science now recognizes that chemical or hormonal changes within our bodies definitely affect how we act.

Maimonides (A.D. 1135-1204): Maimonides was a rabbi, physician, and philosopher. He attempted to codify the Jewish oral law in the Mishna Torah and wrote volumes on religion and philosophy. According to D. B. Klein in A History of Scientific Psychology (Basic Books, 1970), "Maimonides mentions temperament differences in the way of courageous versus craven attitudes, and of cognitive differences in terms of speed learning, ease of understanding, and excellence of memory. Such differences are attributed to inherent differences in the relative preponderance of one of the four humors whose psychophysiological significance had come to be stressed since the time of Galen."

Nicholas Culpeper (1616-1654): With only a few minor modifications, the four-temperament theory remained virtually unchanged since the time of Hippocrates. The first major change came about in the seventeenth century through the writings of Nicholas Culpeper. Culpeper was one of the first—if not the first—to discard the concept of "humors" or "fluids" affecting human behavior. He still used the four temperaments to classify people, but he also theorized that each individual was not one specific type.

He felt there were at least two temperaments affecting our behavior. One was dominant, the other secondary. He described the melancholy-sanguine, for example, in these words: "They are more liberal, and merrier than melancholy persons are, and also, less cowardly, not so pensive nor solitary, neither are they troubled with such fearful conceits, but are gentle, sober, patient, trusty, affable, courteous, studious to do others good. . . ."

Immanuel Kant (1724-1804): The next major contributor to the temperament theory was German philosopher Immanuel Kant. In his book Anthropologies, he popularized the temperaments, maintaining that they could not be overlapped. His writings had a profound influence on other European philosophers.

Wilhelm Wundt (1832-1920): Another German, Wilhelm Wundt, considered to be the father of modern experimental psychology, developed a theory of temperament based upon the four types:

sanguine, melancholy, phlegmatic, and choleric. But he divided the
temperaments into several categories. He also rejected Kant's belief that
an individual could only be one temperament type.

Wundt constructed a graph on which he placed the four temperaments in four sections of a sphere, not unlike that currently used by
Eysenck. He separated the "emotional" temperaments (melancholy and
choleric) from the "nonemotional" temperaments (phlegmatic and
sanguine). He also distinguished between "changeable" and
"unchangeable" personality types. Wundt theorized that people differed
according to strong emotions or weak ones. He observed, "The ancient
differentiation into four temperaments . . . arose from acute
psychological observation of individaul difference between people . . .
cholerics and melancholies are inclined to strong affects, while sanguines
and phlegmatics are characterized by weak ones."

Alfred Adler (1879-1937): Another man who has contributed
significantly to the temperament theory is the Austrian psychiatrist and
psychologist Alfred Adler. Adler developed his own four temperament
types which he described as follows: "The first type consists of
individuals whose approach to reality shows . . . a more or less
domination or 'ruling' attitude (the 'ruling' type).

"A second type—surely the most frequent—expects everything from
others and leans on others. I might call it the 'getting' type. A third type
is inclined to feel successful by avoiding the solution of problems, . . .
tries to 'side-step' problems in an effort thereby to avoid defeat (the
'avoiding' type). The fourth type struggles, to a greater or lesser degree,
for a solution of these problems in a way which is useful to others."
These of course, are almost identical to the traditional divisions of
temperaments into melancholy, choleric, sanguine, and phlegmatic. Adler
believed that few people were one temperament or another, but were a
mixture of two or more. He also believed that our temperaments were
not fixed but were changeable as we grew older.

William Sheldon (1899-   ): The American sociologist William
Sheldon looked at the temperament theory from a different perspective
than others had in the past. Sheldon wondered about the connection
between body type and temperament or character. He postulated three
different body types, each with its own particular temperament. The
three body types were fat (ectomorphs), muscular (mesomorphs), and
lean (endomorphs). And the three personality types were vicerotonia,
somatotonia, and cerebrotonia.

One of the students of somatology became a devoted advocate of the

four-temperament theory after reading some of my books. He had
difficulty reconciling four types with Sheldon's three body types. Finally
he discovered the idea that in Sheldon's triangle there was a fourth
type—a centrist that drew on the other three. He called this middle
type "sensomorphy"—meaning middle or balanced. Interestingly
enough, there are some connections between body build and
temperament. As Arnold Buss pointed out in *A Temperament Theory of
Personality Development,* ". . . evidently there is a relationship between
body build and personality. . . . For example, fat persons are more
sociable than muscular persons, and thin persons are less sociable. At
present no one can explain this relationship between sociability and body
type, and it remains an intriguing fact."

And Louis Kaplan, in *Foundation of Human Behavior,* notes that
". . . studies conducted in Sweden, while not confirming the specific
relationship between temperament and physique described by Sheldon,
showed some definite relations between body build and susceptibility to
persuasion." The athletic types were the most gullible; the tall, lanky
types were more difficult to persuade. But the short and stocky
individuals were far more independent-minded and hardest to convince.

Hans J. Eysenck: Another major contributor to the temperament
theory of behavior is Hans Jurgen Eysenck, a German who received his
training at the University of London. Eysenck, a psychologist, helped
found the psychology department at the Institute of Psychiatry, Maudsley
Hospital in South London. He is one of the most respected
psychologists among European psychologists living today.

Eysenck's greatest contribution to the study of temperaments is his
emphasis on the scientific analysis of individual human differences. In
his research he sought to analyze personality differences using a
"psychostatistical" method. To aid him in his research, he constructed
the Maudsley Medical Questionnaire and the Maudsley Personality
Inventory.

By gathering data from these questionnaires, measuring body build,
and measuring physiological differences, Eysenck has developed his own
theory of personality and temperament based on the concept of people
being "introverts" or "extroverts." Essentially, Eysenck's research has led
him to believe that temperament is biologically based. It is not the result
of external conditioning, but is innate.

Eysenck makes a profound observation in *A Model for Personality*
where he says, "Careful reading of documents straddling 2000 years of
historical development has given rise to some general impressions

which may be useful to newcomers to this field. In the first place, there
is a strong feeling of historical continuity. Galen's and Kant's observations
do not strike the modern observer as ridiculous and outmoded; our own
work may be more extensive, better controlled and statistically more
defensible, but it is recognizably a development of ideas rooted all these
centuries ago."

Building upon the work of Eysenck and others is Arnold Buss, a
professor of psychology at the University of Texas at the time he
and Robert Plomin wrote A Temperament Theory of Personality
Development.

Buss and Plomin also believe there are four temperament types, but
give them different names. As they write, " Our theory suggests four
temperaments: activity, emotionality, sociability, and impulsivity." In their
theory, activity has to do with total energy output; emotionality relates to
the intensity of a person's reaction to events; sociability concerns a strong
desire of an individual to be with others; and impulsivity concerns a
tendency to respond quickly rather than inhibiting a response. These
psychologists believe that inheritance is the most important factor in
determining temperament.

Dr. O. Hallesby: We have briefly covered over 2,400 years of history,
viewing the various secular sources who have theorized about
temperaments. Yet the one author who has had the most profound
influence on my study of temperaments is a Christian, Dr. Ole Hallesby,
who wrote Temperament and the Christian Faith in 1940. Hallesby does
not claim to present a scientific analysis of the temperaments; he is more
interested in describing the temperament types and dealing with the
strengths and weaknesses of each.

In his brief volume he wrote, "Why do we have the different
temperaments? Temperament is what stamps each of us as an individual
and distinguishes us from other people. This individual difference is a
definite part of God's plan. It serves to make life diversified and rich in
all its relationships—in married life, in family life, in friendship, in the
community, and in the circle of Christians. By supplementing and
counteracting each other, the different temperaments give human life
greater fullness and beauty." Hallesby's book, translated into English by
Augsburg Press, introduced the theory of the four temperaments in the
sixties. The one problem I had with his book was the hopelessness with
which he left the melancholy temperament. In fact, I got the impression
he didn't like them very well. By contrast, I had seen many melancholy

people transformed by the ministry of the Holy Spirit and began
incorporating it into my counseling ministry. So I read everything I could
find on the subject of temperament.

In my writings on temperament, it has not been my purpose to delve
into the scientific reasons for temperament differences. It has been my
objective to show that people are uniquely made by our Lord. Each
person has a unique composition of temperaments and is gifted by God
for a variety of functions in the world. It has been my desire to help
people understand who they are and to teach them how to maximize
the positive aspects of their temperament and overcome their natural
weaknesses through God's Spirit.

The most significant contribution I have made to the four-
temperament theory is in applying the strengths of the Spirit-filled
life to the weaknesses of the individual. This is beneficial for self-help or,
as I have used it with thousands of people, as an aid in counseling them
in overcoming their weaknesses.

One of the ways I've tried to achieve this end is by designing the
LaHaye Temperament Analysis. Through this test, an individual can
discover both his primary and his secondary temperament. After the
results of the test are tallied, a detailed report is issued to the individual.
In this report, I discuss the strengths and the weaknesses of the person
and give some constructive suggestions as to what vocation might best
suit his own particular temperament, or where in his church he is most
apt to serve the Lord.

In my opinion, any theory of temperament is useful only if it is helpful
in changing people's lives. One of the most gratifying results from my
other books on temperament is how many people have written me to
express their appreciation for introducing this tool to both improve
themselves with God's help and to enable them to understand other
people. Through the study of temperaments, they have grown to
understand why they behave the way they do and how God has
provided adequate resources in his indwelling Holy Spirit to make them
into the mature fruitful person God wants them to be.

In taking this abbreviated look at the development of temperament
theory, we have seen the amazing continuity through over 2,400
years of history. Different psychologists, physicians, theologians and
philosophers have often given different names to the four temperament
types, but the concept has remained essentially unchanged for centuries.
It is a valid theory of behavior that can greatly benefit those who study

it. And when used in conjunction with the Spirit-filled life to overcome your weaknesses, it can help you reach all the potential God intended for you.

I predict in the future we will see the theory of the four temperaments become the most prominent and respected theory of human behavior used by those who wish to help other people, and you will already know it.

How to Get Your Personalized LaHaye Temperament Analysis

The LaHaye Temperament Analysis is the result of over fifteen years' research and is the most unique test of its kind available today. Each analysis is personally prepared and presented in a thirteen- to seventeen-page letter from the author (depending on your temperament combination and other personal information). It will provide you with the following information in a keepsake leatherette binder which will be of interest to you for years to come.

1. Your primary and secondary temperaments: The 92 percent accuracy level is extremely high. The standard I.Q. test is only considered 80 percent accurate.
2. Your vocational aptitudes, including at least fifty different vocations you could do comfortably.
3. An analysis of your three major vocational weaknesses with appropriate suggestions.
4. Your thirteen spiritual gifts in order of their priority, with an explanation for each.
5. The thirty vocations in your local church to which you are best suited.
6. Your ten major weaknesses, with appropriate suggestions on bringing them into control.
7. Positive personal suggestions on how to overcome your weaknesses.
8. If you're married, some suggestions on how to treat your mate.
9. If single, how to best face life as a single with your temperament combination.
10. If you are a parent, some suggestions on parenting for your type of temperament.

Obviously this test is not for those only casually interested in being the maximum person God wants them to be. If, however, you are really interested in personal self-improvement, you will find this test to be one of the most helpful things you have ever done.

Currently it is not available in bookstores, but can be purchased from Family Life Seminars, P.O. Box 16000, San Diego, California 92116.

As a reader of this book, I want you to have a $10 discount from the regular price of the test. Just send the enclosed certificate along with your check for $14.95,* and your test booklet will be sent by return mail. Allow me one week to process your test, and then you should have your own personalized analysis.

---

*The 1984 price may be subject to change due to inflation in future years.